Joss Whedon FAQ

Joss Whedon
FAQ

All That's Left to Know About Buffy, Angel, Firefly, Dr. Horrible, the Avengers, and More

John Kenneth Muir

APPLAUSE
THEATRE & CINEMA BOOKS
Guilford, Connecticut

Applause Theatre & Cinema Books

An imprint of The Rowman & Littlefield Publishing Group, Inc.

4501 Forbes Blvd., Ste. 200

Lanham, MD 20706

www.rowman.com

Distributed by NATIONAL BOOK NETWORK

British Library Cataloguing in Publication Information available

Library of Congress Cataloging-in-Publication Data available
ISBN 978-1-5400-0079-8 (paperback)

∞™ The paper used in this publication meets the minimum requirements of American National Standard for Information Sciences—Permanence of Paper for Printed Library Materials, ANSI/NISO Z39.48-1992

This book is dedicated to my twelve-year-old son, Joel, who brings joy into my life each and every day, and who has traveled to many wondrous universes and lands with his father, whether in Lego, video game, or action figure form.

And for Ezri, the companion and friend at my side, literally, through the writing of twenty books in twenty years.

Contents

Acknowledgments

The author wishes to acknowledge the help and friendship of his long-time agent, June Clark, and Dean James Minor, of South Piedmont Community College, both superheroes in my life, in their own rights, and without whom this book would not be possible.

Joss Whedon FAQ

Part I

In the Beginning

Who Is Joss Whedon?

(An Introduction to *Joss Whedon FAQ*)

Imagine this story: a longtime geek makes good in Hollywood after two decades working there, finally turning the world to his particular (and peculiar) love of pop culture, comic books, and superheroes. But then, after climbing to the apex of the entertainment industry, the self-same same geek stumbles, and experiences a fall from grace that shakes many of his fans to their core.

In a nutshell, this dramatic tale might be the story of Joss Whedon's writing and directing career, at least if recounted today. In 2019, Whedon remains beloved and renowned as the creator of such cult properties as *Buffy the Vampire Slayer* and *Firefly*, and as the director of the two mega-hit MCU (Marvel Cinematic Universe) films, *The Avengers* (2012) and *Avengers: Age of Ultron* (2015). Throughout a career stretching all the way back to the late eighties, when he toiled on sitcoms such as *Roseanne* (1988–1997), and *Parenthood* (1990–1991) Whedon has utilized his geek passions—his seemingly unquenchable love of comic books, horror movies, and fantasy—not merely to pursue his love and enjoyment of such topics, but to make global audiences gaze at pop culture in much the same the way he does: as smart, even intellectual avenues for stories of feminism, equality, inclusion, or even, simply meta-postmodernism.

Since the mid-nineties, Whedon has strived to both popularize and make more intelligent comic-book movies like *X-Men* (2000), horror films such as *The Cabin in the Woods* (2012), and beloved franchises such as *Alien* (1979–). Although he has not always succeeded, Whedon, in a very real sense, has made many of these properties feel more equitable merely by vetting clever and sharp-tongued stories of female heroes, or "othered" individuals who make good, succeed, or simply save the day. Often,

Portrait of the artist as a young man: Joss Whedon, pre-goatee.
John Muir Photo Archive

Whedon's selections in terms of protagonist qualities are simultaneously coupled with entrenched critiques of established forms or tropes.

Historically, Whedon's movies and TV series have not only redefined formats and characters, but exposed those traditional forms as being out-of-step with changing mores and beliefs.

Buffy the Vampire Slayer points out the inherently misogynistic or at least backward idea of females simply being "damsels in distress."

Famously, his inspiration for this superhero story is a cliched scene he remembers from old productions: a helpless young woman being chased and attacked by a vampire. In Whedon's re-framing of the story, the young woman is not helpless, and she's doing the chasing, not the running. It is the vampire, instead, who should be frightened. He calls it "the Dark Alley Story," but it is a subversion and rewriting of a long-standing horror trope. As he reported on the DVD commentary for *Buffy the Vampire Slayer*, season one, his goal in the genesis of Buffy Summers was to "create someone who was a hero where she had always been a victim. That element of surprise, that element of genre-busting is very much at the heart of both the movie and the series."

Similarly, Whedon's screenplay for *The Cabin in the Woods* takes to task Hollywood horror for being nothing but a repeating set of slightly different formulas. In this world, every terror is but a menu selection, a familiar off-the-shelf product rather than a genuine reflection of human psychology, or a critique of our unfolding world, and the paths it has taken. Whedon told writer Trent Moore at the website *SyFy* in 2015 that the film is a "very loving hate letter" to the genre. And what qualities does Whedon hate about modern horror? "The things that I don't like are kids acting like idiots, the devolution of the horror movie into torture porn and into a long series of sadistic comeuppances." In *The Cabin in the Woods*, the endangered kids make the choice about the future, and decide they no longer want to play the game that society has set up for them.

Even the poverty-stricken, low-tech world of *Firefly* and *Serenity* stands in stark contrast to the "Technology Unchained" paradise imagined by Gene Roddenberry's *Star Trek* franchise. Once more, a Whedon story is best parsed as a subversion of a popularly held viewpoint, in this case that mankind will somehow improve as species with greater technology, and greater access to that technology. In Whedon's rendering, the new frontier is the old frontier, only with spaceships, not stagecoaches. The future is not a better place simply because it is "the future." Man's nature remains the same, both in his desire to control others, and to escape the control of others.

If any of the preceding descriptions read as hyperbole or hagiography, understand that neither quality represents the intent of this text. It is vital, however, to place this artist in his particular historical context.

Whedon's ironic or meta-approach to horror arose in the same decade that artists such as Wes Craven and John Carpenter were thinking very much along the same lines in efforts such as *Wes Craven's New Nightmare* (1994), *In the Mouth of Madness* (1995), or *Scream* (1996). And the feminism inherent in a property such as *Buffy the Vampire Slayer* might also be read as a legitimate development of an important and widely utilized paradigm in slasher films of the 1980s and 1990s: the final girl syndrome developed by scholar Carol J. Clover. At the least, Whedon's worldview seems a distinct follow-on from the feminist approach of low-budget 1980s fare such as Thom Eberhardt's *Night of the Comet* (1984). There are clearly antecedents to his art, and that must be acknowledged.

Yet, by the same token, it would be silly not to similarly acknowledge that Whedon's art has traveled far beyond the precepts of those productions, and thus carried the torch of progress a little bit further. No doubt, the next creator, the next artist around the pike, will pick up where Whedon leaves off, and run the next stretch of this long race.

Whedon's overt feminism and sense of awareness about the limitations of various genres, or formats, only tell part of the story, or this artist's cultural and historic importance. There is a key facet that marks any of his art, even in his early, jobbing script-doctoring days, as belonging uniquely to him. And that facet is, simply, Whedon's persistent theme of disparate, derided individuals coming together, sometimes quite messily, to form a community, and achieve something together that could not have happened had the heroes separated.

"Created family is one of the most prominent themes in Whedon's work," according to Wesleyan University history professor Meghan Winchell, a scholar who studies the artist's work, and even shares the artist's *alma mater.* "Whedon writes for the hero, but the hero cannot prevail without support from friends. He also makes sure that the hero learns this lesson, sometimes the hard way. It is more evidence that Whedon is the right director for *The Avengers*, a dysfunctional family of superheroes with super egos," she reported in "The Wonderful (and Complex) World of Joss Whedon," an article in the *Lincoln Journal Star*, published in April of 2012.

Whether one gazes at *Toy Story* (1995), *Dollhouse* (2009–2010), or *The Avengers* (2012), one sees this same dynamic of "created family" featured over and over. Standing alone, or apart from the group, the members of these messed-up families are weak, and even self-loathing. Together, they form a community that carries the weight of the world on its shoulders. The *Star Trek* franchise is often, and quite rightly, championed as a place of diversity. Gene Roddenberry's universe embodies and puts into practice the Vulcan ideal of IDIC (Infinite Diversity in Infinite Combinations). This is the notion that our differences make us beautiful, and strong, not weak and divided. Yet this idea is also found front and center, loud and clear in *Buffy the Vampire Slayer, Angel, Serenity, Agents of S.H.I.E.L.D.*, and just about any other production where Whedon's creative energies and sensibilities are let out to play.

The second, and perhaps equally vital, aspect of the Whedon mystique involves language, or perhaps more accurately, *communication*. Communication might best be defined as the deliberate or accidental transfer of information. In various Whedon productions, the manner in which his characters communicate with one another proves as vital, no doubt, as the message, or content of that communication. Whedon's sharp-tongued, acid-wit, pop-culture-referencing, intellectual, and sometimes navel-gazing dialogue suggests characters who are fully entrenched in the intricacies and vicissitudes of mass communication. The characters in question are practiced consumers of media themselves.

Accordingly, these Whedon characters contextualize their existence, challenges, and relationships in terms of the myths and stories they have consumed, whether in comic-book form, at the movies, or on TV. So it is not merely that Whedon's heroes, such as Buffy, Angel or Captain Mal Reynolds, find each other and their place in their dysfunctional, sometimes pathological families. It is also that they learn how to interact, and how to view themselves through pop-culture images or ideals. Of course, this facet of Whedon's writing is more pronounced in some work than in others, but it is ever-present. It's really a weird Sapir-Whorf Theory, one might conclude. Only instead of language determining culture, media determines culture, and therefore language. In Whedon's films and TV shows, "language itself gets manipulated to indicate smart but whimsical characters with inarticulate modes of expression, and self-aware pop culture references abound," according to Aja Romano, from *The Daily Dot*, in 2013.

By focusing on those society doesn't always deem valuable or the norm, and by having these characters knowingly position themselves in terms of that larger culture, often alluding to literature and other mass media inspirations, the productions of Whedon take on a particular depth of meaning. Most superhero films or TV series don't set out to acknowledge other superhero productions. Yet in Whedon's work, there may be references to "origin stories," or some character's "kryptonite," or any other trademarks of the genre in focus.

At the same time that a Whedon work of art positions itself as part of an established format, it reminds audiences of the nature of that format, and undercuts it. This has become the go-to approach, actually of the MCU, and is evident in the third Avengers installment, *The Ant-Man* movies, and, especially Gunn's *Guardians of the Galaxy* run.

Perhaps the great tragedy of Joss Whedon involves, again, the historical context in which he exerts his creativity. American culture stands on the verge of a new understanding of how to present his career-long obsessions on screen. Unquestionably, audiences now seek authenticity and diversity behind the camera, as well as in front of it. Therefore, it seems appropriate that a woman take the lead directing a project such as *Wonder Woman* (2016), or that an African-American helm a project like *Black Panther*. It seems wrong to many audiences that white-washing and cultural assimilation, as seen in *Ghost in the Shell* (2015), endures.

So while Whedon has carried the aforementioned proverbial torch quite far in the last twenty-five years, our society's understanding of social progress means that, inevitably, he will put it down, making room for what many deem more authentic or diverse voices. The fact that Whedon's brand was marred, perhaps irreparably, in 2017, when the details of his married life became public, and called into question his credentials as a feminist, does not help his legacy. In fact, that controversy only adds to the perception that Whedon may not boast the same impact on pop culture in the future as he once did.

As this book was being written, Whedon departed from another prominent superhero project with a feminist bent, *Batgirl*, and many in the press speculated that his departure was a result of two things: the bad press involving his marriage, and the apparent demand for more equality behind the camera in Hollywood blockbusters. And, yes, at this juncture, it would be right, too, to note how fast all these changes are coming. In 2012, Joss Whedon oversaw the biggest hit film of the year, and a movie that leapt to the number-three slot on the top-grossing films of all-time list. In the spring and summer of 2018, he grappled with the disappointing financial fall-out from *Justice League* (2017), the lowest grossing DCEU (DC Expanded Universe) movie, and his departure from *Batgirl*.

More books have been written about *Buffy the Vampire Slayer* and its universe (the Buffyverse) than any other media property in history. It

Feminist Icon: Sarah Michelle Gellar as Buffy Summers, Vampire Slayer.
John Muir Photo Archive

is a subject beloved by academia and scholars. Similarly, Joss Whedon himself has often been the subject of scholarly books, whether it is a 2012 biography by Amy Pascale, or companion books that compile his works and draw connections among them. *Joss Whedon FAQ* is not a biography, and does not focus on any personal issues involving the artist, beyond reporting that which is already known. Nor is it an episode guide for all his series.

Rather, this is a text designed to introduce the reader to Joss Whedon's productions and career, and to position both of those things in terms of historical context, and the artist's perennial obsessions. Namely, the two-pronged approach, as enumerated in this introduction. Whedon's art is, overall, a study of disenfranchised people finding themselves through a community of other outsiders, and an exploration of communication in a media-saturated 'Verse.

In exploring these families that we find, or create, and digging into the way we communicate at the end of the twentieth century and beginning of the twenty-first century, Joss Whedon has proven himself, in the words of writer Jeph Loeb, nothing less than a "master storyteller." He stood astride an era in the industry when TV was changing from stand-alone storytelling to serialized storytelling, and in that time and space vetted comic-book stories of dramatic social value and resonance.

"We are long past the age of 'everybody on the internet watches *Star Trek* and lives in their parents' basement,'" Whedon told the *Los Angeles Times*. If *Star Trek* dominated genre thought and scholarship from the 1970s to late 1980s, Whedon's work similarly defines the 1990s and early 2000s. His film and TV efforts reflect the context of the Web 2.0 age, and even the fact that the world is moving beyond this context, where Whedon has been Geek King, is not a reflection necessarily of Whedon's personal or professional failures. Instead, it is a reflection of the fact that the world continues to spin, and change, and evolve.

As it does so, our understanding of storytelling inevitably changes too.

So if one chooses to look at it in such a fashion, *Joss Whedon FAQ* is a study of not only a popular writer and director, but the time and places in which that artist thrives, and has given his audience his best work.

A final note: Throughout this text, the author utilizes the adjective "Whedonesque." Urban Dictionary defines "Whedoneque" as meaning "the sorrow of getting exactly what you want but in such a way that it shatters your soul beyond imagining." That definition goes a long way towards defining the emotional impact of many beloved Whedon productions.

Whedon Repertory Company member, Nathan Fillion, as Captain Malcom Reynolds, in *Firefly* (2002–2003).   *John Muir Photo Archive*

However, this author is going to propose a different definition that goes thusly:

Whedonesque

- A descriptor for a work of art in some way authored (written or directed) by the artist Joss Whedon.
- A descriptor for a work of art that is "in the know" about pop culture and uses pop-culture references in both the discourse, and actual vocabulary of the piece.
- A work of art that involves Joss Whedon's long-standing thematic obsessions: feminism, "found or created" families, and appreciation for diversity, or "the other."

2

How Did Joss Whedon Get His Start?

Family History and Career First Steps

As many biographies point out in their opening sentence, Joss Whedon is actually a "third generation" Hollywood writer. The writer once told *CBS News*, while on a publicity jaunt for *The Avengers* in 2012, that he felt like he "was raised by a pack of wild comedy writers" So writing is clearly in the blood, and represents the family business.

Born Joseph Hill Whedon in June of 1964, Joss Whedon came into a family of writers, and more specifically, a family of TV writers. His grandfather, John Whedon (1905–1991), was a regular writer for *The Donna Reed Show* (1958–1966), and *The Dick Van Dyke Show* (1961–1966), both iconic productions of TV's so-called Golden Age. He even wrote for *Leave it Beaver* (1957–1963), the black-and-white TV series that, rightly or wrongly, has come to represent the 1950s in modern pop culture.

Perhaps more intriguingly for fans of his grandson's oeuvre, the elder Whedon also penned the screenplay for a genre film of another bygone era: the 1970s. During that era, John Whedon authored the screenplay for the obscure Walt Disney movie *Island at the Top of the World*.

Family at the Top of the World

Adapted from a novel by Ian Cameron, *Island at the Top of the World* is a "lost world" fantasy story. This brand of fantasy film proved quite popular in the cinema during the mid-1970s, and typically involved expeditions happening upon, often by accident, prehistoric or alien worlds tucked away from modernity. Some examples of this story type include *The Golden Voyage of Sinbad* (1974), *The Land That Time Forgot* (1974), *At The Earth's Core* (1976), and even Dino De Laurentiis's remake of *King Kong* (1976). John's Whedon's script for *Island at the Top of the World* follows the 1907 expedition of an archaeologist, Professor Ivarsson, played, strangely, by *Good Morning America* host David Hartman, who goes in search of his benefactor's missing son, Donald. The young man has disappeared in the Arctic, near a mythological island that is legendarily a whale burial ground.

As the tale progresses, Ivarsson and his search team embark on this rescue mission, flying a high-tech (for the era) dirigible called the *Hyperion*. The explorers soon discover an isolated land called Astragard that is peopled by primitive and hostile Vikings. The explorers are almost burned at the stake by the local denizens, but manage to escape as natural forces destroy this lost world forever.

Alas, *Island at the Top of the World* tanked at the box office, and a follow-up movie, *The Lost Ones*, was never produced. And yet, if a viewer gazes closely enough at the film, he or she might detect a brand of Whedonesque flair to his grandfather's writing style. For example, the characters are all colorful and memorable, particularly the French captain of the *Hyperion*. Even the very notion of a diverse team of protagonists—a scientist, a French pilot, a concerned father, and a Viking woman, Freja—coming together on one dangerous mission seems at least a bit connected to Joss Whedon's defining ethos. In terms of visuals, the Walt Disney–sponsored film visits ice caves, volcanic lava flows, and a cemetery of giant whale carcasses, and other colorful landscapes. Today, the film is not widely remembered, nor remembered positively by most critics.

Keeping Eclectic Company

Joss Whedon's father, Tom Whedon (1932–2016), also worked regularly in Hollywood as a writer. He was one of the first writers of the CBS (and later PBS) children's series, *Captain Kangaroo* (1955–1984), starring Bob Keeshan, and later went on to work for the Children' Television

Workshop, the company which produced *Sesame Street* (1969–). The company's follow-up series was called *The Electric Company* (1971–1977), and Whedon served as one of the head-writers of this educational and entertaining series.

Comedian and writer Paul Dooley, the talent generally credited with the creation of *The Electric Company*, told this author in an interview in 2004 that "the producers wanted to address actual reading problems, not just A,B,C, 1, 2, 3. They began to realize from *Sesame Street* that kids were learning from it and wanted more. They [the children] were doing so well after one season of *Sesame Street* that they had their alphabet; they had their numbers. They also learned things like fairness and morality."

"The producers started to go further and began to do short words and syllables, and then realized there was a need for another show. *Sesame Street* was for ages three to six, and our show was from ages six to nine, or ten, just when you are learning to read. Research showed them that this was something that kids were ready for, and could make a difference."

The Children's Television Workshop had seven million dollars of funding to produce the first season of the series, but didn't have a title, format, cast, or writing staff, and that's when seven writers, including Whedon, came in to help. With characters like Easy Reader (Morgan Freeman), J. Arthur Crank, and Fargo North Decoder, the children series became a hit, and combined educational entertainment with socially redeeming values. Again, at least a few of those creative elements seem typical of Joss Whedon's writing and directing career, though with less of a focus on actual education, and more detail paid to socially progressive values such as equality and the need (and value) of diversity.

Beyond *The Electric Company*, John Whedon came to be associated with the format where his son would also start his career: the sitcom, or situation comedy. Tom Whedon wrote for the spinoff of the soap-opera parody, *Soap* (1977–1981) called *Benson* (1979–1986), starring Robert Guillaume, as well as *Alice* (1976–1985). The latter series was, for a time, a bit of a pop-culture phenomenon of the disco decade. Based on the 1974 film *Alice Doesn't Live Here Anymore*, the series starred Linda Lavin as Alice, a single mother who moved to Arizona and worked there as a waitress in Mel's Diner, a dive, or greasy spoon.

Barr None

But back to Whedon's formative years in the industry. After graduation, Whedon worked at a video store and authored several spec scripts, including for TV series such as *The Wonder Years* (1988–1993) and a sitcom taking America by storm at the time: *Roseanne* (1988–1997). The latter series, perhaps, has found greater purchase in the cultural firmament especially given its controversial return to the air in 2018.

Roseanne was conceived in the mid-1980s as a blue-collar series about a family matriarch, Roseanne Conner (Roseanne Barr), who, despite a lack of wealth, guided her family with tough love and fairness while living in Lanford, Illinois. In its own way, the ABC series was a feminist series, and concerned Roseanne's close connection with her husband, Dan (John Goodman), and perhaps more importantly, her younger sister Jackie (Laurie Metcalf), and three children. Two of those kids, Darlene (Sara Gilbert) and Becky (Lecy Goranson/Sarah Chalke) were teenage daughters who attempted to navigate adulthood in a difficult world.

Although his first several scripts for the series were heavily rewritten by producers and rendered unrecognizable, Whedon stayed on and became story editor for the series, contributing several well-received teleplays. One episode, "The Little Sister," focuses on the Roseanne-Jackie relationship, and concerns Roseanne's worry for Jackie's safety as she contemplates becoming a police officer. The most fascinating aspect of the episode today, given our understanding of the author's writing obsessions, is a sidebar from the main story about pornography and its impact on female body image. In particular, Roseanne discusses these topics with Becky, and some critics found the moment not just surprising, but topically relevant and "real."

Another *Roseanne* episode by Whedon, "Brain Dead Poets Society" riffs on a then-popular film starring Robin Williams, 1989's *Dead Poets Society*, and sees Darlene grappling with a recitation of a personal poem she has written. At one point in the episode, Roseanne reads her own (old) poetry to her daughter, revealing a new and vulnerable side of the crass-on-the-surface but ultimately loveable character. Some critics saw the episode as a particularly feminist reading of the series situations and characters, and were emotionally moved by the notion of Roseanne, blue-collar Mama, as a one-time poet who had, by economic and life circumstances, been forced to give up her dreams in adulthood. Contrarily, other critics felt that Whedon's high-minded writing felt inorganic to the character, as Roseanne began to name drop obscure poets.

"Brain Dead Poets Society" would not be the last time that Whedon's work would prove divisive. Critics would often disagree on his authorial

Dan Conner (John Goodman) and his wife Roseanne Conner (Roseanne Barr) strike a pose in *Roseanne* (1988-1997), an early series that Joss Whedon wrote for.   *John Muir Photo Archive*

voice and its benefits. Is his trademark wit and intellectual acumen something that fits well with the characters he writes, or an inappropriate
insertion of authorial voice and control in the drama? In later years, in
productions where Whedon exercises more control, he almost universally
features a character that represents his voice, in particular. That voice is
Xander in *Buffy the Vampire Slayer*, or Wash in *Firefly*, for example. But
in *Roseanne*, there is a competing reality: Barr's own voice and character.

Whedon's other episodes for *Roseanne* included titles "House of
Grown-ups," "Chicken Hearts" and "Fathers and Daughters," and author
Ben Joseph at the web magazine *Vulture*, in a 2017 retrospective, categorized Whedon's writing for the series overall in positive terms, as "great."
Joseph writes that Whedon's version of Roseanne Conner is "harsh but
loving, and her meaner moments are written clearly as defense mecha-
nism against everyday life . . . but it's Roseanne's daughters, Becky and
Darlene where Whedon really shines." Joseph praises these young characters, under Whedon's authorial care, as "fully-realized" adolescents with
"distinct personalities." Again, in a limited way, they might even be seen
as proto-Buffy characters. They are adolescents, in high school, navigating the real world at the same time their families grapple with economic
realities.

Roseanne Barr sounded off on Whedon's work for her series in the
year 2013, when he was riding high from the international success of *The
Avengers*. She told Russ Burlingame of the website *Comic Book* that she
thought Whedon has "got a great mind" and that "he can see far ahead."
Roseanne went on to note that she is "so proud of finding him and giving
him his first job when he was only nineteen."

One wonders what Whedon must think of Roseanne Barr today, as
her 2018 revival, while highly rated, went from being an examination
of a blue-collar family to a full-throated supporter of President Donald
Trump. Eventually, Roseanne was fired from the revival series, and the
series itself was canceled, after she posted an overtly racist tweet. (It
was eventually retooled as a series as *The Conners*, featuring the family
members following the death of the matriarch from an offscreen opioid
overdose.)

The seeds for *Roseanne*'s self-destruction may have been evident as
far back as 1989. When celebrating the thirtieth anniversary of the series

on March 19, 2018, Ed Gross interviewed Joss Whedon for the web magazine *Closer* and asked him why he left the series. Whedon's response was diplomatic, but plain: "There were a lot of different factors, but basically the show started to suffer and it was all about *'who's angry at whom?'* And none of it was about what's happening this week on *Roseanne*." In multiple publications and interviews, Whedon has also publicly recalled a meeting Roseanne held with the writing staff. The young Whedon had expected for the meeting to include a pep talk, one pulling the team together. Instead, the meeting was an overt warning from the star of the show for the writing staff to shut up about the behind-the-scenes turmoil on the set, or be fired.

In Between Parents

Before developing his concept for *Buffy the Vampire Slayer*, Joss Whedon was also the staff writer for a short-lived TV series called *Parenthood* (1990–1991), another situation comedy. This is the only iteration of that property, ironically, that has failed to achieve success. The early-nineties TV series is based on the hit film starring Steve Martin, Keanu Reeves, and Mary Steenburgen that, later, became the basis for the hit 2010 series.

Whedon contributed three teleplays to the NBC series: "The Plague," "Small Surprises," and "Fun For Kids," the last with David Tyron King, before its quick cancellation after just twelve installments. The *New York Times* called the first series adaptation of *Parenthood* "one of the most conspicuous failures of the new crop of shows from the television season," and also noted that it arrived during a spell when many movies-to-TV series were failing dramatically. Other notable examples beyond *Parenthood* that season included *Ferris Bueller* (1990), *Working Girl* (1990), *Uncle Buck* (1990), and *Bagdad Café* (1990), all of which were based on successful films.

But while his TV endeavors failed, Joss Whedon was setting his sights on the big screen, and the creation of what remains, to this day, his most well-known character and franchise: *Buffy the Vampire Slayer*.

3

What Was Joss Whedon's First Movie?

Buffy the Vampire Slayer (1992)

Cast

Kristy Swanson:	Buffy
Luke Perry:	Pike
Rutger Hauer:	Lothos
Donald Sutherland:	Merrick
Paul Reubens:	Amilyn
Hilary Swank:	Kimberly
David Arquette:	Bennie
Natasha Wagner:	Cassandra
Candy Clark:	Buffy's Mom
Sasha Jenson:	Grueller
Stephen Root:	Murray

Crew

20th Century Fox Presents a Karzui Enterprises/Sand Dollar Production

Casting:	Johanna Ray
Music:	Carter Burwell
Film Editors:	Camillio Toniolo, Jill Savitt
Production Designer:	Lawrence Miller
Dir. of Photography:	James Hayman

Written by: Joss Whedon
Produced by: Kaz Kazui, F. Howard Rosenman
Directed by: Fran Rubel Kazui
M.P.A.A. Rating: R
Running time: 86 minutes

In a Dark Alley

Buffy the Vampire Slayer is remembered as a franchise that includes a beloved TV series and a spinoff (*Angel* [1999–2004]), multiple video games (such as *Chaos Bleeds*), and a whole series of related comic books. Sarah Michelle Gellar is almost universally identified as Whedon's tough, funny, and vulnerable hero Buffy Summers, the Chosen One. Yet nearly as popular as Buffy herself are the colorful and diverse members of her Scooby Gang: the very proper British watcher, Rupert Giles; the vampire with a soul, Angel; nerdy witch Willow; and hapless, nerdy Xander. This interpretation of Buffy, as well as her sidekicks, however, goes back only to 1997, the dawn of the TV series on the WB.

The first attempt to launch the Buffy franchise actually came five years earlier, in 1992, with a low-budget movie written by Whedon. In 2019, this $7 million movie is not particularly well remembered, even though it can be traced back as the beginning of the concept's core themes, central character, and vocation. It was not until the second attempt to craft *Buffy*, with the TV series, that the concept really connected with audiences. Much in the way that elements of *Alien Resurrection* (1997) play as prehistoric, slightly-off versions of *Firefly*, *Buffy the Vampire Slayer*, the movie, plays as an early, and highly imperfect, variation of a beloved tale.

The origin for *Buffy the Vampire Slayer* is Whedon's oft-told "Dark Alley Story," about a blond girl and a monster in mortal combat, but the monster is the victim, and the girl, the hunter. Whedon was also inspired, while working at a video store, by a film title he saw one day: 1988's *Assault of the Killer Bimbos*. The title of that film, like *Buffy the Vampire Slayer*, suggests female action ("Assault"), power ("Killer"), and a term for females that seems demeaning ("Bimbo"). And of course, like Whedon's later title, *Assault of the Killer Bimbos* boasts a strong element of humor. For a time, Whedon also toyed with another title: "Rhonda the Immortal Waitress."

The Final Girl and the Night of the Comet

In terms of historical context, the time was clearly right in the early 1990s for a female hero whose strength, power, and comedy chops would subvert long-standing genre tropes. The horror films leading up to the early 1990s had already begun to depict women in a very specific, and more evolved, fashion. They had become survivors. In this regard, one might remember Jamie Lee Curtis's Laurie Strode in John Carpenter's *Halloween* (1978) or Heather Langenkamp's Nancy Thompson in Wes Craven's *A Nightmare on Elm Street* (1984). These are the two best-known final girls, but one might also consider Alice (Adrienne King) in the original *Friday the 13th* (1980), or Kirsty (Ashley Laurence) in *Hellraiser* (1987) and *Hellraiser II: Hellbound* (1989). They all survive their particular crises, and prove themselves clever combatants. Scholar Carol J. Clover named this character type as "The Final Girl" and defined her thusly in her landmark 1992 treatise: *Men, Women, and Chainsaws: Gender in the Modern Horror Film*:

> She is the one who encounters the mutilated bodies of her friends and perceives the full extent of the preceding horror and her own peril . . . she alone looks death in the face, but she alone also finds the strength either to stay the killer long enough to be rescued (Ending A) or to kill him/herself (Ending B).

Ironically, the slasher film subgenre was looked at, in the 1980s, as misogynistic, but the final girl theory, from Clover, suggests otherwise. Characters such as Laurie or Nancy are role models, proving to young women that they can navigate the hazards of the world, and overcome them.

Another key step in the development of female figures in horror film came in 1984, with another cinematic influence that Joss Whedon has name-checked in interviews: *Night of the Comet* (1984). This horror

Hero of the Lite Ages: Kristy Swanson stars as Buffy, in the *Buffy the Vampire Slayer* movie from 1992.

John Muir Photo Archive

film, from director Thom Eberdhart, finds two young American women, Regina (Catherine Mary Stewart) and her younger sister, Samantha (Kelli Maroney), surviving an unexpected apocalypse. A comet passes by Earth for the first time in sixty-five million years—ominously, since the extinction of the dinosaurs—and transforms most of the human population into ravenous zombies. Forced to survive and endure in the new world order virtually alone, the sisters take on the apocalypse on their own terms, cracking wise, undercutting authority (represented by some ruthless, surviving scientists), and basically making their way without a patriarchy or established order to tell them what to do.

This author interviewed Eberhardt for the book, *Horror Films of the 1980's* (2007), and learned that the characters of Regina and Samantha in *Night of the Comet* came from the director's interview with two young actresses while shooting a PBS special in the early eighties. The young women he interviewed were thirteen-year-old Valley Girls, and he discussed with them how they would survive an apocalypse. Their answer was that they would "get guns," and they didn't seem disturbed by having to fight for their survival . . . at least until it was pointed out that in the apocalypse, they might not ever get the chance to have boyfriends. The ensuing movie took that idea and depicted Regina and Samantha as fighters, and more than that, heroes. The kind of glib, fun atmosphere evoked in the film feels very much like what Whedon has said he wanted to develop in *Buffy the Vampire Slayer*.

But that's not what happened. At least not at first.

The Myth's First Telling

The 1992 *Buffy* movie concerns a valley girl, Buffy, who lives in Los Angeles with parents who would rather party than raise her right. Even as a big high school dance approaches, a watcher named Merrick (Sutherland) informs the cheerleader, Buffy (Swanson), that she is actually the "Chosen One," the slayer born to destroy vampires. Merrick attempts to acquaint Buffy with her storied heritage, and train her to fight an age-old creature of the night: Lothos (Hauer).

At first, Buffy resists her destiny, but her new responsibilities soon make her old life of shopping, gossiping, and cheerleading feel shallow and empty. All around Buffy, her teenage friends either part ways from the new Buffy, or become vampires themselves. And when Merrick dies tragically at Lothos's hands, Buffy must determine her own destiny.

Helping her out in her big battle is the rebel-without-a-clue, Pike (Perry), and everything comes down to a vampire attack at the senior dance.

Less Than Buff

Budgeted at $9 million, *Buffy the Vampire Slayer* was probably envisioned by those making it not as the next evolution of female figures in the horror film, but as simply a slightly sillier version of the last cinematic vampire hit: *The Lost Boys* (1987). A Sutherland was even cast in each film; Kiefer in *The Lost Boys*; dad Donald, in *Buffy*.

But for Whedon, those making the film simply did not understand, or care, about his vision. He was overruled in terms of casting the role of Buffy, though Kristy Swanson ultimately did a creditable job as the titular character. His ending, which involved Buffy burning down the gym to kill the vampires, also did not make it to screen. And worst of all, the film's director, Fran Kazui, did not seem to understand that the film was not a broad comedy set in a world of vampires, but rather a horror film with some comedic touches. Much of the (absent) heart of the film should have derived from Buffy's relationship with Merrick, her first watcher, and his tragic death. But Whedon found Sutherland rude, and hated his penchant for rewriting his lines, moving away from the script.

"I was there almost all the way through shooting," Whedon told Sarah Dobbs in an interview for *Den of Geek*, in January of 2012. "I pretty much threw up my hands because I could not be around Donald Sutherland any longer."

Whedon knew what was coming: the film received terrible reviews upon its release. Worse, Buffy's potential as a story, and as a character, had not been reached. Indeed, it is difficult to deny, from a modern viewing, that *Buffy the Vampire Slayer* is a flawed film, and more than that, a very flawed carrier of the feminist message Joss Whedon hoped to convey at the time, and later did convey, quite expertly in the TV series of the same.

There is a scene in the film that gets close to the mark, however. Merrick, the Watcher, and representative of the (presumably all-male) Watcher's Council, is dying. Buffy cradles him tenderly in her arms. With his last breath, he tells her something very important: "Do it wrong. Don't play our game."

Thus, Merrick encourages Buffy to embrace her destiny as the Chosen One, but in a manner unique to her. In other words, *she* should be the one who chooses how to be the slayer. The (again, presumably male) establishment has let her, and the other slayers throughout history, down. It has doomed the slayers to a never-ending cycle of life, combat, and death. That cycle means that the slayers are forever denied a "real" life. They are also denied the joys of family, or even of the senior dance, or simple cheerleading. In this moment, with Merrick embracing and encouraging Buffy's own agency, the film lives up to the ideals Whedon has often espoused in terms of his feminism. Female power should not be "ruled" by male power; it should be the province, of course, of those who are female.

Let's go back, again, to "The Dark Alley Story." Joss Whedon has often reported the kernel of the idea that sparked the creation of Buffy. He imagined turning an old horror movie cliché on its head. Basically, he pictured a young, blond woman running, perhaps in an alley, from a famous monster—a vampire, werewolf, or some such thing. But instead of being the victim, the young woman was the hero. She would turn to fight, and she would win. The damsel in distress stereotype would fall away, and in its place a hero would stand.

That noble starting point isn't exactly lost in the film directed by Fran Rubel Kuzui, but the execution of the idea is flawed. There are many reasons for this failure of execution: from budget, to casting, to tone. Although many of Joss Whedon's trademark witticisms hit the mark, such as put-downs ("Get out of my facial") or the comment that a high school student's fashion sense is so "five minutes ago," they are not enough, generally speaking, to support the film or make it something other than a dumb comedy.

In terms of budget, the film's flashbacks to the Dark Ages don't hold up very well, and look like a Renaissance Festival interpretation of Medieval times, rather than a legitimate historical period. Flashbacks on the (also cheap) WB series tend to look much better. Why stress the fakeness of these scenes, in this analysis? They lend an artificiality and distance to Buffy's story. The flashbacks to the lives of previous slayers play like bad community theater and not a "real" memory. This artificiality or theatricality, if one wishes to call it that, only serves to remind one that the movie doesn't, often, feel real.

The casting contributes to this sense of distancing as well. Talented and charismatic actors Rutger Hauer and Paul Reubens play their vampire roles for laughs, rather than menace. A story like this can't work unless the villain is threatening. The audience must fear that the villain could carry the day, and that in doing so, bad things would happen to someone the viewer cares about. Buffy can't be the hero she should be unless she is matched against villains that make her rise to the occasion. The late Rutger Hauer and Reuben are fine actors, of course, but their approach to the vampire characters is all wrong. They don't look good either. In particular, Hauer's usual menace is strongly undercut by bad white-pancake make-up and that hoariest of all vampire fashion clichés: a black-and-red cape. In *Horror Films of the 1990s*, this author described Lothos's appearance as a "creaky visual for a film that should be cutting edge." Ironically, the term "cutting edge" fits perfectly for the ethos of the *Buffy* TV series, with the furrowed "monster" vampire brows, and the depiction of these "demons" as handsome punks, or trench-coated creatures of the night. Surely, the *Buffy* TV productions of the 1990s were the inspiration for the *Twilight*-styled "hot" vampires of the 2000s.

Kristy Swanson is athletic and likable as Buffy in the film, too, but she underplays the vulnerability of Buffy in several key scenes. For instance, during the aforementioned Merrick death scene, she hardly seems to emote at all. The death of the wise old mentor, a key rite of passage in Campbell's Monomyth, should prove the emotional zenith leading up to the third act. Instead, Swanson underplays, and the death scene, including Merrick's advice to Buffy, loses much of its impact. Swanson is a good actress, but she plays a Valley girl who defeats a vampire, not a Valley girl who changes and evolves, and gains some new insight into her identity.

In terms of tone, the film also misses the mark. During the prom set-piece, for example, the high school principal, played by Stephen Root, blithely hands out detentions slips to vampire minions. Again, this "laugh" goes back to the sense of menace the film requires. Instead of presenting the vampires as threatening or dangerous, the film aims for a bad joke, about a principal who can't tell the difference between high school students and the undead. The principal's silly actions undercut the vampires and their reality. And indeed, that would be fine if the aim here were to make a comedy, not a horror film.

Such ill-considered comedic lapses in tone are disturbing, however, because they make the viewer feel like nothing matters, except the jokes. And if nothing matters, then Buffy's heroic journey doesn't matter, either. She becomes, not a great hero, but the center ring at the vampire circus. One can see how Whedon's screenplay aimed for a different tone, but something was lost in translation. This should be the story of the ultimate final girl, Buffy, as she overcomes the monsters in her life. Those monsters make her "woke" to her previous, adolescent self-involvement.

Thanks to Merrick's advice—"Do it wrong"—she realizes she can pursue her destiny in her own way. She doesn't have to be just the slayer. Nor does she have to settle for the callow, empty life of a valley girl. The films should operate on two tracks ably. It should follow Buffy as she conquers the monsters, and as she conquers, literally, adolescence.

Her life is a metaphor for the difficulties of growing up, so Buffy must face the duality of being strong and vulnerable. "You're not like other girls," Pike notes at one point. But, feeling vulnerable, Buffy replies "Yes, I am." She can be the Chosen One *and* want a handsome boy to kiss her, simultaneously. She can rescue the world, and still want to wear a dress. That's what true liberation is, or was fashioned as, in the 1990s, the era of *Ally McBeal* (1997–2002) that some in the media believed was "post-feminism." It's not that a woman can be president of the United States,

Slayer and Beau: Buffy (Kristy Swanson) and Pike (Luke Perry).   *John Muir Photo Archive*

or an astronaut, or a Supreme Court justice. It's that she can do all those things in her own way, without others looking down on her or telling her how to be feminine while doing them. Kristy Swanson is a delightful actress, but she does not project the kind of simultaneous inner-strength and vulnerability that Sarah Michelle Gellar came to master in the TV series. When the SMG Buffy would report she was like other girls, for instance, our collective hearts would break. Here, the same line is just a blip without the same resonance.

The 1992 movie also clearly demonstrates the growing pains of the *Buffy* concept. As fans of the TV series will immediately note, there is no Willow, Xander, Giles, Cordelia, Oz, Spike, Angel, or Hellmouth here. Buffy's only help, after Merrick's death, is the James Dean-ish Pike. Part of Buffy's strength in the TV series comes from her interaction with the Scooby Gang, her "created" family. In the film, Buffy has no truly interesting sidekicks or friends, and so we miss seeing that side of her. The absence of that created family—it's just Buffy and Pike here—may be the defining factor that demonstrates how the movie fails to feel Whedonesque.

Buffy the Vampire Slayer also features some unique touches that aren't carried over to the series. For instance, screen cards tell the audience when it is in the "Dark Ages," and later, in 1990s California, in the "Lite Ages." Similarly, the movie establishes that all slayers are physically recognizable from a mark on their chests, the so-called "Mark of the Coven." The funniest joke of the film is, perhaps, the notion that Buffy mistook the mark for a mole, and had it surgically removed. But slayers such as Kendra, Faith, and the Potentials (in season seven) do not bear the "Mark of the Coven" to identify them. So this idea was dropped from the continuity and never recurs.

Another dropped idea concerns the "early warning system" for slayers when they are in proximity to vampires. As described in the film, this early warning system is, simply put, menstrual cramps. While hunting vampires in a graveyard with Merrick, Buffy feels pain and is unhappy to learn that "PMS" is her "secret weapon." Again, this (bad) joke does not survive the franchise adaptation TV, and that's likely a testament to Whedon's good taste.

Another dramatic shift in the TV series involves the depiction of Buffy's mother, Joyce Summers (Kristine Sutherland). In the TV series, Joyce is a single mom, working hard to provide a stable and loving environment for Buffy. She is a good mother, through and through, even though she is occasionally stern. In the movie, Buffy's mom (Candy Clark) is negligent and completely uninterested in her daughter's life. She would rather live the L.A. party life than parent her daughter.

Buffy (Kristy Swanson) trains to kill Lothos.   *John Muir Photo Archive*

Finally, a key element that made the *Buffy* series so special is the weekly monster-generator: the Hellmouth. Buffy's town of residence in the series, Sunnydale, is on a portal called the Hellmouth. It not only spits out demons and ghouls on a regular basis, but draws other demons and ghouls to the location. So it is a good place for a slayer to remain stationed. In the film, Buffy doesn't truly reckon with a world of the supernatural, only a few silly representative vampires. There is no apparent overarching world, or rather underworld, behind Lothos.

From the mid-eighties to the early 1990s, many horror films sought to walk the line between horror and scares. Tom Holland's *Fright Night* (1985), Dan O'Bannon's *Return of the Living Dead* (1985), and Joel Schumacher's *The Lost Boys* (1987) are a few successful, and memorable, examples. In all those cases, however, the scares outweigh the laughs. Those films don't lose their genre identity. *Buffy the Vampire Slayer* doesn't manage to walk the same difficult line successfully, despite a clever and funny script. What this problem points out, perhaps, is that the best scripts, if not directed by someone who "gets" them, still fall prey to failure. Two of Joss Whedon's earliest, most high-profile films, *Buffy the Vampire Slayer* and *Alien Resurrection*, succumb to this pitfall. The cleverness, the glib dialogue, the gallows humor invoked by the characters are all mistaken, in the wrong directorial hands, as signs of a "comedy."

Although *Buffy the Vampire Slayer* became a name known by horror fans, the movie nonetheless underperformed at the box office. It opened in fifth place, despite showing in nearly two thousand theaters. The film grossed $16 million at the box office, which made it modestly successful. But by and large, critics did not think the mix of horror and comedy was correctly calibrated. *Cinescape Magazine*'s Andrew Hershberger, for instance, noted that in terms both genres, the film "doesn't deliver." John Rosenbaum, the critic for the *Chicago Reader*, felt that the movie was fun, but that it "strained to sell the story," and that Reubens and Hauer were guilty of camping it up as the vampires.

John Bowen, award-winning writer for *Rue Morgue*, saw more of value in the film and felt that "this is one engaging, suspenseful, very funny and sporadically even poignant film," one buttressed by Whedon's "sharp writing."

Over the years, Whedon has not been shy about his displeasure with the 1992 film (and some of its cast's behavior on-set). Like many fans, the creator is not thrilled with this entry, or origin point for a now-beloved (and hopefully immortal) character. In recent years, there have been announcements about a movie reboot of *Buffy the Vampire Slayer*, without Joss Whedon's involvement.

The 1992 film is, to many eyes, a showcase for that kind of folly.

4

Did Joss Whedon Write a "Shitty" *Alien* Movie?

Alien Resurrection (1997)

Cast

Sigourney Weaver:	Ripley
Winona Ryder:	Call
Dominique Pinon:	Vriess
Ron Perlman:	Johner
Gary Dourdain:	Christie
Michael Wincott:	Elgyn
Kim Flowers:	Hillard
Dan Hedaya:	General Perez
J. E. Freeman:	Dr. Wren
Brad Dourif:	Gediman
Raymond Cruz:	Distephano
Leland Orser:	Purvis

Crew

Brandywine Productions, and 20th Century Fox Present *Alien Resurrection*

Casting:	Richard Pagano
Production Designer:	Nigel Phelps
Music:	John Frizzell
Director of Photography:	Darius Khondji

Film Editor:	Herve Schneid
Costume Designer:	Bob Ringwood
Producers:	Bill Badalato, Gordon Carroll, David Giler, Walter Hill
Written by:	Joss Whedon
Directed by:	Jean-Pierre Jeunet
M.P.A.A. Rating:	R
Running time:	109 minutes

Witness the Resurrection

David Fincher's *Alien³* (1992) was not an easy film for audiences to embrace. The third picture in the enduring franchise culminated with Sigourney Weaver's iconic action hero Ellen Ripley committing suicide to save the universe, and then capped things off with no less than three shots of doors slamming, suggesting, metaphorically that the door had been slammed shut on future sequels. Many viewers (including this author) nonetheless love the film for its audacious nature, its ambition, and the fact that it is so far different in tone from its much-appreciated predecessors. What's the fun of a sequel, after all, that hits all the exact same notes, in exactly the same way, as the film that preceded it?

But 20th Century Fox wanted an *Alien* franchise, not *The Passion of Joan of Arc in Space* with Weaver playing a space-age Maria Falconetti, and it was decided that another *Alien* film would be made to make that idea a reality. Enter Joss Whedon, a fan of Ridley Scott's original *Alien*, who was contacted early in the creative process to submit a thirty-page treatment that would have involved, as a main character, the clone of Newt. Newt was Ripley's adopted daughter, in a sense, and a character featured in James Cameron's *Aliens*, but found dead at the start of Fincher's *Alien³*. A clone for Newt would have carried on the franchise's tradition of featuring a female lead, and also offered, at least in a broad way, a connection to the beloved (but dead) Ripley.

Before long, however, a dramatic switch had to be made when Sigourney Weaver was signed on to star in the then-titled "Alien 4," reportedly to the tune of $11 million, and Whedon's script needed to reflect the presence of the cinema's first truly great female action star. Meanwhile, Whedon reported in interviews disparate sources of inspiration for his story of Ripley's clone, including *The Poseidon Adventure* (1972), a tale of cruise-line passengers trapped inside a capsized vessel at sea.

The first *Alien* film to be shot in the United States, *Alien Resurrection*'s budget has been reported as low as $60 million and as high as $80 million, and after directors such as Danny Boyle, Peter Jackson, and Bryan Singer turned down the project, French director Jean-Pierre Jeunet was hired.

The film's shoot was not an untroubled one, with writer Whedon called upon to draft no less than five endings. One occurred on Earth, in a forest. Another also occurred on Earth, though in a junkyard. A third one was set in a desert, and the fourth occurred in a maternity ward. The fifth ending, and the one eventually used in the film, didn't quite make it to Earth, with Ripley battling an alien-human hybrid called a Newborn. This theatrical ending is not of Whedon's making, or preference.

The final film, released near Thanksgiving of 1997, proved a bomb, and quickly became the lowest-grossing film of the franchise (unless one counts *Alien vs. Predator: Requiem* [2007]). It also displeased fans of the franchise who were expecting a film more in the style of *Alien* or *Aliens*.

In 2013, Joss Whedon told interviewer Terri Schwartz at *IFC* that "there is always going to be a shitty 'Alien' movie out there . . . a shitty 'Alien' movie with my name on it." This remark reinforced widely reported comments by the writer from over a decade earlier, in 2005. Whedon had been interviewed for *Bullz-Eye.com* at that point, and opined that it wasn't his script that made the film so poor, but rather the fact that the actors said his lines wrong. Furthermore, Whedon noted that the film was cast, designed, and scored wrong as well.

Whedon has made his negative feelings about *Alien Resurrection* common knowledge, and yet in any study of Whedon's career as a creative artist, it is an important turning point. First, it premiered the same year as one of his great triumphs, the *Buffy the Vampire Slayer* TV series. Second, it forecasted the ironic approach he would bring not only to his heroes, but to other Marvel properties, a decade-and-a-half later. Third, and perhaps most important, *Alien Resurrection* brings to the screen his theme of "created family" in a science-fiction setting.

I heard you ran into these things before.

Two hundred years after Ellen Ripley's death on *Fury 161*, the scientists aboard the military vessel *Auriga* have succeeded in their attempts to clone both Ripley and the alien xenomorph queen growing inside her. The eighth clone of Ripley is the first success in this difficult process. She is seen, however, as a "byproduct," or secondary victory, by the men and women of science. The real value here, according to all, is the birth of the queen. She will be a powerful bio-weapon.

An independent mercenary ship, the *Betty*, brings abducted humans in cryo-sleep to the *Auriga* so they can play host to the new queen's first eggs, which contain the parasitic face huggers. Before long, the *Auriga* is swarming with alien drones, who promptly free themselves from captivity. The crew of the *Betty* attempts to escape from the overrun *Auriga*, but it is on a collision course with Earth.

On the wild ride home, the Ripley clone befriends a synthetic person, Call (Winona Ryder), from the *Betty*, and witnesses the birth of another human/alien hybrid: the Newborn.

No human being is that humane.

It's intriguing to consider how all the *Alien* films differ in tone, approach, and theme or message. The 1979 film from Ridley Scott is all about feelings of isolation and terror in the loneliest, darkest corner of deep space imaginable. Underlying the film is a comparison between three distinctive beings that qualify as survivors: the alien xenomorph, Jones the feline, and, of course, Ellen Ripley, a particularly resourceful human being. Each one of these characters survives or endures a harrowing crisis based on its biological or "natural" make-up (instincts) and individual intelligence.

The reborn Ripley (Sigourney Weaver) listens to Call (Winona Ryder) in *Alien Resurrection* (1997). *John Muir Photo Archive*

By contrast, James Cameron's sequel, *Aliens* (1986), is a gut-crunching, nail-biting war film that forges a space-age comparison to the Vietnam conflict. The Colonial Marines go into a combat situation against a xeno-morph hive with the best technology, the best training, and the finest experience in order to battle an enemy considered "primitive," but which nonetheless challenges their assumptions of technological and intellec-tual dominance. The film also sets up a dynamic battle between maternal figures Ripley and the alien queen.

David Fincher's *Alien³* (1992) categorically eschews thrills and action in favor of a dark, intimate story about Ripley's tortured soul. Is it worth it to survive, personally, if the entire human race is jeopardized by pur-suit of that end? In this case, Ripley confronts her own strength—her innate ability to survive and adapt to difficult scenarios—and judges that there is a higher human value than continued existence. The film serves as a space-age Christ parable, and as an exploration of spirituality and sacrifice.

Unlike the other *Alien* films, Jean-Pierre Jeunet's *Alien Resurrection* is a dark comedy, about, among other things, human folly. The film's main character, a clone of Ripley, stands outside humanity and quips about the circumstances and nature of the failings she witnesses. She is an observer of human nature, but also, surprisingly, a defender.

In case you can't tell, it's all very Whedonesque.

And by that descriptor, one must understand: the film drips with irony. In this case, irony might be defined as an event that seems contrary to what one expects, and therefore proves amusing. Overall, *Alien Resurrection* acts as an observation not about the qualities that separate humans from the drooling xenomorphs, but rather those that connect us or tie us to them. In *Aliens*, Ripley tells Burke that she isn't certain which species is worse. At least you don't see the xenomorphs trying to fuck each other over for "a goddamned percentage."

That statement or observation seems to be the guiding principle, the overarching leitmotif of *Alien Resurrection*. The film goes to some lengths to eliminate the distance, essentially, between aliens and humans, and asks us to put aside moral absolutes or precepts about good and evil, and consider them in more relativistic terms. But the crucial matter to understand here is that the filmmakers undertake this task via Joss Whedon's trademark glib fashion, often through quips, jokes, and moments that puncture the "seriousness" of the enterprise. The humor in the film is not straight-up funny, but rather cold, caustic, and even bitter. The humor arises at a considerable distance from humanity itself. It's as if the Ripley clone—no longer entirely human—wrote the screenplay herself.

Alien Resurrection finds a lot of things about the human race funny, but understands, simultaneously—as Ripley explicitly observes in the movie—that they "aren't really funny at all." No, those things are actually really sad. The things that Ripley sees and comes to understand speak poorly of us as a species. We see humans exploiting other humans. We see humans treating aliens, androids, and human beings as slaves, basically. The only way to express these unpleasant truths involving human nature, therefore, is via the attitude of absurdist humor. Otherwise, the mode of expression will be . . . tears—torrents of terrible, never-ending tears.

The two most human characters in the film, importantly, aren't human at all. *Alien Resurrection*'s protagonist is a hybrid clone, and therefore able to do something neither human nor alien can do: empathize for both sides in the conflict aboard the *Auriga*. And Call is a synthetic android, a human in appearance, but not in nature. Yet Call undertakes her mission to stop the aliens out of the goodness of her (artificial?) heart. The alien terror cannot be unleashed on the galaxy, so Call must take action, must intervene, no matter the cost to her own existence. To some, that might be the very definition of heroism.

Notably, both characters see beyond the human perspective, and appear to the viewer as . . . female. They are women. But they are separate and different from the humans (mostly male) around them, and, in the end, forge a kind of "created family," with Ripley taking on the role of mother figure, and Call, in a way, acting as her child. Separately, Ripley and Call fit in nowhere in corrupt human society, but come to care for

Up close again, Ripley (Weaver) and Call (Ryder) lean on each other again, during the climax of *Alien Resurrection*.   *John Muir Photo Archive*

each other and build a relationship that doesn't factor in "human" as membership for joining.

This description no doubt makes the film sound compelling. Yet the big problem with *Alien Resurrection* is that some touches of humor are downright dreadful, and thereby corrupt the sense of reality one has come to expect in the *Alien* films. By the same token, the dark comedy approach accomplishes two important things.

First, it reflects the aforementioned cynical, caustic view of mankind. The film notes that man is, finally, no better than acid-bleeding, chest-bursting aliens. The gap between species has been bridged. Ripley herself is that bridge, though she has carved out for herself some unique sense of morality, as most humans would understand it.

Second, the attempt to take on an *Alien* movie with a fresh tone (the dark comedy) honors the lineage and tradition of these films. No two in the series are the same; no two cover the same territory.

One illuminating way to view *Alien Resurrection* is as the first movement of an ultimately unrealized second trilogy. The separate setting of the film—two hundred years in the future—the new heroine (not Ripley, but a hybrid clone), and even the enemy (not the Weyland-Yutani Company, but the military), all encourage this reading of the film's attempt to be the genesis of a new series. If a viewer looks at the film in such a way, exploring the interaction of aliens and humans in a much closer, much more intertwined fashion, *Alien Resurrection* is a more gratifying experience.

Indeed, this was actually part of the plan. Whedon was, at one point, planning to write the fifth *Alien* film, which would have featured Ripley battling aliens on Earth. This movie is clearly meant as a preamble to that larger tale. Since this is an intentional "first chapter," it is difficult to judge its success in the absence of the second and third picture in this second *Alien* trilogy.

Alien Resurrection goes a long way toward making the point that "true" evil may not come down to the physical properties that divide species. Rather, the film suggests, an organism who attempts to co-opt the life of another organism for its own agenda is the true face of evil. The aliens, of course, utilize human beings as breeding material for their life-cycle. They do this, however, by instinct, not out of malice. It's *what* they are.

But the humans of *Alien Resurrection* absolutely use other human beings to make money, to make weapons, or otherwise further selfish needs and agendas. They put these ahead of humanity, of human life. Their decision to co-opt other organisms is conscious, determined. It's *who* they are.

This idea is played out in regards to Ripley—now a clone—and the fact that seven previous versions of her were produced and discarded without thought, as merely a means to an end. The clones are just "meat," with no thought given to what they feel or require to survive. Quality of life isn't even a consideration. The Ripley clone is permitted to live only because the scientists on the *Auriga* possess a certain level of curiosity about her.

That's a reason that involves them and their needs, not Ripley or hers. Dr. Gediman (Brad Dourif) and Dr. Wren (J. E. Freeman)—the two characters Whedon has gone on record about as being upset about the casting selections—treat the aliens in much the same way as they treat Ripley: *as meat*. They clone the alien queen, induce her life-cycle (egg-laying), and then attempt to control the behavior of her progeny. The mission of the scientists is to make a new weapon for General Perez (Dan Hedaya), and to control that new weapon with force. No thought is given to these creatures as living organisms. They are bio-weapons, no more.

Even the apparent "protagonists" of *Alien Resurrection*—the crew of the *Betty*—knowingly undertake action for an evil agenda. They steal a traveling spaceship crew in hyper-sleep and sell them for cash so they can get rich. Like the scientists or General Perez, the crew people have decided that their selfish needs are more important than self-determination or quality of life. In particular, Johner derives pleasure from hurting people. He drops knives into Vriesse's paralyzed leg for sport, since Vriess is paralyzed and can't feel pain.

The only person for whom this observation of avarice, greed, and desire is not true is the Ripley clone. She is a creature of two worlds, of two separate physiologies and she doesn't attempt to "use" others for her own purposes. In fact, her mission is often the opposite of that behavior. For example, Ripley elects to burn the surviving clones, one through seven, because one of them begs for death; for peace. Ripley obliges because the creature is doomed not just to pain, but to slavery at the hands of those who would use it. Ripley assesses that such slavery is no way to live, and it is right and noble to obey the clone's wishes and terminate her. At the same time that Ripley can see the humanity of the clones, she can recognize the innocence of the Newborn—another alien/human fusion—and regret its death.

For the first time in the *Alien* series, Ripley is in the position, then, of weighing the two sides of this conflict. In the past, she has always tried to destroy the aliens at all costs, as a danger to mankind and the universe. In *Alien Resurrection*, the plot develops in such a way that it is, finally, crystal clear, that humans are no better than the aliens; that both species are dangerous to the safety of the universe. Consider again, there are no really "good humans" in the film. Call is the most humane character, but she's an android. Vriess and Christie are okay, but they still go along with the mission to hijack the cryo-tubes, don't they?

Consisting of human and alien nature for the first time, Ripley now understands both species, and develops a gallows sense of humor or irony about them. She finds death funny. Not because suffering is funny. But because the behavior of the two species surrounding her has made death inevitable, a predictable punch line to a very bad joke. Essentially, *Alien Resurrection* re-positions Ripley in the drama. In the first movement of an apparent new trilogy, she is not the savior of mankind as she was in the first three films, but the arbiter of values, weighing one side against the other; keeping in check the worst proclivities of each.

And her ultimate determination of evil comes down to a simple choice of control. Evil attempts to control the life of others without any regard for its feelings, suffering, or emotional needs and desires. The Newborn, finally, must die, because it kills without reason. The clones must die, because they have been created not to live, but to serve an end that makes them suffer interminable pain.

Please sense the irony here. Joss Whedon writes the most caustic entry in the series, but also allows, by the same token, for the series to focus on empathy, for the first time. The universe is no longer us vs. them, good vs. evil. Instead, the universe is now riddled with shades of gray, and every creature—experimental clone, human being, or drooling alien—must be taken on its own terms.

So when *Alien Resurrection* is at its cold, bitter best, it is as an examination not of a good species and a bad species, but two species that hurt people and the individuals who are exceptions to the rules. Ripley—the only one who can empathize with both viewpoints—becomes the one to weigh the scales. This idea could have developed further in future films, and it would have been fascinating to see where the idea went had a second full trilogy developed. Imagine two additional films in which the alien and human worlds grow closer and closer, more alike than unlike, and one starts to get a notion of where the material could go.

How are such ideas expressed in the film? Ripley's biology is an indicator of her new position. She bleeds red acid, which signifies her mixed heritage. Similarly, the cartoony, two-dimensional nature of the scientists in the film—one mad (Gediman), one evil (Wrenn)—makes us understand that humanity's villainy has risen to the same extreme level as that of the alien, or even worse. Ripley, "the fast learner" sees the humans for what they are: pretenders to power. And she is, overall, disconnected from human concerns. There really is no human character in the film to like, and that makes the movie's point, but in some way, it also distances the viewer from the players.

Ripley (Weaver) attempts to prove her alien nature to Call (Ryder).   *John Muir Photo Archive*

Ripley's inappropriate sense of humor—"Who do I have to fuck to get off this boat?"—is similarly a signifier that she no longer is exclusively on our side. She finds things funny, but knows they aren't. They are funny to her because her new genetic make-up has changed her very nature. She is now the child (and mother, simultaneously) of the aliens, as well as, physiologically speaking, mostly human.

The *Southland Times* called *Alien Resurrection* "grotesque and captivating" and the "best" of the series (January 9, 1998, page 12). This author agrees with the first observation, if not the second. The film is unbelievably grotesque, perhaps the most of the series. And it is captivating in the sense that we must ask ourselves, for the first time, about Ripley's loyalties and motivations. As the center of the film, she stands as an ambiguous figure, one who could side with either species. *Alien Resurrection* succeeds to the level it does, perhaps, because it is the first film that suggests a balance between human and alien perspectives, and posits a force—the Ripley clone—who can navigate such a balance.

A bitter, caustic film that acknowledges man's fatal flaws, *Alien Resurrection*'s ideas are often superior to the execution of the material. It's one thing to add a certain level of detached glibness to Ripley's mode of expression. It's quite another to go for dumb physical comedy in the body of the film itself. In its ambitious attempt to be a dark, observational comedy about human foibles and transport the series in a new direction, *Alien Resurrection* sometimes makes the characters and world of Ripley and the aliens a live-action cartoon.

Specifically, the frightful power of the aliens has been made a laughing-stock, particularly during the horrendous sequence in which the monster's signature inner jaw pulps the head of General Perez (a grievously miscast Dan Hedaya). Perez stands there, not even unbalanced by the severe impact, and picks out with his fingers the back of his skull and brain . . . presumably while the alien stands there waiting for him to make his next move. The scene is so poorly acted, so poorly presented that one can't tell if it's supposed to be funny or horrific. Instead, it's just a mess. It is a reality-breaking moment that takes viewers out of the film.

Also, the film—forged in the unfortunate and unsubtle era of *Face-Off* (1997) and *Con-Air* (1997)—is mired in stupid, macho BMF-ism. That's Bad Motherfucker-ism, in case you didn't recognize the acronym. Johner is a bad MF. Christie is a bad MF. Vriess, a fellow in a wheelchair, is also a bad MF. Of course, Ripley is a bad MF, too. Viewers are asked again and again to like these characters because they're simply too cool for school. Ooh, look at those big guns. Look at how Christie can ace the ricochet shots! Meanwhile, there's not a single supporting character in the film who deserves to eat at the same lunch table as Parker, Brett, Hudson, Hicks, Bishop, 85, or Clements. They are all walking/talking clichés from the action cinema with only the most basic of "qualities." And, incidentally, they are also pretty clearly the early versions of Joss Whedon's *Serenity* crew.

This point is perhaps the big takeaway regarding *Alien Resurrection*'s importance to Joss Whedon's career: the very clear similarity between the *Betty* and the *Serenity*, and both crews. Both ships are falling apart and deemed primitive, and both ships house mercenaries.

Johner is the same dumb soldier guy/comic relief as *Firefly*'s Jayne (Adam Baldwin). Both are sexist dopes who are good with guns. And the captain of the *Betty*, Elgyn, navigates treacherous terrain with the same sort of amoral, do-whatever-it-takes-to-survive moral compass as Mal Reynolds (Nathan Fillion) does, at least occasionally. Call (Ryder) is the easy-to-dismiss Pixie girl with a secret and inner strength, much like River Tam (Summer Glau).

Even the cockpit of the *Betty* resembles—at least a little—*Serenity*'s command deck. Whedon certainly demonstrated how, in a continuing series, he could take characters painted with such broad strokes and transform them into beloved, nuanced individuals. The crew of the *Betty* doesn't quite get there in *Alien Resurrection*, but it is virtually impossible not to see them as the prototypes for *Firefly*'s dramatis personae.

Here, however, character development is much less pronounced. The macho approach of rampant BMF-ism reaches the height (or, perhaps, depths) of idiocy when Larry Purvis (Leland Orser)—a man carrying a chest-buster inside of him—also ascends to that territory. During his last moments of life, he assaults an evil scientist, Dr. Wrenn, and manages to position his opponent at just the right place, in just the right moment, so that the emerging chest-buster breaks not just through his own ruptured chest, but—conveniently—through Wrenn's skull.

It's a ludicrous, over-the-top moment meant to be intense and manic, but in concept and execution, much like the Hedaya scenes, proves stupid beyond measure. It's difficult to like the film, and its "dark comedy" approach when so many big moments pander to dumb action convention.

Also, some of the verbal humor in *Alien Resurrection* doesn't work in either concept or delivery. "Who were you expecting, *Santa Claus?*" asks Vriess at a crucial juncture, and the moment flat-lines. The humor in the film is so hit-or-miss that *Alien Resurrection* veers between groans and giggles throughout most of its run.

As noted above, Whedon once reported that it wasn't that his script was altered that made *Alien Resurrection* so poor, it was everything that came in the production *after* the script: the casting, the costumes, even the creature design. One can see his point. Winona Ryder is underwhelming as Call, and Hedaya never manages to be convincing as a military general. He could get the job, but he couldn't do the job, to quote his character from *Joe vs. the Volcano* (1991).

In terms of costumes, *Alien Resurrection* dresses all of its evil scientists in—wait for it—futuristic white lab coats, just so the audience understands that, you know, they are scientists. The cartoony aspects of this once-realistic universe have been ramped up to a ludicrous degree. Similarly, the film lacks any driving sense of momentum. *The Poseidon Adventure* (1972) is one obvious template for the story: survivors of a disaster must make their way through a wrecked ship. But there's no sense of how close or how far the survivors are at any given moment from their destination (the hanger bay). There's no sense that they are making progress, either, toward their destination. There's a stop at the clone lab, a stop at the face-hugger lab, an underwater swim, a stop at a chapel, and then a dash for the dock. These incidents feel episodic, and don't build to anything significant.

Similarly, this is the first *Alien* film in which the alien doesn't cast a shadow over the movie even when it is not onscreen. The aliens are missing in action for long spells in *Alien Resurrection*, and audiences just don't feel the danger of their hidden presence. There's no belief that they could be hiding around any corner, waiting to strike.

Conversely, *Alien Resurrection*'s big set-piece is visually arresting indeed. It involves the survivors aboard the *Auriga* swimming through a flooded compartment of the ship in hopes of reaching safety. It's a long swim, too, and the scene culminates with swimming aliens in pursuit. The scene is tense and well shot, as characters struggle to hold their breath and swim for their lives as the aliens, the equivalent of great white sharks, circle in for the kill. And even better, it's all a trap, set to make the oxygen-starved swimmers open up wide . . . in a room of eggs and face huggers. This sequence possesses a surfeit of energy and style, and gives the movie a real kick. If the rest of the movie had lived up to this set-piece, *Alien Resurrection* might be remembered differently.

Perhaps the film's greatest virtue is that it attempts something different in the franchise, and now that particular thing is behind it, one must no longer endure it. The dark comedy and irony angle—the exaggerated colors and characters—has been done, and now the series can move on and attempt another, hopefully more fruitful approach. *Alien Covenant* (2017) somehow still didn't make the grade.

So one can champion *Alien Resurrection* for its decision to, in honor of the series, try something new. But finally, that "dark comedy" is not the most successful approach for the franchise, even considering Joss Whedon's wit. Even acknowledging that judgment, one can't help but wonder what might have been: what a second trilogy—with *Resurrection* as the start point, not a dead end—might have looked like. There are moments and images of greatness in *Alien Resurrection*, but overall, the film doesn't capitalize on them.

Others, though not apparently Joss Whedon himself, disagree with this assessment. On the film's twentieth anniversary, a writer for *VICE*, Frederick Blichert, wrote "'Alien Resurrection' is a Franchise High Point—Fight Me!" and commented on the fact that we can see something from this modern vantage point that, perhaps, was not apparent in 1997.

Specifically, the author writes that nearly "every Whedon project seems to have a woman with special abilities given to her by one shadowy cabal of men or another. Inevitably, she rebels and takes back her autonomy with force." Certainly, this journey can be applied to Ripley in this film as easily as it is to Buffy Summers, Echo, or River Tam. In 1997, some fans of the *Alien* franchise might not have seen "Ripley's rampage" as "patriarchy smashing" (in the words of Blichert) in the same manner as we interpret the actions of these other Whedon characters.

Today, the connection is indeed clearer. Buffy and all the slayers before her were "gifted" (or cursed) by the Watcher's Council, and their slayer powers were to be monitored and controlled. Rossum developed the dolls in *Dollhouse* to be toys, until those toys found the power to rebel. Ripley is the child of ruthless mad scientists, and alien biology, but she chooses her own path (in her created family with Call), rather than kowtow to the authority of the men who "made her."

So in addition to being merely "a shitty" *Alien* movie, *Resurrection* might be remembered as the first big science-fiction project in which Whedon's strong women and created families take center stage.

Part II

The Script Doctor Is In

5

Did Joss Whedon Write a Hit Movie and Not Get Any Credit for It?

Speed (1994)

Cast

Keanu Reeves:	Jack Traven
Dennis Hopper:	Howard Payne
Sandra Bullock:	Annie
Joe Morton:	Captain McMahon
Jeff Daniels:	Harry Temple
Alan Ruck:	Stephens
Glen Plummer:	Richard Lineback
Beth Grant:	Helen
Hawthorne James:	Sam
Carlos Carrasco:	Ortiz

Crew

20th Century Fox Presents a Mark Gordon Production, a Jan de Bont Film

Casting:	Risa Bramon Garcia, Billy Hopkins
Costume Designer:	Ellen Mirojnick
Music:	Mark Mancina
Film Editor:	John Wright
Production Designer:	Jackson De Govia

Director of Photography: Andrzej Bartkowkiak
Written by: Graham Yost
Produced by: Mark Gordon
Directed by: Jan de Bont
M.P.A.A. Rating: R
Running time: 116 minutes

Pop quiz, hot shot.

In Los Angeles, a SWAT team led by Captain McMahon (Joe Morton) is called to a skyscraper when a mad bomber (Dennis Hopper) rigs a bomb to an elevator, threatening to kill its occupants. McMahon's men, including Jack Traven (Keanu Reeves) and Harry Temple (Jeff Daniels), manage to neutralize the threat by rigging a winch on the roof to the damaged elevator. This vexes the bomber, who was holding the city ransom for $3 million.

The resentful bomber sees Jack and Harry awarded medals by the city for their valor and ingenuity during the elevator crisis, and executes his next bombing. After getting Jack's attention by destroying one city bus, the bomber informs the officer (by phone) that there is an explosive on a second bus. The bomb becomes operative when the bus goes above fifty miles per hour. And the bomb will explode if the bus goes below that same speed.

Jack races to board Bus 2525 before the bomb goes live, but only makes it aboard after the bus has reached fifty miles an hour. When the bus driver, Sam (Hawthorne James), is shot during a scuffle with another passenger, a confident but flighty passenger, Annie (Sandra Bullock), takes the wheel for a wild ride.

Now, with Harry's guidance from the office, Jack must figure out a way to defuse the bomb, and save all the passengers aboard. Worse, he is certain that, somehow, the resentful bomber is watching his every move.

I feel the need. The need for . . .

One of the most amazing surprises at the cinema in 1994 was the high-spirited Jan de Bont film, *Speed*. The frenetic, exciting, and infinitely entertaining action film wasn't really on anyone's radar when it opened to strong reviews, and immense audience appreciation. In part, the lack of expectations for the film is a result of the genre, or subgenre, from which it hails. In 1994, it was easy to categorize the film as nothing but "Die Hard on a Bus."

Jack Traven (Keanu Reeves) attempts to stop a runaway bus with a bomb on board in *Speed* (1994).   *John Muir Photo Archive*

But permit me to back up and give a little historical context. John McTiernan's *Die Hard* starring Bruce Willis is, without exaggeration, the movie that launched a hundred or so cinematic and TV knockoffs. This thirty-year-old blockbuster of 1988 so dramatically and thoroughly revolutionized the action genre at the end of the eighties in fact that—for at least half-a-decade—virtually every new entry in the genre was described as "Die Hard in a (fill in the blank)." Die Hard on a Battleship (*Under Siege* [1992]), Die Hard on a Train (*Under Siege 2* [1995]), Die Hard on a Plane (*Passenger 57* [1992]), *Executive Decision* [1996]), and even Die Hard in a Hockey Stadium (*Sudden Death* [1995]).

On TV, even *Star Trek: The Next Generation* presented "Die Hard on a Starship" in the episode "Starship Mine," with Captain Jean Luc Picard (Patrick Stewart) alone on the *Enterprise*, working to stop a team of terrorists from an elaborate theft.

So, in 1994, the concept of "Die Hard on a Bus" hardly seemed special, unique, or even particularly worthy of note. What was noteworthy, perhaps, was the film's creative team. Graham Yost wrote the imaginative script, and Jan de Bont—John McTiernan's go-to cinematographer—was sitting in the director's chair. In front of the camera, the film also had a solid, and, again, surprising cast. Keanu Reeves and Sandra Bullock were not yet superstars at this juncture, and the young talents gave their all in their respective roles of Jack Traven and Annie. And anchoring the film were veteran stalwarts Dennis Hopper, Jeff Daniels, and Joe Morton.

Joss Whedon came aboard the film, originally titled "Minimum Speed," as script doctor, and Yost was pleased at his arrival. Prior to Whedon's arrival, Yost's script had been rewritten by someone else, and he was unhappy with the new draft. In interviews, Yost has termed this period of the film's development as the "dark night" of his soul, until Joss Whedon came aboard to rewrite the script one week before production, and gave it the tonal "bounce" for which his work is famous.

One major change Whedon made to the script involved the tourist character played by Alan Ruck. Originally this supporting character was a rather unlikable lawyer trapped on the runaway bus, but Whedon transformed him into the innocent (but oddly sweet) "yokel" tourist in L.A. Part of the reason, according to Whedon: How many L.A. lawyers do you know who take the bus?

Whedon also punched up the dialogue, and other changes from inception to completion involved Annie's character. At one point she was a stand-up comic. Also, the famous line "Pop quiz, hot shot" (which Whedon apparently hates . . .) was added to the script. Throughout Whedon's rewrite the primary goal was to make the brilliant but fantastic premise work, despite moments that might require excessive suspension of disbelief. An example: the moment when the speeding bus jumps a gap on an elevated freeway successfully, defying physics in the process. For Whedon, this exercise was about knowing "all of the clichés . . . and how to avoid them," according to an interview conducted by Lauren Dica in *The Huffington Post*, on the film's twentieth anniversary. The resulting film, and working experience, was one of which Whedon was proud, and he told Dica he had a "great time" on *Speed*.

Whedon did get studio credit for his work on the film, but the Writer's Guild soon took it away, and his name was promptly removed from posters. Whedon has said in interviews that he has the only copy of the poster that has his name on it, and it's an odd thing to consider. This is a film for which Whedon did much work, and that writing actually survives to screen. Yet he is not credited at all. This is despite the fact that, according to Yost (as reported in 2003 by the *Post-Star*'s Kate O'Hare), that Whedon rewrote roughly 99 percent of the film's dialogue. So *Speed* very much feels "Whedonesque," and it is baffling that his name is not officially associated with the film, a result that Whedon found devastating.

You thought you needed another challenge or something?

There are a number of reasons why *Speed* works so brilliantly, even twenty-five years later. First and foremost, the film's title matches its dramatic approach. The movie is very much about speed, or perhaps more accurately, movement. The screenplay is divided into roughly three events, and three opportunities for tense movement, or velocity. The first act involves an elevator threatening to plummet to its doom. The main body of the film involves that beloved city bus, and its accelerating trek around the city at over fifty miles an hour. And the third act focuses on a runaway subway train, again—like each of the two previous vehicles—spinning out of control. The shifts from elevator to bus to subway make the film constantly feel fresh and vibrant. There is no time for the audience to grow weary of any setting before the film has moved onto the next set-piece and renewed itself, and its premise. Each set-piece involves speed, and each set-piece is dynamic.

From the film's first frames, one can see Jan de Bont is veritably obsessed with this concept of speed. The opening credits are displayed as the camera moves down (quickly) through an elevator shaft, to the beat of Mark Mancina's energetic, pulse-pounding music. Although the shaft is a model or miniature, this fact is undetectable. The movie begins with motion, and never comes to anything approximating a hard stop, until the end credits roll.

But *Speed*'s sense of constant velocity is not the film's only strength. The dialogue moves fast, and is incredibly snappy, and establishes character brilliantly. The gum-chewing, polite-to-a-fault Jack Traven is unlike any other action hero of the era. He's serious, but not grim, dedicated, but not superhuman. He fits in well with the "everyman" mode of action hero popular at the time, which supplanted the Rambo superman mode, but he is not sarcastic, or constantly throwing out one-liners in the manner of a John McClane. Jack's relationship with his mentor, Harry Temple, is a powerful connection, as well, with Harry acting as a teacher, and constantly demanding that Jack not just move, but think. "Do you listen?" "You better think?" "Luck runs out." Harry says all these things to Jack, and in the process, builds up Jack's character. The glory of *Speed* is, in large part, that even though Jack is a muscle-bound hunk, he is also quite the thinker, learning how to take variables "out of the equation," so that lives can be saved. His character, like Whedon's rewrite, applies thought (or wit) to constant motion.

Sandra Bullock's Annie is also a joy, and stands as the emotional heart of the film. At one point, she believes that she has killed an infant, after the bus strikes a baby carriage in an intersection. She breaks down in horror (as does the audience, wondering if the movie will go to that dark place, the murder of an innocent child by another innocent), but it is soon revealed that the carriage was filled with tin cans to be recycled, not a baby.

Moments such as these go far to establish Annie's innate goodness. She is sweet and caring, but also determined, literally "driving" the movie towards its destination. She is the reason that Jack is in the job he is, saving people's lives. She is the good person who represents the overall good of the community.

Through its leads, *Speed* does the near impossible for an action film of this size and scope: it makes its people seem oddly real and affecting.

Jack (Reeves) and Annie (Sandra Bullock) share an emotional moment after escaping from *Speed*'s exploding bus.   *John Muir Photo Archive*

This facet of the drama is crucial when the movie does leap to illogic and fantasy. The freeway gap jump would not succeed if the audience did not care about the characters, and in large part this is because of the screenplay and the performances. The characters aren't generic or familiar, but register as real humans in an unreal situation. While *Speed* features many of the familiar excesses of 1990s action films—big explosions, all extended endlessly via clever cutting, for instance, or a character like Helen, who is a sacrificial lamb, designed purely to create increased audience investment, the film nonetheless boasts an uncharacteristic wit and charm that not only makes it different, but extremely memorable. The last act, seemingly by design, literally goes off the tracks, as if in acknowledgment that there is no more dramatic one-upping of the stakes that can be done at this juncture. But then the film closes in stillness, Jack and Annie wrapped in an embrace, inside an overturned, stalled train car. Everything has finally, at long last, stopped moving and the audience is left with two characters it loves, and wants to see together. It may be a crowd-pleaser, but *Speed* is a brilliantly wrought crowd-pleaser.

It's too bad that Keanu Reeves was not involved in *Speed 2: Cruise Control*, so that the Annie-Jack relationship had an opportunity to continue. Notably, that follow-up film also lacks the light, bouncy touch of Whedon's dialogue and character-building. It was, finally, despite best intentions, just Die Hard on a Cruise Ship.

6

Did Joss Whedon Ever Get Nominated for an Oscar?

Toy Story (1995)

Cast

Tom Hanks:	Woody
Tim Allen:	Buzz Lightyear
Don Rickles:	Mr. Potato Head
Jim Varney:	Slinky Dog
Wallace Shawn:	Rex
Annie Potts:	Bo Peep
John Morris:	Andy
Erik von Detten:	Sid
Laurie Metcalf:	Andy's Mom
R. Lee Ermey:	Sergeant

Crew

Pixar Animation Studios and Walt Disney Pictures

Music:	Randy Newman
Edited by:	Robert Gordon, Lee Unkrich
Produced by:	Ralph Guggenheim, Bonnie Arnold
Story by:	John Lasseter, Peter Doctor, Andrew Stanton, Joe Ranft
Screenplay:	Joss Whedon, Andrew Stanton, Joel Cohen, Alec Sokolow

Directed by:	John Lasseter
M.P.A.A. Rating:	G
Running Time:	81 minutes

You've got a friend in me.

To little Andy (Morris), his beloved toys like the cowboy Woody (Tom Hanks), are things with which to play, and to share adventures. But unbeknown to him, or his mom (Laurie Metcalf) for that matter, all the toys in Andy's room, including Rex the dinosaur (Wallace Shawn), Bo Peep (Annie Potts) and Slinky (Jim Varney) are actually living beings with rich, human, emotional lives.

When not in Andy's presence, these toys come to life, and express their wants, needs, and neuroses. For one of these toys, Woody, the deepest neurosis—jealousy—comes to life and can't be squelched when Andy gets a new favorite toy: the upright, square-jawed space ranger Buzz Lightyear (Tim Allen). Buzz doesn't realize he is a toy, instead believing he is an actual astronaut fighting the evil forces in the galaxy.

Woody and Buzz clash, but the two toys unexpectedly grow close when they fall into the clutches of Sid, Andy's next-door neighbor. Unlike Andy, Sid is rough, even sadistic, with his toys, dissecting and torturing them on a regular basis.

Now the cowboy and space-man buddies must join forces to survive Sid's house of horrors and get back to Andy and their friends. But Andy is moving, and if the toys don't escape soon, they will never see Andy again.

We toys can see everything.

Toy Story, the world's first fully computer-animated film, is today considered a classic and more than that, the gold standard in animation. The film is a rite of passage for every generation of young child raised from 1995 to the present.

However, these achievements might not have been the case, since the film faced a turbulent genesis and development stage in the early 1990s. Pixar's John Lasseter came up with the concept of toys that come to life, which Joss Whedon has termed "gold." But the specific characters were not always the beloved ones we would recognize and love today.

In particular, in early drafts of *Toy Story*, Woody was not likable or kind, but bitter and resentful. Similarly, Buzz Lightyear's dramatic story-arc—his discovery that he is in fact a toy, and not an astronaut—was also something not original to the first iteration of the story. At one point, the film's creators also wanted to make the film a musical, in the vein of something like *The Little Mermaid* (1989), or *The Lion King* (1994), though the idea was quickly dropped.

Overall, the film's screenplay seemed to lack heart, which is difficult to imagine today, given the final shape of the movie. But in fact, the film's script was deemed so poor that Walt Disney Studios threatened to close the project down and move on. By then a successful script doctor, Joss Whedon came aboard for three weeks to do a rewrite, but ended up staying on board for six months, reshaping, primarily, the characters and dialogue in the film. Whedon is widely credited with transforming the character of Woody to make him more likable and less petty, and adding the neurotic dinosaur Rex, a study in contradictions, to the "created family" of toys.

One of Whedon's ideas that did not make it into the film would have marked it as more concretely belonging to his oeuvre. Originally, Whedon wanted Buzz and Woody to be rescued from Sid's clutches by none other than Barbie, a toy deliberately recast in the role of Linda Hamilton's Sarah Connor, from *Terminator 2: Judgment Day* (1991). For Whedon, the radical feminist, Barbie's presence as the hero who saves the day would have been a perfect embodiment of his beliefs. Alas, Mattel did not approve the use of their trademark toy in the film, meaning that other arrangements had to be made. This was unfortunate, in part because Whedon saw Barbie's heroic role as an opportunity to transmit a message of feminism or female empowerment to a young audience, a message in keeping with his later work on *Buffy the Vampire Slayer*, and *Dollhouse*. In retrospect, it's fascinating to watch how Whedon attempted to bring his specific interests (created families and strong female characters) to the projects he worked on, but was stymied time and again.

The changes Joss Whedon made to *Toy Story* helped transform it into the film so many movie-goers love today, and helped make it a box-office hit to the tune of $373 million following its November 1995 release. In addition, it was nominated for Best Original Screenplay, Best Original Score, and Best Song ("You've Got a Friend in Me" by Randy Newman). Those are wonderful accolades for the film, but it seems apparent today, more than twenty years after the film's release, that *Toy Story* is more than a success. It is one of those rare, timeless productions that lives beyond its context; one which translates effortlessly from one generation to the next. Perhaps this is because the characters are recognizable and beloved, or perhaps simply because children still—and always will—play with toys. And at one point in his or her childhood, every kid wonders if a particular toy has feelings, or could possibly be alive.

The later films in the *Toy Story* franchise have only extended the magic of the original 1995 entry, telling tales about friendship, growing up, and finally (in *Toy Story 3*), letting go of the trappings of childhood. Even Sid, the nasty kid from a "bad home," seems eminently recognizable as a real-life, not entirely evil person. Again, we've all known kids who hurt their pets, or didn't take care of their toys, or who spent a lot of time alone, hurting the things and people he ostensibly loves. There is a universality, but also sadness, about Sid.

Toy Story also plays expertly on other common childhood experiences, like misplacing a beloved toy. In the film, Andy loses Woody and Buzz at various points, and is desolate about it. There's nothing worse than putting down a favorite toy, and coming back later to find it isn't there. It is like losing a best friend, in many ways. Writing for *The Guardian* in 2007, journalist Steve Morris presented a new psychological study which proved how children intuitively believe that toys and blankets "possess a unique essence or life force," and that *Toy Story* is very much a celebration of the human ability to anthropomorphize.

Although not solely a product of Joss Whedon's imagination or expert wordsmithing, *Toy Story* is nonetheless well-in-keeping with his work, particularly because it focuses on those interconnected themes he has returned to again and again: that every person matters, and that "created" families can sometimes be more powerful or meaningful than those that are biological. Here, not only is tremendous empathy generated for the mangled, damaged toys tortured by Sid, but their presence and identity matters as they help Buzz and Woody escape a similar fate.

Similarly, the toys in Andy's room—Rex, Bo Peep, Slinky Dog, the Sargeant—are joined together not by biological connection or even by generic toy type, but by fate, forming an ad-hoc family in the process. Woody is the gentle father figure and leader; Bo Peep, the mother figure; Rex is the neurotic uncle who is constantly terrified, despite his physical form as an intimidating dinosaur, and so on. Together, these neurotic, dysfunctional characters form the basis of a family, squabbling and fighting, but also learning to work together and join forces to help one another and the familial unit. It is not difficult to see this very diverse animated group as a dry run for Whedon's handling of another diverse comic-book group: Marvel's *The Avengers*.

In *Toy Story*, there are high-tech (Iron Man/Buzz Lightyear) and old-fashioned (Captain America/Woody) characters, and apparent monsters (The Hulk/Rex) who possess divided or neurotic psyches. The exact mission of each family isn't the same, per se. The toys bond together to save a childhood, namely Andy's. *The Avengers* band together to save our world. But in make-up and nature, these created families are remarkably similar. There is a universe to rescue, in each case; it is only the scale that is different.

Indeed, it's fascinating to gaze at the ad-hoc families of Joss Whedon's career, and explore how the members of the family "matter," in the different settings. *Toy Story* could easily be a young person's first exposure to this theme, before finding it again in *The Avengers*, or *Buffy the Vampire Slayer*. What makes *Toy Story* quite powerful—again like *The Avengers*, or *Buffy*—is the notion that each character in the family must learn where, and how, they fit in with the developing unit.

For instance, Buzz most overcome his belief that he is not a toy, so that he can become a good toy for Andy. He is not the nemesis of Emperor Zurg, but rather a hunk of plastic whose purpose is, finally, to share adventures with the child who loves him. An understanding of his role is not possible until he puts aside the "brand" that society (or merchandisers) have given to him. Again, this is a common theme in many of Whedon's works. Buffy can be both strong and vulnerable, both a slayer and a regular kid. But she has to navigate the space between those roles. Angel can be both a vampire and a hero, but again, he must define his place for himself. There is a recognition, in all these works, that society as a whole labels people, especially outsiders. The key to happiness for these survivors is, if not survival itself, then to overcome those labels within a "created family" so that everyone in that family can see their own worth.

This idea is given powerful voice in *Avengers: Age of Ultron*, when various members of the superhero team, including Black Widow and The Hulk, try to take back the meaning of the word "monster." They constantly call themselves monsters, only to realize that everyone in their created family is a "monster," in his or her own way. If that is the case, then they have to rewrite that term to find meaning in their own lives, and connections with one another. It's possible to draw a straight line back from *Age of Ultron* to *Toy Story*, and see how Whedon perpetually returns to this theme.

Although not a syrupy or sentimental film, *Toy Story* acknowledges that childhood is fleeting, and that children are fickle. Toys don't stay in favor for long. For a child, putting down a beloved toy for a new one is a matter of course. But the film asks the viewer to empathize with the toys; to wonder how it feels to be beloved one moment, and forgotten the next. Again, *Toy Story* is about how easy it is to become an outcast, to be seen as "other," even if you happen to be a toy. If *Alien Resurrection* begins the process of asking audiences to empathize with alien monsters, *Toy Story* continues the process, anthropomorphizing toys and fostering identification for them.

Two generations of toys clash in *Toy Story* and that is part of its unique, timeless magic. Woody is an avatar of a simpler time, the late 1950s and early 1960s, when TV Westerns were all the rage. Cowboys made their own rules, were physical and heroic, and had bonds with the land and nature (whether via their trusty steeds, or the ranches they called home).

The simplicity and tradition of Western toys is contrasted with Buzz Lightyear, a figure of the "space age" (the 1960s and beyond). He is a character who is dependent on technology, who can push a button to don a helmet, shoot a laser, or sprout a glider backpack. Woody is gadget-less; Buzz Lightyear *is* a gadget. *Toy Story* posits these two characters (and eras) in direct opposition. It's the Boomers vs. the X'ers.

This dynamic is canny, because the "cowboy vs. the astronaut" conflict makes the film appealing not just to children, but to parents. But the film also embodies the idea that even that which is amazingly popular, for a time, eventually goes out of fashion. A favorite toy like Woody, beloved by Andy, gets cast aside for something new, flashy, and high-tech. Films are much the same way. At some point, even the MCU will become old hat, and be shunted aside for something new. *Toy Story* seems acutely aware of how children see the world, and move from interest to interest, and there is, in this film, a kind of sad acceptance of that fact. Woody acts badly towards Buzz because he is jealous. And yet the great thing about the script is that Woody does not seem bad, or villainous, himself (as was the case in earlier drafts).

Instead, viewers empathize with the plastic cowboy, because everyone knows what it is like to no longer be the best friend. For a film about toys, *Toy Story* is really about human emotions, and the fear of being cast aside, by a child, a parent, even a spouse, if something better happens along.

As this author wrote in his essay, "This Boy's Bedroom: Product Placement, a New Masculinity, and the Rise of Geek Culture in the 1980s," in Praeger's *We Are What We Sell* (2014), toys in our modern culture have become not mere things to own or possess, simple commodities to play with, but statements about our individual identity, specifically about our created identity.

Who do we choose to be? Who do we want to be? Who do we feel for? Our toys tell us a lot about our dreams and aspirations. When we identify with a brand like Lego, or Kenner *Star Wars* action figures, we are not being "branded" by a corporation, necessarily, but choosing what brand we choose from which to derive meaning. *Toy Story*, a product of the mid-1990s, moves this idea to the toys themselves. Rex is not the fearsome dinosaur he was mass marketed as, but rather a neurotic coward who wouldn't harm the proverbial fly. Woody and Buzz have become, similarly, full-fledged individuals, not mere hunks of plastic. What they epitomize is a simpler time in our lives, and most importantly, a desire to be loved for who they choose to be, rather than who they were marketed as.

The answer to the question posed at the beginning of this chapter is affirmative. Joss Whedon and writer John Lasseter's work on *Toy Story* was nominated for Best Original Screenplay by the Academy.

7

Did Joss Whedon Work on the So-Called Biggest Bomb in Hollywood History?

Waterworld (1995)

Cast

Kevin Costner:	Mariner
Jeanne Tripplehorn:	Helen
Dennis Hopper:	Deacon
Tina Marjorino:	Enola
Michael Jeter:	Gregor
Kim Coates:	Drifter
R. D. Call:	Enforcer
Lenardo Cimino:	Elder

Crew

Universal Pictures, the Gordon Company, Davis Entertainment and Licht/Mueller Film Corporation

Casting:	David Rubin
Music: James	Newton Howard
Film Editor:	Peter Boyle

Dir. of Photography:	Dean Semler
Written by:	Peter Rader, David Twohy
Produced by:	Kevin Costner, John Davies, Charles Gordon, and Lawrence Gordon
Directed by:	Kevin Reynolds
M.P.A.A. Rating:	PG-13
Running time:	135 minutes

You should have stayed underwater.

Waterworld (1995) is a genre film that, upon its theatrical release, was clearly marked in the press as a troubled production, and furthermore, the most expensive film of all time, at $175 million. The creative problems on the picture involved everything from rewrites, to difficult shooting conditions on the water, to the replacement of the project's original director, Kevin Reynolds, by star Kevin Costner.

During the writing of the film, Joss Whedon was hired to punch up the script concocted by Peter Rader and David Twohy. Whedon has since described his stint on the film (to Tasha Robinson at *AV Club*) as "seven weeks of hell" while serving as the "world's highest paid stenographer." He reportedly found the script's concept—a post-apocalyptic film in a future of rapid global warming—good, but the script "generic."

Whedon also informed the same reporter that he accomplished "nothing" on the film, in part because some aspects of the script were cordoned off as sacrosanct by Costner, and therefore untouchable. He diagnosed what he saw as the film's big problem, however. Notably, the writer's concern was that the last forty pages were not set on the water, and the film's central character, the Mariner, was a man of the water. In essence, he became, during the climax, a fish-out-of-water. Whedon's concerns are quite understandable, although historically it is notable that *Waterworld* is not the bomb it is often portrayed as, and actually made a profit after both a successful theatrical run and strong home video sales. The myth of *Waterworld* as financial "bomb" yet lives, even if the facts don't bear it out.

I've sailed further than most men have dreamed.

Waterworld involves a world of the future—a world of ubiquitous oceans—where the silent, rugged Mariner (Costner) seeks to re-supply at a nearby atoll. Unfortunately, he is arrested by the local Elders as a "muto" (or mutant) because he has webbed feet and gills behind his ears. The Mariner's arrest comes at a bad time, because the leader of the eco-unfriendly Smokers, the Deacon (Dennis Hopper) is planning to launch an attack there and grab young Enola (Tina Majorino), a girl with an indecipherable map to the mythical "Dry Land" tattooed on her back.

Enola and her stepmother, Helen (Jean Tripplehorn), free the Mariner from captivity in exchange for passage out of the atoll on his boat. They barely escape with their lives, and the Deacon commits to pursuing them.

On the high seas, the Mariner and his "guests" have difficulty getting along at first, but soon he becomes fond of the women, and they of him. One day, the Mariner takes Helen to the bottom of the sea and shows him man's drowned cities there. That lost world is the only (formerly) "dry land" he knows of, he insists.

When the Deacon captures Enola, it's up to the Mariner to rescue her, and more than that, to lead other ragtag survivors to "Dry Land." Enola's map, properly understood, holds the key to man's future.

Nothing's free in Waterworld.

Eschewing the inside-baseball stats and figures, *Waterworld* plays as a straight-up and not un-enjoyable transplant of George Miller's *The Road Warrior* (1982) aesthetic, only in a world destroyed by global warming rather than by nuclear war. Kevin Costner's gilled, mutant Mariner, in other words, is a wet Mad Max who, like his predecessor, is a variation on Clint Eastwood's Man with No Name, a classic movie character featured in *A Fistful of Dollars* (1964), *For a Few Dollars More* (1965), and *The Good, the Bad and the Ugly* (1966).

In short, this archetype involves a "stranger" who rides into town and becomes involved in a conflict not his own, and who is rather stoic, allowing actions to speak louder than words. Similarly, *Waterworld*'s Mariner is frequently tagged as a silent brooder, and by film's end has even become equated with "Death" Himself for his accomplished—if taciturn—application of lethal force. Beyond the obvious inspiration the film draws from the *Mad Max* mythos, *Waterworld* succeeds mostly because of the reality of the world it assiduously constructs. The film is one of the

Close-up of a Whedon "Other?" Kevin Costner as the Mariner in *Waterworld* (1995).
John Muir Photo Archive

last sci-fi epics to emerge from the pre-digital age of Hollywood block-busters and, accordingly—and for all its apparent flaws—boasts a height-ened sense of texture and verisimilitude.

Everything we witness here had to be arduously constructed and set afloat, and that herculean effort pays off in a visual and imaginative sense. One can practically smell the salt water and the burning fuel. In terms of negatives, *Waterworld* takes an unnecessary dive into sentimentalism, a wrong turn that *The Road Warrior* never falls prey to, though *Beyond Thunderdome* certainly did. Legitimizing Whedon's complaint, the film's final act also consists of one generic action movie trope after the other, from the hero's ability to outpace blossoming fireballs, to last-minute, physically impossible rescues. These almost cartoon-like moments tend to mark *Waterworld* as a product of eager-to-please Hollywood, and make it rather decidedly unlike its spare, gritty, Australian source of inspira-tion. Still, some of the overt sentimentalism and action clichés might be overlooked because of the film's absolutely original setting, and the skill with which that setting is presented.

The film's lead characters—when not grinding the gears of expected generic conventions—are interesting enough to spend two hours with, certainly. Again, the idea of a found or created family has cropped up. By sheer happenstance, likely, the same element is in play in *Waterworld*. The man/fish hybrid, the Mariner, becomes father-figure to Enola, a derided outsider whose tattoo marks her as different. And, in keeping with the tradition of the post-apocalyptic genre, *Waterworld* also makes an earnest statement about man's self-destructive nature.

Undeniably, the quality most admirable about *Waterworld* is its *physicality*. This ingredient might also be described as "texture" or "atmosphere," perhaps, but *physicality* better gets at the film's rugged and powerful sense of setting, of place. The Rube Goldberg–style devices, the trinkets from the "old world" re-purposed for *Waterworld*'s tech, and the sheer mechanical nature of the world combine to create a place of whirring hydraulics, tugging pulleys, fold-out sails, and endless, ubiquitous sea. The tactility and verisimilitude of this world result in many commendable, almost throwaway, touches in the film that are really quite spectacular, and contribute to the idea that "Waterworld" is a real place, one boasting a deep and long history.

In terms of the post-apocalyptic subgenre, *Waterworld* escorts the viewer on an ominous trip to the bottom of the sea, and provides a haunting view of an old metropolis turned to dust at the ocean floor, a clear analog for the Statue of Liberty moment in *Planet of the Apes* (1968) or the "empty cities" of *The World, the Flesh and The Devil* (1959) or *Night of The Comet* (1984). But that's as close to conventional end-of-the-world imagery as *Waterworld* gets, instead setting its action on an unending, dangerous sea, a realm that is both beautiful and incredibly dangerous.

In terms of its narrative, it's plain that *Waterworld* owes a great deal to both *The Road Warrior* and, indeed, the entire Mad Max cycle. The Mariner, like Max, is a man who lives outside of human society and boasts of his disdain for it. Both characters live as scavengers and traders, contacting civilization only to re-supply. Both the Mariner and Max form meaningful relationships, or friendships, with children (Enola, and the Feral Kid, respectively), and both eventually come around to the idea of "helping" an endangered civilization find a new home (either Dry Land, or the gasoline truck's promised land destination in *The Road Warrior*).

Finally, both sagas end with that new home established, but the warrior himself returning to the "wasteland" arena to continue his lonely travels. Mad Max and the Mariner are violent men with a code of ethics, and so they both realize it is better for them to remain "outcasts" in the wild rather than to seek domesticated lives inside a new culture. In *Beyond Thunderdome*, the new city-dwellers light candles for the wanderers who haven't come home; in *Waterworld*, Enola and Helen watch as the Mariner returns to the sea, the realm that nurtured him.

In both *The Road Warrior* and *Waterworld*, a central scenario depicted is the "siege" of an outpost of civilization. Outsiders on a variety of crafts try to "break in" and pillage either Oil City or the Atoll. The beleaguered city, naturally, fights back, but the walls are breached by attacking vehicles, either flying motorcycles or launched jet skis. Both cities eventually fall, leading to a dedicated trek to new home and the beginning of a better society.

These factors—the siege and the trek—make the films' origin stories of a mythic type. As Aeneas had to flee fallen Troy to found Rome, so do Max and the Mariner lead homeless survivors to greener pastures, literally in the case of *Waterworld*. In one moment in that film, the viewer even gets a deliberate mirror-image composition of a famous frame from *The Road Warrior*. There, in the first harrowing action scene, we witness the savage Wez perched on his motorcycle, and another goon seated behind him on the bike, looking at his prey. Audiences see very much the same framing in view here (also in the first action scene), except, of course, on a water craft instead of a motorcycle. Despite the obvious aping of the Mad Max universe, *Waterworld*'s unique, water-bound setting gives it a lot of "juice," at least in a visual sense. The images are so lush and convincing that audiences can make themselves forget, essentially, that the movie is a very expensive pastiche.

As audiences have come to expect from post-apocalyptic films, there is an environmental message in *Waterworld* that suggests man's self-destructive nature. The "Ancients" caused rapid global warming, and now, similarly, the Smokers are running through the last of their oil, trying to sustain an unsustainable lifestyle. Their need to live that lifestyle of

The Mariner (Kevin Costner) braces for an attack on the atoll in *Waterworld*.   *John Muir Photo Archive*

relative *leisure* (replete with cigarettes, electricity, and even automobiles) dooms the Smokers to a life of war and conflict, stealing what they need from other nation-states/atolls at the barrel of a gun.

The fact that the Smokers inhabit the Exxon *Valdez*, a poster-child for environmental irresponsibility, pretty much says it all. And this too is America›s fate, if it doesn›t tap alternative energy sources. The nation will have to fight resource wars to maintain the culture›s high standard of living. Even the film's villain plays into this leitmotif. At one point, the Deacon attempts to flick a lit cigarette into an open oil tank, an act which could have instantaneous, catastrophic results were he successful. The message is clearly that he is self-destructive, but there's more. By wantonly, thoughtlessly using up the Earth's resources, we're essentially lighting a spark that could destroy everything we hold dear.

"We outgrew it," one Smoker says of the Exxon *Valdez*, and indeed that's precisely the fear of many environmentalists. What happens when we outgrow the planet's capacity to sustain us? Interestingly, Joss Whedon's *Serenity* features an opening scene that explains how humanity will react when there are too many of us on the Earth, and it can no longer sustain us.

Waterworld's environmental message is leavened somewhat by the film's many action sequences, which grow progressively less satisfying and less convincing as the film continues. The opening battles on the sea and at the atoll are genuinely awe-inspiring, and feature death-defying stunts. By the end of the film, however, rear-projection and cartoonish explosions dominate the proceedings, sacrificing the element of reality in the process.

Although much of the popular press still terms *Waterworld* a bomb (despite eventually making back its budget and then some), this is hardly a terrible science-fiction film, nor is it a great one. *Waterworld*'s biggest problem is that the film's first half elaborately sets up a world and characters of tremendous interest, and then the last half spends all its time blowing things up, hence Whedon's disparaging comment about the script seeming "generic."

In short, this film is a lot like many other examples of mainstream 1990s filmmaking. And yet, the film doesn't open that way at all. In fact, *Waterworld*'s opening is a kind of brilliant "screw you" to conventional standards and decorum. How many Hollywood blockbusters can you name that open with a shot of an established star, like Costner, pissing into a cup, refining his urine, and then drinking it?

At least in terms of last shots, *Waterworld* finishes strong. The Mariner heads off to the next horizon and the next mystery. Perhaps it's the mystery of his very creation, or the mystery of the end of the world. It's kind of a shame that audiences never got to see that second adventure. Mad Max and The Man with No Man each got several attempts to get their equation right.

Too bad Whedon never got to write a sequel.

8

Did Joss Whedon Write an Animated Film?

Titan A.E. (2000)

Cast

Matt Damon:	Cale Tucker
Bill Pullman:	Korso
Drew Barrymore:	Akima
Nathan Lane:	Preet
Janeane Garafolo:	Stith
Ron Perlman:	Sam Tucker
Tone Loc:	Tek
Jim Breuer:	Cok

Crew

20th Century Fox Presents a Fox Animation Studios and David Kirschner Production of a Don Bluth Film

Casting:	Marion Levine
Music:	Graeme Revell
Film Editor:	Bob Bender, Paul Martin Smith, Fiona Trayler
Production Designer:	Philip A. Cruden
Story by:	Hans Bauer, Randall McCormick
Written by:	Ben Edlund, Joss Whedon, John August

Produced by:	Don Bluth, Gary Goldman, David Kirschner
Directed by:	Don Bluth, Gary Goldman
M.P.A.A. Rating:	PG
Running time:	94 minutes

My scanners are showing a veritable cornucopia of nothing.

Titan A.E. tells the story of the first generation of humans who live in space, and not by choice. The film begins in the thirty-first century, the year 3028 AD, as a vicious attack by aliens consisting of pure energy, called "the Drej," launch a final attack on Earth. Mother Earth is destroyed in the attack, though survivors manage to evacuate the planet. One child, Cale Tucker (Damon), is separated from his scientist father during the assault. His father, however, is trying to save the human race, and manages to launch a ship called the *Titan* that is rumored to be the savior of all mankind.

Fifteen years later, Cale is a displaced adult working in squalor on a remote salvage station at Tau 14. There, he covets a ring his father gave him, and tries not to make trouble with the aliens with whom he works, who view humans as a primitive, lower life form. Then one day, a captain called Korso (Pullman) comes to find Cale and help him find his father on a heroic journey. The way to find his father, and the *Titan*, is to activate a "map" inside a ring that Cale's father left him. Unfortunately, the Drej also covet the map, and seek to destroy the *Titan*, so the human race can never again assert itself in the galaxy.

Cale joins the ragtag crew of Korso's ship, including the alien gunslinger Preet (Lane), the heroic alien Stith (Garafalo), and the beautiful engineer, Akima (Barrymore). Cale finds himself attracted to Akima, and learns that Korso has sold him out, and the entire human race, to the Drej. As the search for the *Titan* continues, Cale sees the wonders of the galaxy, including Sesharri, a planet of bat people, and encounters "wake angels," strange space whales. Eventually, the *Titan* is located, frozen over, in a nebula of giant ice crystals.

As the Drej move in for the kill, Cale realizes he can restore Earth using the *Titan*'s generator, and populate it with animals from a vast DNA bank that his father left behind. In the end, Korso experiences a change of heart, and helps Cale and Akima activate the *Titan*'s generator, creating a new Earth. And so, in the year 3044 A.E., as the humans of the drift colony learn of the new world's existence, mankind has a new home in the stars. Cale names the planet . . . Bob.

I don't think this future thing of yours exists.

Produced on the then-exorbitant budget of over $75 million, this animated science-fiction film from Fox Studios is another outer-space bomb found in Joss Whedon's CV, at least if one chooses to rely only on the numbers. *Titan A.E.* combines CGI and traditional animation under the guidance of *Secret of NIMH* (1982) director, Don Bluth, and it grossed less than $40 million at the box office. Today, *Titan A.E.* is revered by many as an under-appreciated cult movie.

This project came along shortly after director Don Bluth and producer Gary Goldman had an unexpected hit in the animated film, *Anastasia* (1997). Their next effort, *Titan A.E.*, has been termed "The first animated science-fiction film," according to its press kit, and the film broke new ground with its revolutionary combination of 2-D and 3-D animation. Roughly 80 percent of the film is computer generated, mostly the backgrounds, both interiors and exteriors. The other 20 percent of the film—mostly the characters themselves—are hand-drawn, or 2-D animation.

Titan A.E. originated with a story by Hans Bauer and Randall McCormick, and then several writers set to work doctoring the script, including Ben Edlund, the creator of *The Tick* (2001–2002) and a writer on *Angel*. Next, Whedon came aboard, and then, finally, John August took a turn. Whedon, who was working on *Buffy the Vampire Slayer* TV series at the time, completed significant work on the project, and much of it remained in the finished product.

Bluth described the concepts of the film in the following way, according to the movie's press kit. "The movie, to me, is about the indomitable

Cale (Matt Damon) takes the helm of the Valkyrie in *Titan A.E.* (2000).   *John Muir Photo Archive*

Akima (Drew Barrymore) contemplates the future in *Titan A.E.*   *John Muir Photo Archive*

human spirit and the search for an identity. It asks, What are we about? Are we worth saving? Can we ever have a home again?"

For Whedon, the key to the story was finding the emotional connections Cale makes with others, and how these change him. "Among other things," he is quoted in the press kit as saying, "I wanted to explain how his bitterness and conflict with the memory of his father would express itself." Those emotional connections that Cale makes with others are, for lack of a better term, about a person fitting in with his created, or found, family.

I happen to be humanity's last great hope.

At the time of its release, *Titan A.E.* received mostly negative reviews. The general consensus among critics is that the film didn't know its audience. Was *Titan A.E.* a cartoon space opera for adults, or was it an adventure film for children? Some of the creature designs seemed too coarse and childish for adult approval, while other scenes featured shocking amounts of violence and blood, making the film seem less than suitable for children.

Critic Roger Ebert, writing on June 19, 2000, however, found much to praise in the pre-Pixar epic. "Here's the animated space adventure I've been hoping for," he enthused, "a film that uses the freedom of animation to visualize the strangeness of the universe in ways live action cannot duplicate, and join its vision to a rousing story."

Long after the film's failure at the box office, something typical in Joss Whedon's career occurred: a critical re-examination. In 2013, an article in *IO9* was posted by Meredith Woermer; it is titled "Why '*Titan A.E.*' is an Underappreciated Masterpiece." The article concluded not only that the film was "Whedon funny," with good "banter on the ship," but that the dialogue qualified as "one of the most endearing qualities of the film." The author also concluded that the Bluth film, co-written by Whedon, "pulls off wonder without have to bathe a gape-jawed actor in blue light."

If anyone seemed nonplussed by this newfound appreciation for a sci-fi opus that most of the moviegoing population had ignored, it was Whedon himself. In a 2015 interview conducted by Rob Leane of *Den of Geek*, Whedon put a stop to the "ahead of its time" narrative by characterizing the movie as "behind the times." Although Whedon acknowledged that some of the film "played beautifully," he also suggested some of it was a "little . . . old school."

Today, the film seems like a crucial, early piece of the *Firefly* puzzle, much in the same way as *Alien Resurrection*. Here, for instance, walls on spaceships are decorated with Far Eastern writing, suggesting that Western culture alone won't dominate the stars in the distant future. This is a touch carried over into both *Firefly* and *Serenity*. Similarly, there is a dystopian ideal at work here, of humanity as a minority in a very diversely populated alien universe. That is different, of course, from the all-human future of *Firefly*, but audiences are introduced here, as they are in virtually all of Whedon's work, to a team of misfits who come together to achieve something magnificent: the founding of a new Earth.

Titan A.E. is an odd mix of dystopia and heroic journey, forged from equal parts optimism and pessimism about the human race. That odd mixture seems unique to Whedon, and in a way that is familiar from both *Firefly* and *Alien Resurrection*. While the film introduces characters

Poster art for *Titan A.E.* featuring a Drej warship behind Cale (Damon) and Akima (Barrymore).
John Muir Photo Archive

From *Titan A.E.*, a battle on the unusually visualized world of Sesharrim.   *John Muir Photo Archive*

who tell the audience that "the human race is out of gas" and "circling the drain," a team of misfits work together to bring the human race a new future, even in the face of impossible odds.

Much of the film's dialogue captures both the existential angst of the characters, and their quick wit in the face of the struggle.

"Are you homesick?" one character asks Cale.

"You have to have a home first," Cale responds, grimly.

The film thus explores the concept of diaspora, the dispersion of people form their homeland, and in a significant fashion. If the Whedon canon is all about those found families, then *Titan A.E.* illustrates that, wherever they are, they also make a home—at least in the absence of a homeland.

In some ways, the most successful parts of *Titan A.E.* are those showcasing the life of the human race in the in-between-time After Earth and Life on the planet Bob. Cale is eking out a living with strange aliens on a salvage station, eating unpalatable food, and having no real sense of purpose or drive. "There aren't many of us left," one human notes glumly, and mention is made of life in the poverty-stricken drifter colonies. It doesn't sound appealing. In losing Earth, these human refugees have lost that which made it special, and that which made it *feel* special. This predicament is Whedonesque in its attempt to craft empathy for the real-life refugees here on Earth, now, in our time. To be without a home is indeed a horrible thing, and that is the fact that drives so much of the film's action. For the human race to get its mo-jo back, it needs a new home, but the galaxy is either indifferent or hostile to the possibility.

This idea is referenced with an allusion to a similar initiative of the 1970s: Gerry Anderson's *Space: 1999* (1975–1977). This series involved a group of 311 humans stationed on the Earth's moon when it was blown out of orbit during an explosion at an atomic waste dump. The series found the moon traveling the galaxy, in search of a new home for those lost humans. Both *Titan A.E.* and *Space: 1999* are origin stories; tales of the sojourn from an old, lost home, to a new one, where the people can re-establish themselves.

Titan A.E.'s connection to *Space: 1999* is not merely thematic, but visual. One of the strangest and most distinctive planets that Moonbase Alpha visited in *Space: 1999* was called *Piri*, and featured in the episode

"Guardian of Piri," by Christopher Penfold. It was depicted as a world of strange quasi-mechanical trees that possessed glowing orbs and wire-like vines. No planet in the history of television had ever looked like that signature world. Yet *Titan A.E.* resurrects the distinctive look of Piri with its red hues and orb-shaped "Hydrogen Trees." So in some ways, this origin story of human refugees is a call-back to an earlier one, which may be why Whedon termed the film "Old School." While the combination of 2-D and 3-D animation may have been new, many visuals were drawn from earlier sources.

The presentation of the Piri-like planet, as well as the ice crystal nebula, give *Titan A.E.* a tremendous visual lift in its last act. The mix of CGI and old-school, hand-drawn animation doesn't always feel right but these worlds are depicted in jaw-dropping format, and the imagery lingers in the memory long after a viewing of the film. The climactic sequence with the Drej ship (which resembles a jeweled crown, or human head), the *Titan*, and the ice crystals, is beautifully rendered.

It should be noted that critics certainly had a point when commenting that *Titan A.E.* fails to determine for just whom this space opera was intended. Some of the character renderings, particularly of the aliens, seem cartoonish and silly. Stith, for instance, walks on big, fat, indistinct legs that are patently unreal. On the other hand, the audience sees cute alien creatures, like an insectoid bug, get shot and splattered into a million chunks and pieces on camera, which doesn't seem appropriate for young viewers. Likewise, there are many instances of human blood spatter in the film, suggesting an adult approach to the material.

Thus far in his career, Whedon has toiled on three space operas, all set in dystopian futures. Notably, *Alien Resurrection*, *Titan A.E.*, and *Serenity* failed at the box office. In some ways, they appear to stem from a very dark place. In one, man is just a "resource" on which the government (and military) can experiment. In another, man is an unwelcome minority in a universe of hostile aliens. And in the third, human freedom has disappeared, and totalitarianism attempts to take the sky "away" from the individual, like Mal Reynolds. *Star Wars* is a dark story, too, of civilization's fall and authoritarianism's rise, and yet it does not feel nearly as dark as the imaginings of Whedon in this genre. His signature myth-building and hero building occurs in a darker, more violent, less hopeful world, and that fact may limit the appreciation of his space operas to a "cult" fringe, rather than an enthusiastic mainstream.

It is also true that in the case of *Titan A.E.* and *Alien Resurrection*, Whedon's words were interpreted by directors who did not have the same love or understanding of science fiction (or space opera) as the writer in question. *Serenity* is the only one of the three films he has directed, and the best space opera in his canon, even if pieces of its success can be detected in the earlier works.

In an interview following the release of *Age of Ultron*, Whedon was asked which joke was the greatest he had ever written. His response: "*Titan A.E.*" Some read that, sincerely, as a comment that there was a joke in the film he wrote, which he liked. He may have been talking about the naming of the new Earth "Bob." However, others saw his comment as the ultimate put-down of the underappreciated space opera; that the film itself had become a joke to Whedon.

9

Is There a (Script) Doctor in the House?

Or: On What Other Films Did Joss Whedon Work as Script Doctor?

A script doctor is a consultant and writer who works on a film project, usually without credit, and often without glory. There are very specific rules about how writers get credit for their work in these "triage" situations, when they function as sort of the cinematic equivalent of the literary ghost writer.

The Writer's Guild of America establishes that for a script doctor to receive credit for his or her work, they must contribute 50 percent of original material to a screenplay, or 33 percent of an adaptation. These are high thresholds to overcome, which likely account for the reasons that script doctors, though often appreciated by producers and director, are underappreciated by the Academy.

Today, Joss Whedon is widely known as a writer, director, creator of franchises, and mastermind even, of creative fictional universes, like the Buffyverse. Throughout the 1990s, however, he served as one of Hollywood's script doctors, applying his sense of story, characterization, and trademark humor to some of the industry's biggest—and most notorious—film projects.

In some films already discussed, including *Speed* (1994) and *Toy Story* (1995), Whedon's creative energy and artistic hand is more apparent. In others, Whedon himself counts his contribution as less than meaningful, or limited to a specific line of dialogue, or action. This short chapter serves as an overview of Whedon's lesser-known work as a script doctor.

The Quick and the Dead (1995)

In the mid-1990s, the Western genre was achieving its first legitimate comeback in years, with the likes of *Young Guns 2* (1990), *Unforgiven* (1992), *Tombstone* (1993), *Posse* (1993), *Bad Girls* (1994), and Kevin Costner's *Wyatt Earp* (1994). Some were notable for being more diverse in characterization than previous generations of Westerns, which means that they featured non-traditional protagonists. Some of the Westerns were feminist in nature, featured African-American stars, or Gen-X actors transplanted to the familiar frontier.

A similar project was Sam Raimi's *The Quick and the Dead* (1995), featuring Sharon Stone as a vengeful gunslinger called "Lady," out to take revenge on John Herod (Gene Hackman), the despot of a small town called Redemption. The cast also includes Leonardo DiCaprio, Russell Crowe, and cult favorite Lance Henriksen as the flamboyant Ace Hanlon. The script was penned by Englishman Simon Moore, who had written and directed *Under Suspicion* (1992) starring Liam Neeson.

Once Stone, Crowe, and Hackman were on the project, rewrites were demanded, and the script began to undergo drastic change to accommodate the demands, and egos, of the various actors. Moore told this author for *The Unseen Force: The Films of Sam Raimi* (2004) that "one of the rules of Hollywood is that the nearer you get to production, the more anxious everyone becomes. There's really only one thing you can keep changing, and that's the script."

Hence the demand for script doctors.

At one point, John Sayles rewrote the film to make it seem more authentic, but his changes were largely jettisoned in what Moore describes as a "completely fucking pointless exercise." In other words, Moore wrote a script, the actors wanted changes, and Sayles rewrote the script. But the studio executives didn't like the rewrite, and had Moore fix it by basically removing the majority of Sayles's material. So it was back to square one.

What was Joss Whedon's role in all of this? In 1994, he met with Sam Raimi, reportedly for "one afternoon," according to Joel Stice at *Uproxx* in 2014, and resolved some problems with the film's climax. Raimi reportedly appreciated Whedon's help in improving the film's ending.

Twister (1996)

In 1996, Joss Whedon worked on another blockbuster that doesn't carry his name: the tornado-chasing, disaster-action film *Twister*, from *Speed* director Jan de Bont. Whedon worked on the $90 million film in the spring of 1995, following in the footsteps of scribes Michael Crichton, Anne Marie Martin, and Steve Zaillon. Whedon was on-and-off the project at least twice, once for illness (bronchitis) and once following his wedding to Kai Cole. After his final departure from the Bill Paxton and Helen Hunt starrer, writer Jeff Nathanson continued Whedon's work. There is apparently very little of Whedon's effort left in the final film, except for the sequences at Aunt Meg's house.

X-Men (2000)

For many longtime superhero fans, the age of the "modern" crime fighter in film truly began in the year 2000, with the release of Bryan Singer's *X-Men*. The mid-1980s had seen the Christopher Reeve Superman series collapse into silliness with Cannon's low-budget *Superman IV: The Quest for Peace* (1987), and the Batman age, which had been ushered in by Tim Burton in 1989, fell into disrepute with the widespread critical and commercial failure of Joel Schumacher's *Batman and Robin* in 1997.

Despite its lack of fidelity to the yellow suits of the X-Men mutants, Bryan Singer's *X-Men* at least felt like a serious, committed attempt to give the beloved Marvel heroes their due. Still, the film was not without many, many problems. *Entertainment Weekly*'s Owen Gleiberman wrote in June of 2000, for instance, that the film is "an awkward, de-personalized piece of hackwork, and a rather earthbound one at that. This is a movie that was shot in Toronto and looks it. As directed by Bryan Singer, it has a diffuse, stop-and-go rhythm that makes it hard to tell where dystopian ominousness leaves off and sluggish amateurism begins."

Apparently, those working on the film were not X-Men fans, or comic-book fans in general, which may account for the occasionally scattershot approach to the material. As is typical for big-budget studio films—and there was $75 million at stake for his comic-to-screen adaptation—a number of writers were brought in to make the script work, including Ed Solomon and *Gladiator* (2000) scribe John Logan. Joss Whedon was another name associated with these uncanny mutants and their first film. He was brought in, ostensibly, to punch up the film's climactic battle sequence. However, as a fan of the property, Whedon saw more problems, as he told reporter Craig Seymour in the May 10, 2000 issue of *Entertainment Weekly*: "I didn't think the script was any good, so I did a major overhaul."

Apparently, Whedon's rewrite was more in keeping with the tongue-in-cheek mode of *Buffy the Vampire Slayer* and, according to the same article, this "clashed" with Singer's more serious approach to the material. So what of Whedon's contributions remain in the finished film?

Possibly the worst joke in superhero history.

In particular, in the final battle at the Statue of Liberty, Storm, played by Halle Berry, quips to the villain, Toad (Ray Parks): "Do you know what happens to a toad when it gets struck by lightning?" The answer: "The same thing that happens to everything else."

This line was a groaner for audiences, and has since been immortalized at sites like *Den of Geek* as one of the worst lines in genre, nay, cinema history. Whedon has explained that the line is not necessarily bad; it was Berry's self-important, grandiose reading that killed it. The line was supposed to be nonchalant, but Berry, according to Whedon, played it like she was in *King Lear*.

Fortunately for Whedon, and *X-Men* fans, Whedon got a second chance to demonstrate his chops by working on a comic with John Cassady in 2006, *Astonishing X-Men: Gifted*.

Part III

The Cult Creator

10

Buffy the Vampire Slayer (1997–2003)

Cast

Buffy Summers:	Sarah Michelle Gellar
Willow Rosenberg:	Alyson Hannigan
Xander Harris:	Nicholas Brendon
Rupert Giles:	Anthony Stewart Head (Seasons 1–6)
Cordelia Chase:	Charisma Carpenter (Seasons 1–3)
Angel:	David Boreanaz (Seasons 1–3)
Spike:	James Marsters (Seasons 4–7)
Anya:	Emma Caulfield (Seasons 4–7)
Dawn:	Michelle Trachtenberg (Seasons 5–7)

Crew

Presented by Mutant Enemy, in association with Kuzui Enterprises, Sandollar Television, and 20th Century Fox

Created by:	Joss Whedon
Theme Song:	Nerf Herder
Main Title Design:	Montgomery/Cross
Executive Producers:	Sandy Gallin, Gail Berm, Fran Rubel Kuzui, Kaz Kuzui

Into every generation a slayer is born.

In the mid-1990s, Joss Whedon brought his beloved and inspiring heroine, Buffy, back to life, this time for television audiences, and the second time was truly the charm. Virtually everything that the 1992 movie got wrong, the TV series got right. Not only did Buffy evolve to become a strong, if vulnerable, heroine, this time around details were added to the "world" to make her story much more logical, or appear more deeply grounded in reality. Whedon added the concept of "The Hellmouth," a supernatural portal that was located in the happily named burg of Sunnydale, and this gateway had the habit of spewing out new supernatural threats for Buffy to confront. This portal thus fostered the series' "monster of the week" format. So while the story was often serialized, there were also opportunities for stand-alone episodes.

What truly improved the *Buffy the Vampire Slayer* concept, however, was the fact that Whedon populated Buffy's world with the Scoobies, or the Scooby Gang, a diverse group of sidekicks who were fully developed as unique and memorable characters. In the 1992 movie, Buffy had only her pseudo-boyfriend Pike to help her hold supernatural evil at bay. During its seven seasons on the air, the new team of regulars supported Buffy in brightest day and darkest night.

Among the new characters were Xander Harris (Nicholas Brendan), a typical teenage geek with a crush on Buffy and a Chandler-esque (from *Friends* [1994–2004]) sense of humor and line delivery. And then there was Willow Rosenberg (Alyson Hanigan), a tech-savvy "shy" girl who is brilliant both with science and magic. Over the course of the series, Willow found her confidence, came out as gay, and developed a loving relationship first with Tara (Amber Benson), and later the slayer-in-training named Kennedy (Iyari Limon).

Also joining the team was the requisite shallow Valley Girl, a comic-relief "type" filled first by rich cheerleader Cordelia Chase (Charisma Carpenter), and later by Anya, a former wish-demon, portrayed by Emma Caulfield.

Playing Buffy's father-figure and mentor was Rupert Giles (Anthony Stewart Head), a character considerably more sympathetic and caring than Buffy's cinematic watcher, Merrick. Unlike Merrick, Giles seems to

Scoobies at the Library. Giles (Anthony Stewart Head), Buffy (Gellar), Angel (David Boreanaz), Willow (Hannigan) and Oz (Green) on-set during production of *Buffy the Vampire Slayer*.

John Muir Photo Archive

truly have a tender heart, and intriguingly, a dark past involving the supernatural.

However, nothing transformed the universe of Buffy more than the addition of two other characters: first, the vampire Angel (David Boreanaz), and later, the vampire Spike (James Marsters). Angel was a two-hundred-year-old vampire with a soul, one who would fall hard for Buffy, and vice versa. He had roamed the Earth as a monstrous sociopath for decades, until a gypsy curse gave him a soul, so he could feel remorse for his actions.

Why was this single change so impactful? Angel offered Whedon and his writers the opportunity to tell a story of not just first romantic love, but of star-crossed, or tragic, romantic love. Despite their feelings for each other, Buffy and Angel can never be together, and they both know it. This fact makes their relationship all the more haunting, and powerful. The third season episode "The Prom" explores the idea that Angel and Buffy are both in denial about their future together, and sees them go, sadly, their separate ways. Their relationship is perfectly expressed in Buffy's dream sequence. She imagines her wedding day, with Angel. But she burns up, like a vampire, while he watches in horror. The idea here is that Buffy will grow old and die, turning to dust, while Angel remains young and handsome for all eternity.

Also, belying a new viewpoint, Angel is a vampire, the very thing— the very evil—Buffy, by dint of her title, is supposed to "slay." Suddenly, the lines of battle become unclear. The conflict is no longer as simple as humans vs. monsters, or good vs. evil. Instead, even the monsters on *Buffy the Vampire Slayer* are treated as people. In fact, many of the demons on the series, from Angel to Anya to Spike, are simply "others," individuals with different natures and backgrounds.

As Joss Whedon informed author Barbara Lippert in *New York*'s "Hey There. Warrior Girl" in December of 1997, the series is really about "disen-franchisement, about the people no one takes seriously." This tenet applies not merely to an unsung titular heroine, who is tougher and more heroic than her fashion sense suggests, but to creatures of the night as well.

The character of Spike—a punk-rock vampire—also grows in popular-ity over seven seasons, eventually becoming Buffy's second love interest. He is a fascinating choice, less concerned with romantic love and, well, more overtly sexual. If Angel represents the romanticism of young love, Spike's role is largely to reveal how Buffy has evolved fully into an adult, sexual relationship, one in which she has to define her own lines of behavior. Spike eventually redeems himself because he truly loves Buffy, but she seems to see him as more of a physical plaything, or sparring partner. The Buffy/Spike relationship is not without controversy. It takes center stage in season six, the first episodes on UPN, a storytelling choice apparently not favored by Sarah Michelle Gellar. Regardless of one's pref-erence in leading men, the viewer sees two very different male vampires, and two very different relationships.

It is likely that these relationships would not have proven so powerful and relevant without the central performances of Sarah Michelle Gellar as Buffy. Where Kristy Swanson was athletic and sarcastic, more like Cordelia than Buffy, Gellar was able to tap into a different side of the heroine. This iteration of the character is less sassy, more three-dimen-sional. She can still kick ass, but there is something vulnerable and sweet about this Buffy; a human side that is overlooked in favor of comedy and physicality in the unsuccessful feature film. Quite simply, Sarah Michelle Gellar anchors the series, portraying a consistent character with wit and charm, and by fostering constant empathy. *People Weekly*'s Tom Gliatto writes that the actress plays the role with the "right degree of put-upon resentment," but that is not quite a strong enough statement.

Gothic Heroine or Modern Feminist? Sarah Michelle Gellar stars as the Chosen One in the TV adaptation of *Buffy the Vampire Slayer* (19973–2003).
John Muir Photo Archive

It's not so much resentment that one sees in Buffy, but the fact that she just wants to be a normal kid instead of spending her nights in sewers or cemeteries, killing monsters. Just once, she wants to be like everyone else. It's resentment, perhaps, but also the recognition that a certain kind of life will always be denied her because she has been "chosen" to carry on the slayer legacy. The family that Buffy finds in the series makes all the difference for the character. They provide her with a network of support that her absent father, and well-meaning mother, simply cannot.

Frederic C. Szebin, writing in *Cinefantastique*, noted that "Sarah Michelle Gellar as Buffy may have finally kicked asunder that tired cliché of the screaming maiden in distress. Here is a heroine who can be sexy without being trashy, tough without resorting . . . to machismo, and funny without the forced goofiness prevalent in today's society." The miracle of the TV incarnation of *Buffy the Vampire Slayer* is that Whedon's creation, coupled with great writing and Gellar's performances, redefines heroism (and perhaps even super-heroism) beyond the typical terms associated with "super" men. Buffy doesn't have to be male or act male to be a fantastic heroine. She is not "fighting for her rights, in her satin tights," to use the phraseology from 1977's *Wonder Woman* TV series, which still viewed the heroine in sexist terms, but rather a fully developed person, and woman, and also, the most heroic of all crusaders.

Structurally, *Buffy the Vampire Slayer* follows the same formula throughout its seven seasons on the air. Like *The X-Files* before it, the series features monster-of-the-week stories, wherein Buffy and the Scoobies defeat momentary threats to Sunnydale's safety. Among the more interesting threats: vampire motorcycle gangs, an alien from outer space, a demon called "The Judge," a praying-mantis woman, and, of course, Dracula himself.

But these tales are interspersed throughout the series run with what Chris Carter terms Myth-arc stories: ongoing or serialized tales that depict a larger story. In the case of *Buffy the Vampire Slayer*, each season sees Buffy going head-to-head with a character type that Whedon calls a "Big Bad," a kind of supernatural boss.

In the first season, Buffy and friends battle a Nosferatu-like ancient vampire called "The Master," who is trying to harvest all the blood of Sunnydale. In the second season, the vampire trio of Spike, Drusilla

Late cast additions Emma Caulfield, Michelle Trachtenberg, and James Marsters join series stalwart Head for a group hug.   *John Muir Photo Archive*

(Juliet Landau), and a soulless Angel (again, "Angelus" in this form) were the Big Bads. Their plan is to open a portal to hell in service of a demon god called Acathla.

In the third season, a renegade slayer, Faith (Eliza Dushku), teams with the demonic mayor of Sunnydale (Harry Groener) as he seeks to "ascend" to a form of incredible power. For many fans, this season, and this Big Bad's character arc, remain the high point of the series. Everything comes down to graduation, as Buffy, too, must ascend (from high school).

The fourth season of the series witnesses Buffy leaving the high-school milieu behind, and going away to college. Here, the series unexpectedly blends science and the supernatural with the addition of a government/ military organization called "The Initiative," which seeks to tag and control the monsters of the Hellmouth. This season sees the Initiative succeed with some monsters, installing a chip in Spike's head, and thus effectively neutering him as a menace. Buffy also gets a new boyfriend this season, the Iowa farm boy, Riley (Marc Blucas).

Season five sees Buffy fight her most powerful nemesis yet, an acerbic blond god called Glory, who is attempting to bring her Hell Dimension into our reality. Shockingly, the final battle sees Buffy lose her life. This is also the season that gave Buffy a sister born from mysticism, Michelle Trachtenberg's Dawn. The decision to add Dawn so late in the game was (and remains in some quarters) a controversial decision. Some fans objected to retooling the series to include a sister, while others saw it as simply another brilliant and surprising turn of events.

Once more revealing a multi-faceted sense of reality, the series' sixth season features Buffy battling three "Nerds of Doom," a trio of anti-social, derided white boys who feel they are overlooked and underappreciated by society at large. For the first time in the series' history, the villain arose not from the supernatural, but from our mortal, world. The same season also sees Willow's lover, Tara, killed by something very real: a stray bullet; it was also the season of Buffy's aforementioned torrid sexual affair with Spike. The sixth season fiercely divided fandom, with some fans (including this one) finding the series more immersive and addicting than ever, while others felt it went too far to the dark side.

Perhaps in response to such a step away from the norm, the seventh season finishes off the series with a return of the supernatural "Big Bad," in this case a monster called "The First Evil," from the dawn of time. As the series comes to a stirring conclusion, Buffy and Willow rally the power of the slayer to activate all potential slayers around the world. This plotline is unapologetically feminist in nature, reminding all women everywhere of their potential to be as strong and committed in their lives as Buffy is to her final (on TV, anyway) battle.

Although the filmed pilot was not very good, and the first season feels pretty hit-or-miss in terms of quality, *Buffy the Vampire Slayer* quickly proved incredibly popular with adolescent viewers, but also with scholars and academicians, primarily for the clever allegories and stories it vetted throughout its run. For the first three seasons, the story is basically "High School is Hell" on a weekly basis, a concept to which anyone who remembers those years will relate. While growing up, Buffy and her friends must deal not only with the responsibility of doing well in their studies, and taking their next steps to adulthood, but battle monsters who expose some modern aspect of teenage angst.

For example, an early episode called "Out of Mind, Out of Sight," involves an unpopular female student, Marcie Ross (played by Clea Duvall), who grows so accustomed to feeling invisible that she actually becomes invisible. Marcie's inability to be seen and noticed by her class-mate results in her becoming a monster as she enacts revenge on all her tormentors, including Cordelia.

Another *Buffy the Vampire Slayer* episode, "Beauty and the Beasts," aired in the stellar third season, involves the idea of an abusive boy-friend and the girlfriend who just can't seem to escape from him despite his violent treatment of her. The boy in this case, Pete (Phill Lewis), is more than an abuser. Like Marcie before him, he is also a literal monster, having created a formula to make him more macho. Instead, he has only turned himself into a monster, one who sees no problem hurting Debbie (Danielle Weeks), a woman he ostensibly loves. In short, Pete's story is that of Dr. Jekyll and Mr. Hyde. But the focus here is not on the nature of the monster, but rather the women in the monster's orbit who enable his behavior.

The "B" story in "Beauty and the Beasts" actually mirrors this power-ful idea, with Buffy learning that Angel had returned from hell (following his demise in the second-season cliffhanger), but as a wild, feral beast. Once learning this, Buffy hides his existence from her friends, fearing their judgment of her. Buffy's behavior in this episode reveals that it isn't only the weak-willed Debbie who is willing to tolerate the presence of a monster in her life, but our hero as well.

"Earshot," another third-season installment, takes on the concept of school shootings in America, and proved so on-point about the subject it that the WB delayed the episode's original airdate until the following fall. In "Earshot," Buffy gains the ability to read the minds of her peers after exposure to strange demon blood. She soon hears someone planning to commit murder at the school, but can't tell who it is. Her investiga-tion ultimately leads her to Jonathan (Danny Strong), one of the Nerds of Dooms, who has gone up to the bell tower on the school campus, armed with a rifle. Tired of feeling unloved and unseen, he seeks to strike out. But in a surprise twist, he is planning only to commit suicide, not kill others. The real killer is someone else.

Still, this episode is a trenchant look at issues of teen self-esteem, and was intended to be aired in April of 1999, the same month that saw the devastating school shooting at Columbine High School in Littleton, Colorado. "Earshot" was simply deemed so powerful that it didn't finally air until five long months later.

Buffy the Vampire Slayer very quickly succeeded in the ratings, and became a success both as striking entertainment and as a series that had something to say about what it means to be a teenager, particularly a teenage girl, in modern America. *Time* magazine termed the series "a post-feminist parable on the challenge of balancing one's personal and work life," and *TV Guide*'s Matt Roush called the series a "literal scream and a hoot. Better yet, it's smart with unfailingly glib dialogue."

As the series grew more confident over the seasons, it began, under Joss Whedon's auspices, to take greater risks. For instance, the fourth season features a silent episode called "Hush," that is widely loved and admired, and the sixth season brought a musical episode, "Once More, with Feeling," that is likely the direct antecedent to *Dr. Horrible's Sing-a-long Blog*.

The fifth season also features a heart-wrenching episode called "The Body," written and directed by Whedon, which involves the non-supernatural death of Buffy's beloved mom, Joyce (Kristine Sutherland). The stunning story explores Buffy's reactions, in a moment so real it hurts, to the discovery of her mother's corpse, and proved to be an emotional highlight of the series.

Looking back, perhaps the most amazing thing about *Buffy the Vampire Slayer* is the fact that it was able to combine horror ("Hush") superheroes ("The Gift,") drama ("The Body") and comedy with such skill that it never feels like a tonal mishmash, or that any element is off-point, or a mistake. The Buffyverse is such a remarkable place to visit because its characters speak with wit, charm, and individuality, and the stories are engaging, terrifying, inspiring, and recognizable to us all. We have all lost loved ones, endured high school, or felt invisible. Whedon's work always involves both social commentary and the deconstruction of clichés, and Buffy is perhaps the best, most shining example of that approach.

The TV series is a paean to female strength, without being a polemic. It is funny without descending into camp or tongue-in-cheek antics, the downfall of its film predecessor. And the show is effortlessly scary without depending on feelings like disgust or over-the-top gore. It's the ultimate comic book, consistent, even as it manages to be four or five different things at once. *Entertainment Weekly*'s critic called *Buffy the Vampire Slayer* a "slam bang series that prides itself on its blithe knowingness and sarcasm, and just keeps getting better at juggling hilarity, gothic romance and horror."

The same critic also noted that no series other than *Seinfeld* loves "the language of the conversation" more, and that's another thing that makes Buffy so remarkable an artifact. "Buffy Speak," is a unique, culturally relevant form of expression, whether it involves Buffy and Xander discussing "Muldering" through a crime investigation and evoking *The X-Files*, or Willow remarking of an alternate universe doppelgänger that she is evil, skanky, and "kind of gay" ("Doppelgängland"). The on-point dialogue is knowing about its characters, their manner of relating, with the writers knowing how to turn a phrase so that it proves unforgettable.

A reboot of the series was announced at San Diego Comic-Con in July of 2018, an idea that met with some resistance from fans. This is because via *Buffy the Vampire Slayer* and *Angel*, the Buffyverse is a well-populated place. It would be great to have a new series with an African-American vampire slayer as the lead. But to "reboot" Buffy herself means to *un*write the masterful universe that captured a generation of fans (and academics), from 1997–2005, essentially. That nearly decade-long time period is about more than a heroine. It is about her world, her friends, her victories, and her dream for the future. So a reboot threatens to unravel all that world, just to retell the same heroine's story.

If it's not broken, why fix it?

11

What Are the Five Best Episodes of *Buffy the Vampire Slayer*?

B uffy *The Vampire Slayer* (1997–2003) ran for 144 episodes, and it is no easy task picking only five "best" episodes. It would be much easier, for instance, to pick the "best five" for each season. There is much fan consensus about the high quality of episodes, such as "The Body," "Hush," and "Once More, with Feeling," but that only leaves two slots, so many great episodes won't get a shout out.

Here goes.

#5. "Pangs." Written by Jane Espenson. Directed by Michael Lange. Airdate: November 23, 1999

In this holiday installment, from the series' fourth season, Buffy (Sarah Michelle Gellar) and the Scooby Gang investigate a murderous demon after the buried Sunnydale Mission (believed to have been destroyed in the earthquake of 1812) is accidentally unearthed. Or rather, Xander discovers the mission by falling into a hole during the dedication and ground-breaking ceremony of U.C. Sunnydale's new and expensive "cultural center." Unfortunately, by breaking into the sealed subterranean chamber, Xander accidentally releases the vengeful spirit of a Chumash warrior named Hus (Tod Thawley).

Hus's Native American people suffered imprisonment, forced labor, and terrible disease when the white man arrived from Europe and quickly populated the American continent. Now, the demon's first order of business is "re-creating the wrongs" done to his native people all those years and centuries ago. Translated, this means that the demon curses Xander with malaria, smallpox, and syphilis. "I am vengeance," declares Hus. "I am my people's cry."

As Buffy tracks down the vengeful and murderous Hus, she broaches another challenging undertaking. She prepares a traditional, home-cooked Thanksgiving meal at Giles's apartment. A nostalgic Buffy recalls the happy holidays from her youth and—during her first year away at college—desires to recreate that experience. She talks meaningfully and wistfully in the narrative about the "sense-memory" of Thanksgiving that occurs every time she smells a roasted turkey.

The socially minded Willow is upset, however, because she believes Thanksgiving is really just a celebration of "one culture wiping out another." It's a "sham," Willow complains, upset by Buffy's buy-in to the myth. Buffy's response? "Perhaps it is a sham . . . but it's a sham . . . with yams."

Giles and the recently neutered Spike (with a behavior-modification chip lodged in his noggin) are bothered by Willow's unflattering description of the autumnal holiday. They both see the situation more plainly. "You had better weapons . . . and you massacred them," Spike tells Willow of the Native-American population. Simple as that.

Or is it?

The debate raises an important question. Is it right for Buffy to "slay" Hus when he has a legitimate grievance against Sunnydale's ancestors? What's worse, isn't he right to be upset that—*on his people's former land*—the conquering people are now building a "cultural center," in effect a celebration of the genocide of the indigenous folks?

On top of all these moral questions, Angel makes a surprise appearance in Sunnydale, and doesn't tell Buffy.

What remains so terrific and funny about "Pangs" nearly a full two decades after its first airing is that Buffy's attempt to host a happy holiday dinner is undercut at every turn by grave philosophical and political disagreements in her family, a unit which certainly includes the demonic Spike at this point. The topic turns overtly political after a fashion, and everyone who has ever returned home for a family holiday knows very well that politics is the source of much indigestion at real-life gatherings.

This fact of life seems especially true in the Trump era, when so many families are split down the middle over political issues. And yet, as this episode points out, the Thanksgiving meal is a time when one is supposed to be gracious and happy about togetherness. In-laws who hold different viewpoints are suddenly thrust together for a meal at the same table—and there's usually alcohol involved—and the sparks can really fly.

The particular philosophical discussion underlining "Pangs" concerns a question not unfamiliar to most of us in modern American culture. Can a wrong in the past be repaired by a wrong in the present? This idea has been discussed much, especially near the end of Clinton's second term (when *Buffy* aired), specifically in relation to America's ignoble history of slavery. Should apology be policy? Are modern Americans responsible for their ancestors' misdeeds?

In terms of the Native-American genocide, the same question is raised in "Pangs." And if reparations forced upon a blameless current generation don't feel particularly just either, does a simple apology to the families of the wronged feel like enough? Is that the best we can muster?

Obviously, there are no simple answers to such deep questions of American history, but *Buffy the Vampire Slayer* takes the context of Thanksgiving and holiday gatherings and then makes the dramatis personae debate the conflicted nature of the holiday, each according to his or her own personal beliefs. Nobody is bad. Nobody is evil (well, nobody besides Spike). Everyone just boasts a different perspective on what remains a controversial subject. What the episode is, then, is an intercultural communication event, over the American holiday table.

Here—treading deeper into the quagmire—some hurtful comments are even made about a "minority" living in Buffy's modern, diverse Sunnydale: *demons*. Xander lays down the law, and it sounds perilously like bigotry. "You don't talk to vengeance demons, you kill them!" he stresses, angry and sick.

Well, of course, this remark hurts Anya's feelings. She's a demon, after all. Not all of them are evil, are they? What about Oz? What about Angel? And on and on. Is killing them on sight the answer? Today, "Pangs" seem to be a statement not only about politics, but racism, and perhaps most importantly, the diversity of those who sit together at this aforementioned

American table. At Buffy's table sits an Englishman, a Jew (Willow), a slayer, a vampire, a demon, and a geek.

And so they are all going to see things differently. But the important thing is that these characters, whether they admit it openly or not, also love one another. Their differences can make things awkward, but Thanksgiving is a time of family, and "Pangs" proves itself brilliant by making the audience understand that as diverse as it looks, the people seated around this holiday table are Buffy's family. It's a found, or engineered, or created, family, messy and messed up, but a family nonetheless.

Finally, Hus and a "raiding party" of demons arrive at Buffy's Thanksgiving meal, and a colossal battle occurs between the slayer and a demon she has zero interest in killing. Buffy would prefer to offer an apology, rather than fisticuffs. To the direct-minded Spike, however, this approach is folly. "You exterminated his people," he reminds Buffy of Hus.

An apology ain't gonna cut it.

Finally, Buffy's "political correctness" must give way to the practical. She does fight, and with lethal force, and the implication seems to be that some hurts, some breaches, simply can't be resolved peaceably. Ultimately, even the politically correct Willow feels like something of a hypocrite by episode's end. When the Native-American demon spirits attack, she's among those who pick up a shovel and fight for their lives. As we all surely would under the same circumstances.

But the coda in "Pangs" involves hope for the future instead of a conflict over the past. In the episode's last scene, the threat of Hus is nullified, and Buffy and her friends (including Spike) sit down together—demon *and* human—for an enjoyable "family" feast. The mere fact that these diverse folks *break bread at the same table may provide the key to moving past old wounds.* Perhaps enemies old and new must share a Thanksgiving table and a special meal together, and start fresh. Build new, better memories. Let go of the angers of the past, even if they are justified.

Otherwise, as Hus learns, the only possible future is death. At least breaking bread, and passing the cranberry sauce is a start. As Xander happily notes at the conclusion of "Pangs," it's the perfect Thanksgiving in Sunnydale after all: "a bunch of anticipation, a big fight, and now we're all sleepy . . ." It's a Thanksgiving recipe every American family understands.

#4. "Innocence." Written and Directed by Joss Whedon. Airdate: January 20, 1998

"Innocence" is a crucial turning point in the second season of *Buffy the Vampire Slayer*. Up until mid-season, Angel has acted as a loving boyfriend, and a trusted ally in the fight against evil. Yes, he is a vampire, but he has shown restraint about his appetites, and true loyalty and love for the slayer. He is the most trustworthy guy one can imagine.

Then, at the end of the episode "Surprise," which immediately precedes "Innocence," Buffy and Angel have sexual intercourse for the first time, and he experiences, during that event, a moment of true happiness. However, he has been cursed with gypsies who want revenge for his murder, decades earlier, of one of their own. If Angel is ever to experience true happiness, he will lose his soul, and become the murderous Angelus. That's what happens in "Innocence." Angel is transformed into Angelus, and he remains Angelus throughout the remainder of the season.

There are other details in the plot for "Innocence" that bear repeating. Spike and Drusilla (Juliet Landau) have assembled a monstrous demon, The Judge (Brian Thompson), who by touch can burn the humanity right out of a person. This is the powerful nemesis Buffy and Angel are fighting when they retreat, hide, and then make love.

However, more important than any of these details, perhaps, is the subtext or parallel track running throughout "Innocence." Buffy has just had sex for the first time, and immediately after doing so, her boyfriend changes, and not for the better. *Buffy the Vampire Slayer* is a series always at its best when it draws parallels between the supernatural and the experience of adolescence, and that is what Whedon accomplishes with this story. Angel is suddenly "that guy," the one who is no longer attentive and caring, once he's had sex with the girl of his dreams. All that came before in the relationship—the attention, the friendship, the ardor—was just preamble for sex, and now that he's gotten what he wants, he doesn't care at all about his girlfriend's feelings.

Angel is that guy on steroids, actually. He is mean and condescending to Buffy about their first time, and he acts like it is no big deal, when it means the world to her. And then, when she doesn't understand the change in his behavior, he acts like *she's* the one with the problem; that she's making too big a deal out of what happened. He even calls her, essentially, a whore, telling her: "I thought you were a pro." Finally, Angel gives her the ultimate brush-off. "I'll call you," he tells Buffy, when he clearly has no intention of doing so. This is gaslighting in the extreme.

What's fascinating about "Innocence" is that it functions on more than the supernatural/adolescent tracks. The story is actually one about betrayal, or more specifically, about men betraying women. As noted above, Angel takes Buffy's heart, and then betrays her, seeking to destroy her with cruelty. But while Buffy's story unfolds, Willow simultaneously discovers that Xander and Cordelia have been kissing and carrying on together in secret. Willow has been in love with Xander since the start of the series, and not only has he been dishonest with her about his feelings for Cordelia, he has chosen as a girlfriend a person Willow hates. "You'd rather be with someone you hate than be with me," she tells him, in tears.

Finally, Jenny Calendar is betrayed by men in her life, too, and "Innocence" points that out. In particular, the gypsy leader (Vincent Schiavelli) is at fault. He calls himself "faithful" in terms of his family, and his plan for revenge. But, in fact, his curse—and his commitment to the curse—has loosed a monster that can't be controlled, and that ultimately kills Jenny. "Uncle, this is insanity," she begs him, but he won't change from his course, any more than Angel or Xander change from theirs.

Taken together, "Innocence" is about the loss of something precious. It is not about the loss of virginity, necessarily, but the realization, on the part of Buffy, Willow, and Jenny, that even though they feel love and affection for others, that does not mean they will live happily ever after. The have lost the innocence of believing that they will be loved and treated well by the men in their life. Instead, they are "all fools," just as Jenny tells her uncle at one point. They have realized they should not give their trust to men so easily.

"Innocence" is also a great episode because of the Scooby Gang's inventive way of defeating the Judge, a villain who grows so powerful that he will soon be able to "reduce people to charcoal with a look." The prophecy regarding the Judge reads that no weapon forged can destroy him. Thus, after Xander and Cordelia steal a missile launcher from a local army base, Buffy blows the Judge to pieces with a weapon that was never forged. The reaction shot of Buffy after she has fired the weapon is amazing, and would eventually be incorporated into the series' opening credits. It is sweet revenge for her to foil Angelus's plan and bring an end to the Judge's reign of terror.

"Innocence" also ends on a strong note that reinforces the episode's themes. In the coda, Buffy and her mom watch a musical on television, 1936's *Stowaway*. This is a Shirley Temple film, in which she sings "Goodnight, My Love." That song could be the epitaph for Buffy's relationship with Angel.

#3. "The Body." Written and Directed by Joss Whedon. Airdate: February 27, 2001

If any episode of any TV series could be described as "too real," Joss Whedon's fifth-season entry "The Body" fits the bill. This episode is heartbreaking, all too familiar, authentic. The episode came about because of Whedon's own experience as a young adult with sudden death in his family: he lost his mother. The author used the truths he learned during that tragedy to craft an unforgettable episode that, in some ways, completes Buffy's journey to adulthood.

"The Body" involves the unexpected and not-supernatural death of a beloved character: Buffy's mother Joyce, who had been played for four-and-a-half seasons by Kristine Sutherland. As the episode begins, Buffy returns to her home, thinking all is well. She enters her house and shouts out, "Hey, Mom!"

For her, everything is normal and happy, but behind her, in the background of the shot, Joyce is on the sofa, dead, the victim of a brain aneurysm. From here, the episode adheres closely to the stages of grief as diagrammed by Elizabeth Kübler-Ross. Those stages are denial, anger, bargaining, depression, and, finally, acceptance.

Denial is Buffy's immediate response. She calls 911 for help, and as the EMTs work on her mother, the audience slips into Buffy's thoughts. In this fantasy, Joyce wakes up, and it's a "beautiful miracle." Then, Buffy and Dawn are with an awake and happy Joyce in the hospital, noting she is "good as new," and that Buffy saved her life by coming home when she did. It's desperate, wishful thinking that ends back in the real world, with

Joyce still unresponsive, and cold, now on the living room floor, as the EMTs fail to bring her back.

The opening scene in "The Body" is extraordinary not only for capturing Buffy's immediate reaction, denial of death, but the feeling that life is somehow now unreal, as she contends with the unthinkable. For instance, there is a brief close-up of Buffy's telephone in the scene, as if the keys which she should dial (to call Giles) are indecipherable. At one point,

A family affair: Dawn (Trachtenberg) joins Buffy (Gellar) in the fifth season of *Buffy the Vampire Slayer*, a span that brought stellar episodes such as "The Body."

John Muir Photo Archive

Buffy stands outside the house and there is no music on the soundtrack, only the distant sounds of wind-chimes and children playing. It feels like an extended moment of unreal time. Even the EMT, when he first approaches Buffy to tell her that there is nothing he can do to save Joyce, is out-of-focus. These strange moments capture how disconnected life feels when something terrible has occurred. Buffy's off-kilter responses (like her almost mindless comment to the EMTs, "Good luck") visually and aurally capture the notion that Buffy has slipped into another dimension, one that is catastrophically real and irreversible.

The stage of anger in the grieving process comes into the episode with Xander's presence. Xander comes from a very unhappy family life, and Joyce is, in some ways, the mother he wished he had. When Joyce dies, Xander goes off the rails, blaming the doctors who took care of Joyce for not preventing her death. He is so angry that he punches through a wall in Willow's dorm room, and literally can't pull it out. When he does manage to retract his hand, it is bloodied, and he has hurt nobody but himself. As in life, the reaction to tragedy here is to look for someone responsible, someone to blame. Anger is easy; acceptance, hard.

Bargaining is not a stage of the Kübler-Ross model focused on in detail here. Buffy doesn't attempt to seek a supernatural remedy, for instance, for her mother's death. She does not promise to be a "better daughter" before the eyes of God, either, if only her mother is returned to her. However, it might fairly be stated that Willow and Anya go through aspects of the bargaining process. Anya will be a better human being, she hopes, if only someone can explain to her what "death" is. As a vengeance demon, she did not know mortality, or death. It is something new to her, and therefore something terrifying. She keeps awkwardly seeking answers about Joyce's death, apologizing for her lack of tact and knowledge, as if to "know" will make it easier. And Willow considers that she can't "even be a grown-up" because she can't choose the right wardrobe for the family's visit to the morgue. It's as if dressing correctly will somehow make Willow mature, appropriate, and able to help Buffy. And, of course, that isn't the case.

The fourth stage in the model is depression, and this might best be expressed in the latter half of the episode, in moments that involve both Dawn and Buffy. At school, Dawn is seen crying over a slight from a classmate, and then attending an art class in which the subject of the day is the use of "negative space" in painting. Buffy takes Dawn out of class to tell her what has happened, and director Whedon makes an interesting visual choice. Instead of following the grieving sisters out into the hallway, where Buffy reveals the truth to Dawn, the camera stays planted in the classroom.

The Buffy–Dawn scene is observed only from a distance, through a window, and the audience cannot hear what is said. It can only witness the impact of the news, as Dawn collapses into tears. Perhaps this is Whedon's way of acknowledging that no one can truly "feel" the death of another's loved one until it happens to their own loved ones. The audience sees Dawn's pain, but it is somehow distant, something observed and felt from afar.

At the hospital, Buffy is quiet and withdrawn, both qualities of depression. It is here that Tara attempts to explain to Buffy about her own experience with the death of her mother. She tells Buffy not to feel bad about "thoughts and responses" that she might not understand. In other words, there is no wrong way to grieve, no guidebook for dealing with such a tragedy. The sad thing here is that Buffy may not be able to hear Tara's words due to her own depression and grief.

The final stage of grief, acceptance, comes in the episode's final composition. Buffy has just had to slay a vampire in the morgue to save Dawn. Dawn has fallen backwards, near Joyce's body. She pulls the white sheet off Joyce's face, and we see, without question, that her mother is dead and gone, just as Buffy said moments earlier. The episode cuts to black on that recognition. There is no arguing with death. Acceptance of it isn't a matter of degrees. On seeing the corpse, Buffy and Dawn have no choice but to accept Joyce's death. Their mother is gone.

"The Body" is a harrowing episode, in part for how it deals with the swirl of emotions (and stages of grieving) brought on by a sudden, and senseless, death of a loved one. The episode features almost no background music whatsoever, and this absence of a soundtrack makes the story feel all the more real. In real life, soundtrack music doesn't reveal or illuminate human emotional states. Instead, silence is real, awkward, and ever-present in grief. The silence here represents, perhaps, the absence of the deceased's voice. No other sound will possibly suffice, and yet it will never be heard again.

Another brilliant aspect of "The Body" involves the return to a frequent series theme: Buffy's duty and obligation to be the slayer. Here, she cannot even grieve her mother in peace. She can't stop being the slayer long enough to feel what she must to continue going, to care for her sister. Instead, she still must kill a vampire; must still be "on the job." And this predicament is oddly truthful. Loved ones die, and yet the world does not stop spinning to account for grieving. Bills still must be paid. One must still go to work, or raise children (or siblings), or even attend school. Although a death in the family feels like the end of the world, the world just keeps turning.

For how it handles the grieving process, for how it treads into real pain, and does not use supernatural tropes to alleviate it, "The Body" is a one-of-a-kind episode of this series, and one of the finest episodes in the canon.

#2. "Hush." Written and directed by Joss Whedon. Airdate: December 14, 1999

One of the most ambitious and audacious episodes of *Buffy the Vampire Slayer* is the "silent movie" episode titled "Hush." A silent TV episode might sound like a gimmick to some readers, but when this author interviewed Mr. Whedon in the early 2000s, he affirmed to me that the idea was far from a ratings stunt. "The fact is, the silent episode made sense in that world, as horror," Whedon observed. "To be unable to scream is a terrifying thing, and it made sense in *Buffy*. What was interesting about it was when I started to write it at first, I was just terrified. I thought, At least I know Buffy is going to have sex with her boyfriend. That's two minutes I know they don't have to talk, and we'll watch. Then as we went through the season, I realized it was too early for them to have sex, and was like, 'Oh, I lost my crutch. I'm a dead man. I'll never be able to do this.'"

"But what was interesting was that I came to the realization that the show was really about communication," Whedon explained, "about the fact that when we stop talking, we start communicating. [It was] the idea of language getting in the way of real communication. When I realized that, everything became very interesting."

Indeed, what "Hush" truly concerns is the potency of non-verbal communication, and how our body language reveals our true selves, even if we do not wish it to. Every person in the world is, in fact, a "one-person band," an orchestra, giving off a variety of signals every single moment. Each person uses expressions and eye contact, body movement or gestures, physical artifacts, even space, time, and touch, to convey and communicate their needs and wants. By taking away language, "Hush" is all about the ways the series protagonists reveal themselves, albeit inadvertently, to their friends.

In "Hush," Buffy experiences a creepy dream sequence set in her college psychology class. At the end of the dream, she is told by a young girl that "the Gentlemen are coming" and that they need to "take seven." Who are the Gentlemen, you may ask? Only one of horror TV's most terrifying monsters, right up there with *X-Files* (1993–2002) monsters of the week, such as the Fluke Man from "The Host" or The Peacock Family in "Home." The Gentlemen are floating, smiling, bald creatures who delight in stealing the hearts of their victims. They are, perhaps, among the images that inspired the creation of Slenderman in the late 2000s. They share that creepy-pasta's formal manner of dress, as well as his chrome-dome.

The Gentlemen arrive in Sunnydale and steal the voices of all its residents, including Buffy, her Scooby Gang, and her new boyfriend, Riley. At this point in the continuity, Buffy and Riley are keeping secrets from each other. Riley is a soldier who is part of the Initiative, a scientific/military project "tagging" supernatural creatures for some unspecified (but presumably dark) purpose. And, of course, Buffy is no average college student, but rather the slayer. So when Buffy and Riley attempt to get closer and talk, they can only speak in half-truths and lies. Their conversations become a "babble-fest" and actually gets in the way of their developing relationship.

But now, the Gentlemen have taken away their voices, and Buffy and Riley are revealed through their actions. They both discover that their significant other is not just an ordinary person, but a protector, a soldier. After their voices are restored, and the truth is revealed, Buffy and Riley note that they "need to talk," but fall into awkward silence. Where do they start? Their non-verbal communication has revealed more about their true natures than any spoken conversation could. The honesty in their non-verbal communication has left them speechless!

"Hush" is a key text in the *Buffy the Vampire Slayer* catalog, and a daring one. Consider that Joss Whedon is the man known for his talk; for his witty language. His use of a glib tone, pop-culture references, and Valley-girl slayer-slang are the very things that mark him as an artist, and earn him the admiration of critics. In "Hush," the artist must get away from all of that, and tell a story with very little dialogue. At the same time, the story must still feel like a natural part of the series, and develop the characters simultaneously. Yet Whedon manages to translate the humor and ironic nature of their characters to body language, which is no small feat. One of the best moments reveals Buffy acting out the process of "staking" the bad guys, though with just her fist, and no stake. This looks, as she quickly realizes, like the act of male masturbation. The baffled responses from those around her is priceless.

Similarly, Buffy's response to Giles's stick-figure drawing of the slayer, with wide hips, sells her displeasure with the inaccurate rendering. The entire episode is filled with canny, clever touches like these that make one realize the efficacy of non-verbal communication.

As Whedon has noted, sometimes when people start talking, they stop communicating. "Hush" not only communicates through the terrifying presence of the series' most memorable villain, or monster of the week, but through its dramatis personae understanding of how to harness their inner "orchestra," and really transmit ideas and emotions to one another. In most supernatural series, the brilliant conceit of non-verbal communication as the essential mode of learning and communicating would be enough to earn "Hush" the number-one spot in a top-five list. *Buffy the Vampire Slayer*, however, had one even more audacious experiment to undertake, in "Once More, with Feeling."

#1. "Once More, with Feeling." Written and directed by Joss Whedon. Airdate: November 6, 2001

Although there are many outstanding episodes of *Buffy*, it is "Once More, With Feeling," the all-singing, all-dancing musical episode, which shines today as something truly amazing, and transcends both its genre and the medium. Critic David Klein called this 2001 installment "absolutely captivating," and "like nothing" he'd seen on regular series television, which he's watched and written about for more than twenty years. He wasn't exaggerating.

Buffy the Vampire Slayer has been called a "post-feminist parable on the challenge of balancing one's personal and work life," and a "literal scream and always a hoot." "Just about the best horror show on television," according to *Cinefantasique*, *Buffy* has also been praised for the fact that "no other show balances so many elements as deftly, without a trace of corniness or melodrama." "Once More, with Feeling" reflects all those strengths, and more.

Some background: For its sixth season, *Buffy the Vampire Slayer* moved from its longtime home at the WB to UPN. In the fifth-season finale, Buffy died while saving the world from an evil god named Glory, and for the sixth season she was resurrected by her friends (including Willow and Xander), but something went terribly wrong. Our stalwart slayer had been pulled out of a heavenly afterlife—not a hell dimension, as her friends feared—and now this mortal coil was all pain and suffering for Buffy. She felt disconnected, alone, and out of touch, but the gallant Chosen One just couldn't express these uncomfortable emotions to her friends, and so she bore the pain in silence and isolation.

At least until, that is, "Once More, with Feeling," a musical treatise about communication, about the songs we sing to ourselves, about the secrets we hide and yearn to share. So if "Hush" was a dissertation on non-verbal communication, "Once More, with Feeling" was about how song and dance can also reveal character.

"Once More, with Feeling" features original music and lyrics by Joss Whedon, with songs produced and arranged by Jesse Tobias and Christopher Beck. Choreographer Adam Shankman was responsible for not just fight scenes in graveyards, but the dance numbers too. The episode's action starts when a demon called Sweet (Hinton Battle) arrives in Sunnydale, summoned by someone close to Buffy. He casts a spell on the town that makes every inhabitant sing and dance about their inner-most emotional issues. That doesn't sound so bad, except that the urge to release the singing and dancing also happens to cause murderous spontaneous combustion, resulting in townies dropping like flies.

Buffy and her friends—including the lovelorn vampire Spike—investigate the crisis, but all the while sing their own tunes. Spike sings "Rest in Peace," imploring Buffy to stop toying with his emotions, or leave him alone. Buffy sings "Going through the Motions," about her detachment from the world. Giles (Anthony Stewart Head) croons about holding Buffy back ("Standing"), and Xander and Anya sing a duet, a 1930s-style "pastiche" called "I'll Never Tell," that reveals their fears about their romantic relationship and marriage plans.

Alyson Hannigan and Emma Caulfield, behind the scenes on *Buffy the Vampire Slayer.*   *John Muir Photo Archive*

In the end, Buffy's secret emotions about being brought back to life are revealed in the final confrontation with Sweet, and her friends know, at last, what is up with the slayer. The honesty and hurt evidenced in this crescendo is practically jaw-dropping. Devastating, but in the style of the old-fashioned movie musical, the episode climaxes not with psychology, but with a kiss and curtain dropping. "Where do we go from here?" the cast sings, as viewers of this fascinating series know that, again, the characters are headed to new and dangerous places. Nothing on *Buffy* remains static; everything changes, and "Once More, with Feeling" is a turning point not only in the continuity, but in the series' legacy, as viewed nearly two decades later.

"The thing about musicals," Joss Whedon told me in an interview for my 2004 book, *Singing a New Tune: The Re-birth of the Modern Film Musical* (which features a chapter on "Once More, with Feeling"), "is you sing what you can't say. In the same way as shutting up [in "Hush"] caused everybody to open up in ways they hadn't before, singing did the same thing. The heart of the matter—what the person is feeling, what they need to communicate, the great revelation, the denouement, whatever it is—all of this should be expressed through song."

Buffy the Vampire Slayer has always concerned language, and how characters use it to conceal, dissemble, reveal, lie, deny, or express love. How the Scoobies sometimes look at Buffy (as a superhero) and themselves (as sidekicks) in dialogue ("Avengers Assemble!" Xander quips in one episode) is one of the perpetual joys of the program, and "Once More, With Feeling" takes the characters in exciting new directions and lays bare their emotions in another manner of communication—not psychologically adroit patter, but the simplicity and elegance of song. It's a bit amazing that an episode this good—boasting a dozen full-fledged musical numbers—could be made on a TV budget and within production limitations. Yet every single song in "Once More, with Feeling" brings out new facets of the characters, and gives the series a wind behind its back for the remainder of the sixth season, one of this author's personal favorites. The sixth season remains controversial because of the sometimes degrading, perverse nature of Buffy and Spike's sexual relationship, but it is an ambitious season too, in which "Life," not some made-up demon, is the "Big Bad."

The musical is a form that's perpetually out-of-fashion in the twenty-first century, but Joss Whedon did the seemingly impossible here. He made the artificial, theatrical art form not just palatable to an increasingly "reality"-obsessed world, but actually irresistible—especially to genre fans. "Once More, with Feeling" is not only the finest and most involving episode of *Buffy the Vampire Slayer*, it's one of the great hours in TV history, with a brilliant soundtrack to match the action on screen.

"It's such an alchemy," Whedon explained to me. "It's so hard to get it right, but if a musical really does hit people, they'll love it more than any damn thing in the world. Because music speaks to people more than anything else does . . . . When you put in exciting lyrics, characters you love, and all that good stuff, everything heightens. It takes you to another level of existence." Fortunately, the cast was up to the challenge and took on the difficult challenge of singing.

"I knew Tony was my ballad guy. I knew James was my rock-and-roll singer, and Michelle wanted to dance a little. I knew what everybody's strength was," Whedon told me. "What I didn't know was how good Emma was going to be. That was a revelation, but I knew she was my musical-comedy girl."

"Once More, with Feeling" proves Whedon's thesis in spades. It is an installment of *Buffy* and genre television that transcends standard episodic television, and just about everything else out there. Of course, just because *Buffy* was a success as a musical, that did not mean Whedon wanted to apply the genre formula to his other TV series.

"I was asked, 'Do you want to do a musical episode of *Angel* or *Firefly*?' And I said, 'Not in a million years.' Those shows don't lend themselves to it. The thing about *Buffy* is that you do the musical episode without violating the reality of *Buffy*. That's the most important thing to me. What's hilarious about working in fantasy is that you can say, 'The evil twin thing? That's not reality, that's bullshit! Who buys that? But the dwarf growing out of someone's head is fine.' . . . You have this seemingly arbitrary, but in fact very strict sense of what can go on in this world. And *Buffy* is so sophomoric, romantic, colorful, tense, sexual . . . I think half the episodes feel like they're about to burst into song anyway . . . . So, to say a demon has come [to Sunnydale] who causes musicals makes perfect sense in that world. It doesn't make sense in the *Angel* world to me. It definitely makes no sense in the *Firefly* world. It's a different kind of choice."

One might note that *Angel* is Whedon's neo-noir, and *Firefly* his neo-Western. If that's the case, then *Buffy* is his musical: a series characterized by big emotions, colorful performances, and carefully choreographed action. If this is so, then "Once More, with Feeling" represents, actually, *Buffy*'s great act of "becoming" what it was always meant to be.

12

Angel (1999–2004)

Cast

David Boreanaz:	Angel
Alexis Denisof:	Wesley Wyndham-Pryce
J. August Richards:	Charles Gunn
Charisma Carpenter:	Cordelia Chase (Seasons 1–4)
Glenn Quinn:	Allen Doyle (Season 1)
Andy Hallett:	Lorne (Seasons 2–5)
Amy Acker:	Winifred Birkle/Illyria (Seasons 2–5)
James Marsters:	Spike (Season 5)

Crew

Mutant Enemy, Greenwoolf, Kuzui Enterprises, Sandollar Television, 20th Century Fox Television

Casting:	Anya Colloff, Jennifer Fishman, Amy McIntyre Britt, Barbara Stordahl, Angela Terry
Costume Designers:	Chic Gemarelli, Shawna Trpic, Jessica Pazdernik, Enid Harris
Production Designers:	Stuart Blatt, Carey Meyer
Music:	Robert J. Kral, Christopher Beck
Cinematography:	Ross Berryman, Herbert Davis
Executive Producers:	Gail Berman, Sandy Gallin, David Greenwalt, Fran Rubel Kuzi, Kaz Kazui, Joss Whedon, Tim Minear, Jeffrey Bell

At the height of *Buffy the Vampire Slayer*'s popularity during its third season airing on the WB, serious talk of a spinoff series to highlight David Boreanaz's brooding vampire-with-a-soul, Angel, began in earnest. By the following fall, *Angel* (1999–2004) had its own prime-time berth, Tuesdays at 9:00 p.m., even as Buffy Summers started her freshman year in college (and gained a new boyfriend in Marc Blucas's Riley).

Co-created by Joss Whedon and David Greenwalt, *Angel* quickly proved a stark change of pace from its predecessor. Where *Buffy the Vampire Slayer* concerns navigating adolescence and adulthood, with the high school years serving as the equivalent of a supernatural "Hell," *Angel* is deliberately crafted as a noir, a "dark" enterprise. Where *Buffy* is sunny (right down to its choice of locales, Sunnydale), *Angel* inhabits the night.

As TV curator David Bushman notes in an interview with David Greenwalt, "[F]or the spinoff they moved him [Angel] to that great blanc/noir setting, Los Angeles—home to both Disneyland and the Manson murders (or, as scholar Benjamin Jacob has termed it in deconstructing the series, "Los Angelus")—and made him a private eye. The early seasons of *Angel* in particular have a real noir vibe to them, which, as Greenwalt says in this interview, was the intention from the start, as he and Whedon sought to distinguish the show from its forerunner.

The film noir genre originated in America of the post–World War II era (circa 1946), and is known for a number of distinctive elements, virtually all of which one can detect in any close reading of *Angel*. First and foremost, the protagonist in a film noir is often a private eye, or investigator, one working outside any official bureaucracy and with few resources. This private dick is often scraping by, eager for his next job. This description perfectly suits Angel's world in turn-of-the-millennium Los Angeles, as the series commences. He works to help the hopeless in Los Angeles, but forms a very low-budget agency with the help of another Sunnydale transplant, Cordelia Chase (Charisma Carpenter), and Doyle (Glenn Quinn), a human-demon hybrid with prophetic visions.

Although some critics, including *Variety*'s Laura Fries, considered the "help-for-hire angle" a little "dicey," it is part and parcel of the format that *Angel* apes. The hero (or anti-hero) of the noir must always stand outside any establishment or form or authority. The first-season episodes of the series reek of desperation. Cordy has failed in an acting career, and must steal food from a party she attends. And Doyle and Cordelia are reduced to shooting a (terrible) video commercial to publicize Angel's services. Angel, meanwhile, broods in his basement.

Beyond the private-eye hero, the noir must always feature an urban setting: city streets, bars, nightclubs, and alleys. These are the places where the lowest of the low, from petty criminals to gangland bosses, operate in secret, under cover of night. *Buffy the Vampire Slayer* is set in Sunnydale, a suburbia that happens to rest on a Hellmouth, but a place of high school, caring parents, and commerce (like the Magic Box magic store). Angel is set in the so-called City of Angels, and a metropolis of extreme contradictions. In L.A. there is simultaneously great wealth, and great poverty. There are popular movie stars who live there, and desperate people chasing stardom. There is the reality of police violence, and the "romance" of police TV shows and films, which glorify authority, standing side-by-side. Tinsel Town is also the area of riots and social unrest in the 1990s, the era of the series. And the history of the noir format is not only an urban one, but one about social unrest, of social commentary.

Film noir is a complex genre, and *Angel* reflects and transmits that complexity through Angel's ongoing negotiation of various realities, dimensions, and hierarchies. Throughout the series, he must contend with capricious (and often haughty) higher beings. Some are known as the Powers-That-Be. Others are known as Oracles. Some are known simply as the Senior Partners (at the wealthy law firm Wolfram and Hart). And then there are the Old Demons, like Illyria, who dwell in a "hole in the world," but look for ways to re-insert themselves into the ebb and flow of the human world.

Angel possesses no real power among these various hierarchies, even if he is, at times, awarded the trappings of power (like an office and staff at Wolfram and Hart). He is a "new player in town," as "City of Angel" establishes, but not a power player. This idea, too, is very noir. As Jennifer Fay and Justus Nieland write in *Film Noir: Hard-Boiled Modernity and the Culture of Globalization* (2009), noir concerns an "understanding of the American citizens neither as totally free agents nor as passive victims, but rather as a member of various population groups whose interests were represented by a complex web of interlocking and competing national bureaucracies."

In other words, Angel stands up not only for the little guy, but in a real sense he's a little guy, too. He may be known variously as a savior or "Promised One," or as the subject of the "Shanshu" prophecy, but this merely means he is a pawn of the demonic hierarchies, to be moved around on a game board, and fulfill destinies he has not written for himself. Metaphorically, he is always in that basement, and there is always a (guarded) elevator going to the "top floor," where the decisions of the powerful are unseen, but felt.

They help the hopeless. Angel leads his team in Los Angeles in Joss Whedon's *Angel*. From left to right: Fred (Amy Acker), Wesley (Alexis Denisof), Angel (David Boreanaz), Cordelia (Charisma Carpenter) and Gunn (J. August Richards).   *John Muir Photo Archive*

Joss Whedon has reported that conventions of film noir define what *Angel* is, as a series, and that fact is clear, too, from the other elements of the form the series revives for interpretation. For example, noirs are known to often feature flashbacks, and *Angel* is a program rife with flashbacks. Not only does the series feature flashbacks to Angel's long life and turmoil two centuries earlier, but to his time in other decades of the twentieth century as well. In "City of Angels," the vampire with a soul notes that he was in Vegas during the Great Depression, and other episodes place him in tales during the Second World War ("Why We Fight"), and even during the McCarthy hearings of the 1950s ("Are You Now, or Have You Ever Been?").

Angel's past is part of the "thing" he is running away from but can never escape, and the frequent flashbacks to his time as Angelus, a murderous vampire who feeds on humans, is a constant reminder of how far the road is that he must travel to be redeemed. Audiences see, for instance, his history with Darla (Julie Benz), his sire, in 1760, as well as his previous, bloody encounters with a vampire hunter, Holtz (Keith Szarabjka).

Uniquely, it is not just Angel who is the subject of personality-defining flashbacks throughout the series. An early episode, "Hero," reveals how his friend Doyle failed to help other demons of his kind, before coming to terms with his own nature as a half-breed. And "A Hole in the World" opens with Fred's (Amy Acker) flashback to her last days at home with her parents, before moving to Los Angeles. Her parents feared she would be traveling to a den of inequity and evil. She assured them that that was not the case. But, ironically, she spent the next five years living in a cave in a dimension called Pylea, scraping by as a slave. And the same episode, "A Hole in the World," features Fred's possession by the Old One, a demon named Illyria. She literally dies, becoming a devil in the process, thereby validating or at least justifying her parents' earlier concern for her soul. In the case of all these characters, the past is a constant presence in their lives, coloring their decisions.

Films noir are also beloved for their downbeat, pessimistic, or even bleak endings. *Angel*'s final episode, after five seasons, titled "Not Fade Away," ends in that precise fashion. If not downbeat or pessimistic, one might conclude, at least, that it is highly ambivalent. Angel and his friends face down an army of evil in an alley, and the audience has no idea what happens to them. Do they win? Lose? Die? Surrender? It is not unexpected at all that a noir series would go out on such an inconclusive, tragic note.

Furthermore, *Angel* features a number of deaths among *Angel*'s heroic team, throughout its run. One quality Joss Whedon is famous for, at least among longtime fans, is killing off beloved characters. In *Angel*, major characters never survive for long. Doyle, Cordelia, Wesley Wyndham Price (Alexis Denisof), and Fred all die during a five-year spell.

When one cuts out all the bells and whistles, a film noir is truly about the private investigator, and his search for his own identity. The cases he navigates are ones that reveal something not only about the participants and their world, but about their souls. This fact is also abundantly true of *Angel*, as a series. Angel grapples throughout all the episodes with his own self-loathing, loneliness, and weakness. His vampirism plays as a metaphor for alcoholism; the habit he can never quite beat. And his resistance to corruption is never a given.

In the fifth, and final, season, for instance, he makes a deal with the "Devils" at Wolfram and Hart, and in some way compromises his morals. When Cordelia reminds him that he has become CEO of "Hell Incorporated," he must find who he is, again, and reckon with the fact that people like him "just don't get to" have happiness. Even when doing what he is destined to do—fight evil—he is "miserable." Over the course of the five-year run, Angel loses the woman he loves, Cordelia, and must give up all connection to his son, Connor (Vincent Kartheiser). His lot in life is to be perpetually unhappy, even as he fights for the rest of us, for the human race.

It is, finally, the noir qualities one finds in *Angel* that grant the series "an atmosphere entirely different from *Buffy*'s," according to critic Ken Tucker's in his 1999 review of the series in *Entertainment Weekly*. If *Buffy* is about growing up to face the world, then *Angel* is about an adult reckoning that the world is a place of moral compromises and transience.

In terms of quality, *Angel* is not nearly as consistent a series as its celebrated predecessor. The series goes through dramatic cast and location changes during its five years on the air. Angel Investigations moves from the hole-in-the-wall urban office in the first season, to a haunted

Los Angeles hotel, The Hyperion, in the second season, to the modern offices of Wolfram and Hart in the fifth. The characters change radically over the span too, and there are two ways to gaze at these changes. The first involves inconsistent writing. Cordelia goes from being a sarcastic, ignorant, superficial character to nothing less than Saint Cordelia in the span of four years, and Wesley goes from being a namby-pamby by-the-book Watcher to a streetwise fighter of the supernatural in short order. These transitions are sometimes whiplash inducing, and feel awkward or contrived.

On the other hand, one might argue *Angel* is a series about second chances, and second acts. Angel gets a second act. He is no longer hiding in a crypt, lurking in the shadows to protect "The Chosen One." He is actively seeking redemption here. Likewise, Cordelia is no longer the smug, parochial rich brat the audience met in Sunnydale, but someone who gets to know suffering and pain, primarily from her supernatural visions, and failed acting career. Wes, through his at-first-unrequited love of Fred and then her devastating loss, comes to be fully human and relatable, right down to his heartbreaking final moment.

Even the addition of James Marsters's Spike during the fifth season gives that character a second act. He moves beyond his love for Buffy Summers, and begins taking steps to become a champion and defender of good in his own right.

Angel is the second Buffyverse series but it is really the "second act" series, and one can apply that leitmotif not just to the main characters listed above, but even recurring characters such as Eliza Dushku's Faith, who shows up in *Angel* for a run of episodes.

Still, no matter how one parses these second acts, the tone and direction of the series often seem to change radically. The series pushes the Cordelia and Angel romance, and then drops it. And then the series drops Cordelia altogether. The series moves from its standard gallows humor to outright silly fantasy in the Pylea stories that end the second season ("Through the Looking Glass," and "There's No Place Like Plrtz Glrb").

The series also mirrors some of the same plot developments as those featured on *Buffy the Vampire Slayer*. In its fifth season, that series introduced a fully developed (supernaturally created) sister for Buffy, named

Dawn. In *Angel*, the vampire with a soul ends up with a fully grown son, Connor, by Darla, whom he never raised. Wesley ultimately reveals a dark, cold-blooded side, just as Giles did in stories such as "The Dark Age" and "The Gift." These storylines feel a little too familiar.

Structurally, too, the series are similar: with each season building towards a battle with what Whedon has called "Big Bad," general-type villains who threaten to bring about the apocalypse, or otherwise end the world.

Finally, although it may be impolitic to write this, David Boreanaz, the series lead, never proves as interesting or as multi-layered as Gellar did on *Buffy the Vampire Slayer*. He plays deadpan and broody well, but that is not always enough to carry the series. As the center of this series, it seems difficult for writers to find other characters to effectively play off Angel, which may be why there is such a revolving door of supporting performers. One can compare this to *Buffy*, again, where the initial chemistry was perfect, and then the second round (involving Anya and Spike) only enhanced it.

Angel also aired on different nights during its run—Tuesday, Wednesdays, and Mondays—and the characters moved their base of operations frequently. From Angel's original office, to the Hyperion, to Wolfram and Hart, over five years. These shifts in location often don't seem to come about organically, and often make the series feel as though it is jumping, willy-nilly, from one unsuccessful revamp to another while it attempts to find its own unique voice, apart from *Buffy*.

Perhaps the saddest thing about *Angel* is the sense of a lost opportunity. The fifth-season revamp at Wolfram and Hart produced the best batch of episodes, and finally molded the cast into the best group yet, adding Illyria and Spike to the mix. Fans mourned when the series was canceled on its cliffhanger note, leaving, perhaps, the best yet to come. The results of the final battle in that alleyway were not revealed until Joss Whedon took up the writing mantle for an *Angel* comic book which picked up where "Not Fade Away" left off.

Others disagree with this author's assertion that *Angel* is the lesser Buffyverse series. As writer Joshua Rivera notes in *Entertainment Weekly* in 2014: "If *Buffy the Vampire Slayer* is a show about becoming, then *Angel* is about something far more challenging: *existing*. There is a rot to the world, one that threatens to infect us all—not in grand, dramatic ways, but mundane ones. Entropy and inertia are the natural order of things."

Perhaps one's sense about these series comes down to philosophy and disposition. *Buffy the Vampire Slayer* is the sunny and funny series, the one that views the world as a place of danger, but teamwork and hope and love. *Angel*, fitting in with its time period (the fin-de-siècle age that also gave rise to Chris Carter's dark but brilliant masterpiece, *Millennium* [1996–1999]), is all about fighting the good fight, even when all seems hopeless.

13

What Are the Five Best Episodes of *Angel*?

Angel is often a hit-or-miss series, with tonal, location, and character changes that don't always seem to arise organically from the narrative. The five episodes below, however, represent the series at its finest, and that means at its darkest, at least for the most part. Two of the episodes selected as best in the tally below feature the deaths of major and beloved characters. One story is about the destruction of innocence, via the television industry. Another concerns a cycle of harassment and abuse that lasts beyond linear time, and never ends. In these stories of reversals and existential angst, the series found its true and most powerful voice, in some ways as the anti-*Buffy*.

Some other possible contenders for best episodes include Cordelia's heartfelt curtain call, "You're Welcome," and the series finale, "Not Fade Away."

#5. "City of . . ." Written by Joss Whedon and David Greenwalt. Directed by Joss Whedon. Airdate: October 5, 1999

In the premiere episode of *Angel*, the intent to create a dark television counterpart for *Buffy the Vampire Slayer* is plain. Angel, the vampire with a soul, is now living in Los Angeles following his departure from Sunnydale in the *Buffy* episode "Graduation Day Part II." Here, he encounters a half-human, half-Brachan demon named Doyle, who tells him of a prophetic vision, one involving a young woman who needs help.

That woman is Tina (Tracy Middendorf), a waitress and aspiring actress who has now become the abused plaything of a rich, sadistic investment banker named Russell Winters (Vyto Ruginis). While on the case, Angel learns that an old friend from Sunnydale, Cordelia Chase, is also in danger of falling into Russell's orbit. Angel promises to help Tina, but she is suspicious of anyone trying to help anyone else in Los Angeles, a town she views as cutthroat. Angel proves his worth to Tina, but not before Russell, a vampire, murders her in cold blood.

Fortunately, Angel is in time to save Cordelia from suffering the same bloody fate. He also contends with Russell Winters personally, when he learns the investment banker is untouchable before the law. Angel goes to the law offices of Winters's attorney, at Wolfram and Hart, and kicks the vampire out of a high-rise window into the burning sunlight. After Angel does so, Wolfram and Hart learns that there is a new, and dangerous, player in town.

"City of . . ." immediately makes the audience aware that it has left Sunnydale, and entered the twilight world of Los Angeles, populated by vampires of all sorts. The episode's first scene, replete with a noir-ish voice-over narration from Angel, finds the titular character stopping two vampire thugs (one played by *Lost*'s Josh Holloway) from attacking girls in an alley. He saves them, but goes all "vampire" on them, terrifying the innocents, an acknowledgment that Angel is eternally combatting his own nature as a lapsed blood-sucker (read: alcoholic).

For all the talk about a "Dark Alley Story" in relation to Buffy, it is ironic that *Angel* begins with a literal return to the old trope, and finds a man rescuing a damsel in distress in, of all places, a dark alley. It can't be a coincidence, right?

Later, the episode proves even darker when Angel is unable to rescue his first client, the sweet and desperate Tina. Tina is a young blond woman, with some of Buffy's pluck and energy, and even with all his strength and cunning, she is doomed, a statement, again, about the Big Bad here: the city itself. If Angel's ongoing thirst for blood is the first clue that this series seeks to be a more adult look at the Buffy-verse, then Tina's tragic death in the first episode is a powerful reminder that this will not be a series of hope and happy endings. All Tina wants is to go home, to return to Missoula. But the bloodsuckers of L.A. won't even let her do that.

Even the episode's denouement is brutal and shrouded in darkness. Angel realizes that Russell's money and connections make him impervious to the law. "Guys like him can get away with anything," according to the teleplay, and even Russell believes in his own invincibility. He reports, at one point, "I can do anything I want." Angel's response is classic. He asks Russell if he can fly. And then, without missing a beat, he kicks him out a plate-glass window. As Russell falls, he burns up in the sunlight.

Although the episode features a strong Batman vibe, right down to Doyle's joke about the "bat cave," early on, Batman is not usually a murderer. He is a vigilante, certainly, but he doesn't kill often. Angel, our "dark avenger" according to another episode, "Hero," commits murder in the very first episode of the series, and does so without regret. His

David Boreanaz stars as Angel.   *John Muir Photo Archive*

act feels justified, given Tina's death, but it sure as hell doesn't look like redemption. Rather, it looks like Angel is lost in Los Angeles.

"City of . . ." is a perfect introduction to Angel's world because the teleplay by Greenwalt and Whedon takes pains to separate this setting from Buffy's. His is a place that lures "people . . . and other things," according to Angel's opening narration, and this episode makes plain that it will be the playground of the series. In small ways, the episode also pays homage to Angel's history. At one point, he calls Buffy on the telephone and hangs up, but not before the audience hears her answer. At another point, the audience gets caught up on Cordelia's story. She tells Russell about her family's problems with back taxes and the IRS (an arc dramatized during *Buffy*'s third season), but even this sob story is not enough to warm the heart of the sadistic Winters.

"City of . . ." also points the series toward its future continuity, discussing one of the many byzantine hierarchies of the supernatural realms, the "Powers-That-Be," and makes mention of Doyle's half-breed status (he's human on his mother's side). Doyle's demon heritage becomes a key aspect of the character's self-esteem and self-loathing, and plays into his demise in the episode "Hero."

Finally, this episode involves Angel's first encounter with the "full service" demonic law firm, Wolfram and Hart, and one of its most ambitious young attorneys, Lindsey (Christian Kane). The firm and the characters are mainstays of *Angel*, despite all the changes in cast and settings over the next five seasons.

#4. "Hero." Written by Howard Gordon and Tim Minear. Directed by Tucker Gates. Airdate: November 30, 1999

Poor Doyle, we hardly knew ye.

"Hero" is the ninth episode of *Angel* aired in 1999, and the story famous for dispatching Glenn Quinn's beloved half-breed demon to the nether world. It is also the episode which saw Doyle's ability to receive visions from the Powers-That-Be transmitted to Cordelia Chase.

In "Hero," Angel Investigations is again floundering. Business is bad, and pay is non-existent. Cordelia hopes to shoot a commercial called "The Dark Avenger," with Angel acting as a kind of superhero who helps the hopeless. When Angel doesn't want to be involved, she shoots the commercial with Doyle, an "everyman," instead. He reminds her, however, that it may not be wise to advertise on TV an agency with no investigator's license.

Soon, however, Angel, Doyle, and Cordelia become enmeshed in a case involving innocent demons hiding in Los Angeles. These refugees claim that they are hiding from "soldiers of darkness," and that they want to travel to Ecuador for sanctuary. These "oppressed demon people" also have a prophecy of their final days. "The Promised One," whom they believe to be Angel, will deliver them from an "army of pure-blood demons" called the Scourge. The Nazi-like demons march on the streets of Los Angeles by night, killing all impure bloods (including vampires). This conflict makes Doyle feel every bit the "mongrel" the Scourge consider him to be, as he has never fully accepted his demon heritage. In fact, he has kept it a secret from Cordelia, with whom he is in love.

Angel attempts to infiltrate the Scourge, even as he and Cordelia arrange for the innocent demons to escape by ship. But the Scourge has developed a weapon called the Beacon. The weapon's cleansing light can destroy any demon flesh tinged with humanity. When the Scourge finds the ship with the innocent demon aboard it, they plan to expose all aboard to the Beacon. Remembering Angel's words that "you never know your strength until you are tested," Doyle sacrifices his life to save Angel, Cordelia, and the other demons from the terrifying weapon. Before he dies, Doyle kisses Cordelia and transfers his power of prophecy to her.

If the preceding description sounds like a tear jerker, it is no mistake. At this point in *Angel*'s history, Doyle is perhaps the most relatable character of all: a slightly cowardly everyman who is in love with a woman out of his league, and contends with self-loathing regarding his nature. He is neither human nor demon, and fits into neither world. As is written elsewhere in this text, Joss Whedon is famous, or if one prefers, notorious for killing off beloved characters, and Doyle seems to die almost out of the gate on this series. The audience has already grown to love the character, and believed that "seeds" were being planted for his long-term development, including his love for Cordelia. Instead, Doyle's journey ends heroically and tragically in "Hero," making the episode one of the most unforgettable in the canon, not only because of its content, but because of its early placement in the episode chronology.

None of this commentary, however, is meant to suggest that "Hero" isn't a strange episode. Many episodes of *Angel* are dark, but "Hero" seems set in an alternate universe of extra-special gloom and doom. Here, the streets of L.A. are overrun by demonic Stormtroopers who wear quasi-Nazi uniforms, and own the night. These demons who seem drawn from human evil have never been referred to before in the series, and are never referred to again, after this episode, which is an oddity. This army of pure-blood demons even has a kind of ultimate weapon that, like its owners, is not resurrected in future episodes. Continuity-wise, the episode seems weird. Angel, Doyle, and Cordelia run desperately in the night, hiding innocent demons from the Nazi Scourge, and are seemingly terrified of the hate group. It's like the episode is occurring in Nazi Germany, at the height of the Third Reich. There's no one to help the innocent, save for Angel. Neither the Powers-That-Be nor the Oracles (in "The Nether World of Eternal Watching") step in to prevent the Dark Evil from rising. The Scourge exists, and dominates the L.A. nighttime for this one episode, and this one episode alone, just long enough for Doyle to die.

It sounds hopelessly contrived, no doubt, but "Hero" sets up a powerful atmosphere that overpowers questions about continuity or demon politics. The Scourge are terrifying, often lensed in silhouette, or emerging from fog and mist, and they refer to their enemies as "vermin." They are heartless and soulless, an example of prejudice and racism eclipsing decency and humanity. Their victims, meanwhile, hide in squalor and anonymity, in a part of Los Angeles that resembles a German ghetto, circa 1936.

Adding to the grim mood, Doyle recounts the story of another time the Scourge came, and he didn't help another family of Brachan demons who were endangered. That past "sin" is resolved here, as Doyle achieves the redemption denied Angel, by sacrificing his life. He finds his inner hero, and rescues a group of innocents from a dreadful fate. The story connects Doyle's "demon" nature to the word "hero" and that's important. If more everymen had stepped up to fight against Hitler's Germany, the

Holocaust may not have occurred. What *Angel* seems to suggest is that for evil to triumph, good men (and women), must simply do nothing to stop it. The episode felt weird and dark and piped in from an alternate universe in 1999, yet feels highly relevant in 2019. With immigrants being scapegoated by certain figures in authority, and the same authority figure comparing them to an "infestation," the Scourge's war against "vermin" no longer feels so distant, or unconnected to reality.

Serious, and seriously disturbing, "Hero" feels, paradoxically, like *Angel* both at its grimmest, and most optimistic.

#3. "Smile Time." Written and directed by Ben Edlund. Airdate: February 18, 2004

"Smile Time" is absolutely, utterly ingenious. There's no other way to describe it. Written and directed by Ben Edlund (from a story by Joss Whedon and Ben Edlund), this is one of those amazing Buffyverse signature stories. If you are a fan, you know the ones I'm talking about: the installments so gloriously conceived and so bravely executed that when you find time to stop laughing, gasping, or crying, your jaw just hits the floor at the elegance and audacity of it all. These episodes go by names like "Hush" (the silent episode of *Buffy* featuring the Gentlemen), or "Once More, with Feeling," the musical episode in which the characters sing the things they can't bring themselves to say.

"Smile Time" is in that league, and if this author were trying to convert anti-*Angel* folks to an appreciation of the series, this is the episode he would recommend. Especially if a viewer has a finely developed sense of the absurd.

"Smile Time" finds Angel's gang (working at Wolfram and Hart) investigating a children's epidemic that is mystical in origin. Eleven children have collapsed in Los Angeles, all in front of the television; and all between 7:00 a.m. and 7:30 a.m. That happens to be the time slot of an *"edutainment"* puppet show called, you guessed it, *Smile Time*. One character on this series is a big, fat, purple blob with a horn for a nose, called "the Grumpus" (any resemblance to the Grimace is purely unintentional, we assume). The Grumpus, by the way, communicates entirely in honks. The children, all between the ages of five and eight, have been found unconscious, but with huge smiles frozen on their faces, and bulging, focus-less eyes.

The episode opens with a deeply disturbing prologue worthy of *The X-Files* in which a boy named Tommy, staying home from school due to an illness, vegetates in front of the TV, only to watch as a puppet on the screen approaches the "edge" of the tube and tells him to touch the television. *"You don't want to be a bad apple, do you, Tommy?"* the *Sesame Street*–style puppet asks. Well, Tommy *doesn't* want to be a bad apple, so he touches the TV and the puppet promptly sucks out his life-force. When Tommy›s mother walks into the room, she finds her pajama-clad son on the floor, his little body contorted, his neck twisted at a grotesque angle. There's a gruesome smile etched on his youthful features; his eyes are wide and dead. *Yikes!* This is a potent and psychically scarring image, especially for parents of young children.

Back at Wolfram and Hart, this case is just what Angel needs to take his mind off Nina, a hot blond woman who also happens to be a werewolf and is spending full moons at the law agency (in a jail cell) to avoid hurting anyone. She and Angel have begun to develop romantic feelings for each other, but Angel has been trying to ignore the signals because he fears achieving a moment of *"perfect happiness"* (read: orgasm). Because, if he does so, a gypsy curse will take away his soul. So Angel investigates the studio where *Smile Time* is produced. In a splendidly creepy scene, he discovers a dank, secret chamber, a hole in the wall behind a file cabinet that descends into an underworld. There, a fat man (with a towel over his head) sits silently, a mystery. Above this quiescent figure hangs a weird "nest egg" of glowing light (a repository for the souls of children). It flares suddenly at Angel, and before you know it, our champion—*he who helps the hopeless*—has been transformed into a tiny puppet.

And this is the *raison d'etre* for the episode: to turn our stalwart hero into a creation who *"has the proportionate excitement of a puppet his size."* As much as Angel is embarrassed by the transformation, it also helps him deal with some of his personal issues, especially with Nina. And the scene in which Angel›s friends and co-workers first see him in his new form is very funny. *"Oh my God, Angel,"* says Fred, at first sounding disturbed, *"you're so . . . cute."* Even better is the moment wherein Spike, Angel's rival for Buffy's affections (and for the title of *Shanshu*, or vampire with a soul), sees his nemesis in puppet form. *"You're a bloody puppet!"* Spike exclaims, and then it›s on. The two vampires engage in a knockdown, drag-out fight in the lobby, staged by the stunt coordinator as though it is a serious combat between two colossal fighters. *Only one of them happens to be made of felt.*

After some initial embarrassment, Angel tells Nina what has happened. (*"Nina . . . I was turned into a puppet last night,"* he explains seriously), and it is here that the makers of *Angel* turn truly wicked. In the jail cell, pacing in front of Nina, Angel—*after five frickin' seasons of being the strong but silent and sullen type*—engages in a wonderfully written, self-reflective monologue about his feelings. The tender, human, emotionally vulnerable side of the tortured, brooding vampire is excavated here at last. But all the while, we're watching a puppet emote. If that isn't pure, self-reflexive genius, the author doesn't know what is. Sometimes, it takes a puppet to say what's in a person's heart, one supposes.

Soon, it's time to take out the evil soul-sucking puppets at *Smile Time* before they can destroy Los Angeles's entire child population (turns out that pure, innocent life force is a hot commodity in some demon dimensions these days). Gunn conducts some research and learns that these demons have struck before ("Anyone see the last few seasons of *Happy Days?*" he asks, seriously, by way of exposition). So with Angel's portentous declaration, *"Let's take out some puppets,"* the group marches into battle. Once more, this moment is splendidly staged and orchestrated. The audience is treated to a Michael Bay–style *Con-Air* (1997)/*Armageddon* (1998) "bad MF"/"hero walk" shot replete with slow-motion photography.

Armed for battle, Fred, Gunn, and Wesley march toward the camera, looking grim and dedicated. In front of them . . . just a little lower . . . but nonetheless leading the charge is Angel, a puppet with a sword braced across his shoulders. It plays as perfect parody of solemn action movies, and serves as a great visual joke; one that invites giddy laughter and exposes how silly this clichéd shot really is.

Just when one thinks the episode can't possibly get funnier, the audience is treated to a *battle royale* at the studio between the heroes and the troop of sinister puppets. Among the highlights of the battle are a puppet decapitation by sword (and the puppet is a cute puppy!), a volley of "macho" action-movie one-liners *("I'm going to tear you a new puppet hole, bitch!")* and a slow-motion dispatch of the villain as the puppet ringleader is sent hurtling across the studio and killed. We see his dying puppet legs twitch. Also unforgettable are the death throes of the Grumpus, after Wesley rips out his horn-nose.

The episode's puppet production numbers, such as "Self Esteem is For Everybody," and the educational skit, "Action Math," are also a lot of fun, and what remains so deeply admirable about *Smile Time* is that it punctures and pokes fun at its own serious nature. *Angel* is a dark, brooding series about "redemption," with a mostly taciturn hero leading a pack of committed supernatural fighters against the dedicated forces of evil. *Smile Time* reveals how—with simply one element altered (our hero as a puppet)—the whole enterprise can be viewed as absolutely ridiculous. This episode serves as a parody of itself. It makes one wonder if *Con Air* wouldn›t have been made entirely more palatable if Nic Cage had been a puppet. In some ways, this is the same equation wrought by Trey Parker and Matt Stone in *Team America: World Police* (2004), only here the joke must sustain forty-five minutes of drama, not ninety minutes, and thus never has the chance to get old.

There's also a unique subtext in "Smile Time" about how television sucks the life out of your child. The episode literalizes the old canard from moms about how sitting too close to the TV can harm you. Well, little Tommy finds out that's true in this story. Television here is depicted as a portal of evil since the hellish soul-sucking procedure is transferred via a hidden carrier wave piggy-backing on the show *Smile Time*, effectively making the boob tube a two-way conduit. Or some such tech talk.

There are so many great lines and images in "Smile Time," it is difficult to tag them all. There's a great ghoulish moment involving guest star (and producer) David Fury, wherein we learn a puppet has its hand lodged up *his* back, not vice versa. There's also a good B-story involving Gunn going through a personal transformation of his own. Specifically, he is losing the education/intelligence that he was implanted with when becoming a hot-shot attorney. Here, he makes a deal to keep his ill-gotten brains (think: *Flowers for Algernon*) and that decision will carry repercussions in future episodes.

"Smile Time" reveals that *Angel*, the series, has big fat brass (puppet) balls, and is surely one of the best episodes in the canon.

Final note: Drew Massey, the puppeteer behind *Greg the Bunny*'s Count Blah, does an amazing job of making Angel the puppet utterly convincing as an extension of the Angel we had grown to know and love over a five-year period. The pint-sized puppet even broods like David Boreanaz.

2. "Waiting in the Wings." Written and Directed by Joss Whedon: Airdate: February 4, 2002

Angel buys tickets for himself and the gang—Fred, Gunn, Cordy, and Wesley—to go see a visiting old world ballet company that he first saw in 1890. At the show, however, Angel comes to the realization that nothing has changed; that the dancers, including the prima Ballerina (Summer Glau) are the same ones he saw dance 110 years earlier.

Angel and the others investigate this strange phenomenon, only to learn that a "temporal shift" is involved. The man who runs the show, Colonel Kerskov, once learned that his lover, the prima ballerina, was no longer dancing for him, as he wanted. Worse, she had fallen in love with another man, and planned to run away with him. Rather than lose her, Kerskov trapped the dancer in a repeating time loop, making her dance the same show, *Giselle* (1841), every night . . . just for him.

Angel and Cordelia are briefly swept up in the love triangle. Every time they step into the prima ballerina's dressing room, they are possessed by the spirits of the dancer, and her lover, Stefan. They realize that they must break the curse and destroy Count Kerskov's power source, so the ballerina can be free.

Written and directed by Joss Whedon, "Waiting in the Wings" is a story of jealous love, applied to the main characters, as well as the "ghosts" at the ballet company. As Angel and the others uncover the story of the dancer, Kerskov and Stefan, a modern love triangle forms between Gunn, Fred, and Wesley. Fred and Gunn are in love, and Wesley, it seems, could play the role of the jealous Kerskov. Meanwhile, Angel and Cordelia find themselves in similar roles, especially in the episode's coda, when Angel discovers he possesses a rival for Cordelia's affections, Groo (Mark Lutz) from the alternate dimension, Pylea. The idea seems to be that in any love triangle, one lover waits (and plots?) in the wings, seeking an advantage.

The idea of waiting in the wings also applies specifically to the prima ballerina who, every night for over a century, dances *Giselle* for a man she despises. She realizes that she keeps giving the same performance, and tells Angel that "I don't dance. I echo." She has resigned herself to the fact that there is no escape from her fate, or her relationship with Kerskov. "Waiting in the Wings" becomes a story of female empowerment in an abusive relationship, however, when Angel reminds the dancer that she possesses agency. "It's not too late," he tells her. "You can change things."

The episode succeeds on an intertextual level as well with the featured ballet, *Giselle*. This work of art is the story of female supernatural figures who hate men. The *wila*, or *nymphs*, resurrect a wronged woman, Giselle, to help trap her lover. But Giselle's love for the man who wronged her is too strong. "Waiting in the Wings" concerns, similarly, Kerskov's hatred for the woman who betrayed him. Angel and Wesley, likewise, see their women lost to rivals. And like Giselle, they don't strike. Their love for Fred and Cordy, respectively, is stronger than that.

"Waiting in the Wings" is beloved by *Angel* fans who are shippers for Cordelia and Angel, since the episode features a great deal of sexual innuendo and chemistry between the characters. At one point, Angel even has to strategically hide an erection from Cordelia. But the episode is also beloved by intellectual fans who enjoy Whedon's literary approach to the story. His love of ballet as an art form shines through in every scene, and he manages to make "Waiting in the Wings" a dramatic response to *Giselle*, a meditation on the perils of obsessive love, and perhaps most satisfyingly, a story of female empowerment; of a woman rediscovering her ability to fight back against an abuser. The series pilot, "City of . . . ," showcases Angel failing to save another abused, harassed woman, Tina. In "Waiting in the Wings," the prima ballerina fights back and wins, escaping from a trap of her lover's making.

1. "A Hole in the World." Written and directed by Joss Whedon. February 24, 2004

The very best episode of *Angel*, from its fifth and final season, not only imagines a "hole in the world," but puts a hole in the heart of every loyal viewer. In this tale, written and directed by Whedon, Angel and his team are still working at Wolfram and Hart, attempting to suss out the plans of the Senior Partners. Fred, meanwhile, finally works up the courage to tell Wesley about her attraction to him. He has long since given up on having a relationship with her, and so, at first, is shocked. Soon, they both realize they were meant to be together.

Their happiness, however, is not to be. An ancient sarcophagus arrives at Wolfram and Hart, and is brought to Fred's laboratory there. It opens, spraying "old mummy dust" at her, and changing everything. Carried in that dust is an original demon, an Old One called Illyria that existed on Earth millions of years before humankind. Transported in a mystical parasitic agent, Illyria is beginning to hollow out Fred's body, liquefying her organs. Soon, Illyria will destroy her soul, and walk about in her body in a plan "set in motion millions of years" earlier.

The whole process of the possession will take just a matter of days, leaving Angel, Spike, Gunn, and Wesley precious little time to find a cure, whether scientific or mystical. While Wesley tends to the rapidly ailing Fred, Angel and Spike travel across the world to a place called "The Deeper Well." There, in a "place of madness" are the sarcophagi of all the surviving Old Ones, resting in what Spike calls a "hole in the world." The two vampires with souls learn from the well's guardian that Fred can be saved, but if the demon is called back from her body, it will travel the world, and possess thousands, perhaps tens of thousands, along the way. The horror Fred faces will become one, instead, multiplied around the world. And Fred would never want that to happen.

This is an eventuality Angel must ponder, but he is too late to save his friend. At Fred's bedside, Wesley watches the love of his life die, lamenting her own exit from this mortal coil, and watches in horror as a blue-eyed, blue-haired demon, Illyria, takes over her body.

"A Hole in the World" is the cruelest, darkest, and most upsetting episode of *Angel*. In it, Fred, a joyous innocent, is lost, just as she has worked up the courage to inform her soulmate, Wesley, that she loves and desires him. Everyone on Angel's team races to save her, but it is too late. Evil wins, and in some sense, it is the fault of Fred's friends. Gunn, working illegally to keep a brain chip that makes him a "legal eagle," signed the customs form that brought the sarcophagus into the country. And Angel, once again, is unable to protect a woman he cares deeply for; just like Tracy ("City of . . .") or even Cordelia ("You're Welcome").

And the loss here is total—and devastating. Fred doesn't merely die inside her own body, to be replaced by a demon. Her eternal soul is extinguished as well, denied an afterlife and, therefore, peace. Fred doesn't just expire in "A Hole in the World," she is erased from existence—all planes of existence. It's the darkest fate for a beloved character possible. Doyle and Cordelia died in heroic efforts to save their friends, and set them down the right path.

Not so, Fred.

What makes this bitter pill even harder to swallow is that the episode opens with a flashback. The audience sees Fred's parochial parents in an argument about her leaving for L.A. They are afraid of what will happen to her in the City of Angels, a city they believe is filled with sin and depravity. "A Hole in the World" validates their viewpoint, as their daughter is possessed by a demon, her soul wiped from existence.

Angel is a series that is at its best when its characters suffer the most, and face recriminations for their actions. Wesley, Angel, Lorne, Gunn (and, I suppose, Spike too) fail their friend Winifred Burkle most egregiously in this episode, and the momentum of that failure is what carries this series into its final, tragic chapters.

Why does Joss Whedon hurt his fans like this? He has said in interviews, more than once, that in any series in which there is a war between good and evil, there must be casualties, or suspension of disbelief will be lost. There always has to be a cost for light's victory over darkness. "A Hole in the World" is first a desperate race to save Fred, and then a reckoning with the fact that there is no way to save her, and that the cost of Angel's ongoing battle is high.

"A Hole in the World" is a devastating episode of *Angel*, and because of that, the most unforgettable installment. Fred is so much more than a token sacrificial lamb, and she deserves so much better than the harsh fate she receives here. If *Angel* is the dark flip-side to *Buffy the Vampire Slayer*, then this episode must be Exhibit A as to why that is the case.

cannot be escaped. The Reavers not only create victims; their violence propagates their madness, and numbers. The film *Serenity* reveals the true story of the Reavers, and it differs a bit from the "gossip" reported above, though not significantly.

In more personal terms, *Firefly* is the saga of Captain Malcolm "Mal" Reynolds (played by Nathan Fillion), formerly a sergeant in the Independent Army. His side lost the war against the Alliance six years before the commencement of the series timeline, and now he captains

Profile in courage: Captain Mal Reynolds (Nathan Fillion) of the spaceship Serenity.   *John Muir Photo Archive*

the battered Firefly class transport vessel *Serenity*, named after the valley where the Alliance won the war.

Mal's ragtag crew includes his former lieutenant, the no-nonsense, by-the-book soldier Zoe (Gina Torres); her husband, the wisecracking ship's pilot, Wash (Alan Tudyk); and the "muscle" of the group, the obnoxious Jayne (Adam Baldwin). His favorite gun is named *Vera*.

Young but blunt-talking Kaylee (Jewel Staite) runs the ship's systems and could probably fix any machine in the galaxy. And finally, there's lovely, dignified Inara (Morena Baccarin of *Homeland*). She's the *Serenity*'s foremost citizen, "an ambassador" called a *companion*. This descriptor means she's a combination psychologist/courtesan. Many *Firefly* episodes involve Mal's inability to accept Inara's choice of profession as a legitimate one. He also strongly disagrees with Inara's description of the profession as empowering to women.

In the age of #MeToo, Inara has been re-examined by many scholars, audiences, and fans. Is she a character representing women choosing their own destiny (even if it involves sex work?), or is she just an old-fashioned male fantasy: a high-class call-girl with a heart of gold? In "'Tis Pity She's a Whore: Postfeminist Prostitution in Joss Whedon's *Firefly*?" by Dee Amy Chinn (published in Feminist Media Studies in 2006), the author writes that "on the surface, *Firefly* may suggest the rehabilitation of the prostitute with its insistence on Inara as one of the most respectable inhabitants of the spaceship *Serenity*. . . . Nevertheless [the series] draws on a patriarchal and colonist discourse to reinscribe the body of a woman of color as the site of white (predominantly male) hegemonic privilege."

In a 2009 blog, this ain't livin', author S. E. Smith asks, "Is Joss Whedon a Feminist? The Women of *Firefly*/*Serenity*." The debate has continued since, without a definitive answer. The author also asked, in the same blog: "Has Whedon created a world in which very problematic and sometimes shortsighted depictions of women can be used as a starting point to talk about feminist issues, thereby bringing women's issues to the attention of people who might otherwise ignore them? Or are the gaping knowledge and cultural gaps in *Firefly*/*Serenity* just another example of antifeminist norms on television?"

What remains so intriguing about the Mal/Inara romance is that Mal is the perfect embodiment of an independent person, wanting to be left alone and leaving others alone to live their lives. Yet he cannot accept Inara's choice to be a companion, and to have intercourse with different lovers. He imposes his parochial view of sex and relationships on her, and tries to dictate how she should live. This is part of the character's inherent contradiction. He demands total freedom from Alliance rule in his life, but then turns around and declares that his ship is *not* a democracy, and that others must obey him.

Regardless, if some of *Firefly*'s main characters seem familiar from all these descriptions above, it may be because the *Serenity* crew looks very much like the mercenary crew of the *Betty*, from Joss Whedon's script for *Alien Resurrection* (1997). *Firefly* makes these "types" real people, with more notable foibles and greater depth. Mal may be a capitalist working to make a living, but he is also a man who knows a just (and perhaps "lost") cause when he sees one. River Tam is a woman with a secret, not unlike Call, but again, she is given a social circle—a more developed "found family"—and history that the synthetic human from the movie franchise is largely denied. Overall, the characters here are stronger because they have been rethought.

Except for Jayne. He's pretty clearly just Johner, from *Alien Resurrection*, the rude, ignorant man with a big gun who generally serves as comic relief.

In the first two-hour episode of *Firefly*, titled "Serenity" the crew makes a pit-stop on the planet Persephone after a scavenging operation gone wrong, and picks up new passengers, including the mysterious man of God, Shepherd Book (played by Ron Glass), and Simon Tam (Sean Maher), a once-promising young physician. Without the crew's knowledge, Simon has smuggled aboard his sister, River (Summer Glau), a slightly unhinged psychic genius. She's long been held hostage by the Alliance at "the Academy," and seems to harbor dangerous secrets.

As the adventure continues, *Serenity* becomes a marked ship because the Alliance and its deadly operatives demand River's return. In particular, she knows some important and buried details about their plans for the citizenry, and they are determined to protect knowledge of it from the unsuspecting masses. Once more, this plotline comes to fruition in the film, *Serenity*. But over the course of the series, River is hunted by blue-gloved operatives of the Alliance, as well as a determined bounty hunter in "Objects in Space."

In each episode, the crew attempts to make money, often illegally (in episodes like "The Train Job"), and often unglamorously (visiting a "Mudder's" world in "Jaynestown" and transporting livestock in "Shindig"), while simultaneously evading the authorities. Many of these missions involve Mal's particular and personal code of honor. There are some lines of morality even he won't cross, and some lines he deliberately blurs to get what he wants. Mal boasts a self-destructive quality, and sometimes lets his pride get the better of him.

One of the best and most memorable aspects of this unique sci-fi series is its fashioning of a "lived in" future world wherein the characters speak in

A *Firefly* family portrait (L–R): Jayne (Adam Baldwin), Inara (Morena Baccarin), Kaylee (Jewel Staite), Captain Reynolds (Fillion), Wash (Alan Tudyk), Zoe (Gina Torres), Dr. Tam (Sean Maher), Shepherd Book (Ron Glass) and River Tam (Summer Glau).   *John Muir Photo Archive*

un-translated Chinese idioms, and must scrap and struggle just to survive. This is definitively not a universe of plenty, where "technology unchained" (the mantra of *Star Trek: The Next Generation*) has created a veritable utopia, rather an evolution of Whedon's work from *Titan A.E.* The Firefly class ship is always just a few dollars away from falling apart, or running low on fuel, and so the Whedon-created series is the determined opposite of romantic views of space adventuring that fans have come to expect.

Some longtime sci-fi fans have noted *Firefly's* similarity to the British cult-TV favorite *Blake's 7* (1978–1981), which also features a group of criminals on the run from a totalitarian Federation. Those similarities exist, but *Firefly* is its own unique animal, focusing less on a resistance movement and more on a group of disparate individuals who, by necessity, must form an ad-hoc family. It's clear in *Blake's 7* that the Federation is a malevolent totalitarian state, but the Alliance of *Firefly* is not yet as far down the line on that continuum. It is certainly getting there. (Both governments, for instance, use pacification gas to quell their populations, in an effort to maintain control.) But on the surface, *Firefly* looks more like a high-tech capitalist state, with areas on the frontier where control has not yet been reached.

In terms of thematic metaphor, *Firefly* is very clearly and deliberately a reflection of the post-American Civil War milieu. There, the Union (the Alliance) soundly defeated the Confederacy (the Independents), with overwhelming technology and numbers. Many veterans of the Confederacy later moved to the wide-open frontier of the Old West, in hopes of establishing something new and "free."

Mal, the son of a rancher in the inhospitable world Shadow, abundantly fits this description on the series. He is still sensitive about his side losing the war, and frequently makes comments that, for him, the war has not ended, and indeed will never be. In "The Train Job," he quips to his (Alliance) enemies that he believes the Independence Movement "will rise again," a clear reflection of the popular refrain that the South shall one day rise again. This is basically "The Lost Cause" argument, only in the future and in space.

Firefly's Reavers—those murderous and bloody space savages existing on the frontier of space—symbolize, at least on the surface, another part of the American history allegory. They take on essentially the same role as American Indians once did in the Western movie genre. They are "the other" that is feared by civilization and gossiped about; known and feared for their strange, savage ways. Had the series lasted longer, one wonders if the Reavers might have been portrayed in a less villainous, more three-dimensional light, given their obvious inspiration in Native-American culture. Instead, their story comes to fruition in *Serenity*.

In both design and behavior, it must be said, the Reavers also very closely resemble the Martians of *John Carpenter's Ghosts of Mars* (2001). Both races are self-mutilators, and both are berserkers. The Martians in that film are possessed alien barbarians, while the Reavers are psychologically disturbed barbarians, but they look and sound very much alike.

Regarding visual technique, *Firefly* pioneered the use of the camera "zoom" in vast outer-space shots, a facet of the series that was promptly appropriated and popularized by the Sci-Fi Channel remake of *Battlestar Galactica* in 2003. The series also apes the style of Kubrick's *2001: A Space Odyssey* (1968), making certain that there's no sound in the vacuum of space. These qualities help differentiate *Firefly* from the big space operas such as *Star Wars* or the aforementioned *Star Trek*.

Intriguingly, there are no alien races featured in the series. In fact, the *Firefly* aesthetic always reminds this author of that great tagline from 1981's space western *Outland*: "Even in space, the ultimate enemy is man." That movie is basically *High Noon* in Space (though starring Sean Connery, not Gary Cooper), and *Firefly* might aptly be described as a space western as well. This lands the property in a select group of films and TV program like *Battle Beyond the Stars* (1979), an outer-space version of *The Magnificent Seven*, or *Cowboy Bebop* (1998–2003), an outer-space Western anime series.

"I believe we are the only sentient beings in the universe, and five hundred years from now we will still be the only sentient beings around," Whedon told the *Post-Gazette's* Rob Owens in 2003. "Aliens are something everyone else is doing."

As any review of the series' creative structure indicates, *Firefly* is a genre drama with a great deal on its mind. But at its core, the series is a dedicated meditation on personal freedom. Even the theme song, written by Joss Whedon, strikes this particular note, observing that one can take a person's "land" but can't take the "sky" from them. Thus, the series serves as a paean to the pioneer spirit, reflecting these settlers who just want to be left alone to live how they choose.

One gets the sense that Mal would hate any government (or religion) in power, because it would seek to control his destiny. And that is a control he will simply not tolerate. Yet, as noted above, he has trouble granting Inara the same freedom he cherishes, at least in terms of her choice of profession (and clientele). Critics have compared Mal to Han Solo from the *Star Wars* films, but he's far more complex than Solo is, if only because audiences get the opportunity to spend more time with him, and see how he reacts in many, far more varied situations. Mal often plays the role of scoundrel or brigand, it's true, but this is a mask. He was once a soldier, and so it is clear that he understands duty and responsibility . . . and sacrifice, quite well. When he pretends to be the scoundrel, it is to cover his bruises from having lost the battle—and cause—of his life.

That trademark Whedon linguistic aesthetic—snappy, Hawksian dialogue and outstanding, non-traditional roles for female characters—is on full display in *Firefly*. Like *Buffy the Vampire Slayer*, the mechanics of language and the art of the put-down are primary considerations of the drama. Character and personality are exposed by the way people speak to one another; by the very words they choose, and how they express themselves. And that fact alone lands *Firefly* head-and-shoulders above most of its brethren on network TV. One fascinating aspect of the series is the way it blends Western and Eastern language, English and Mandarin, specifically.

This two-pronged language of the future is explored in the blog TLF Translation, in a post by Joseph Philipson on January 1, 2015, titled, "Language and Culture in Science Fiction: *Firefly* and *Serenity*. The blogger writes: "In the *Firefly* universe, the two main languages are not perfectly distributed, with one language being favored over the other depending on where you are. . . . As well as the shared dominance of English and Mandarin, there are obvious dialectical differences depending on where these languages are spoken. In the case of English, the variety spoken on the central planets differs from the way the language is employed on the outer planet." The author goes on to write about "Core Language," and "Frontier Slang," and one can learn much about the characters by which language they speak.

In short, it is easy to enumerate *Firefly*'s best qualities: a coherent, believable future mythology; a language all its own, fascinating, realistic characters whom we grow to love, and entertaining, rip-roaring space adventures stories to boot.

Where *Firefly* has grown increasingly controversial in its second decade of life is in its ever-harder-to-ignore "Lost Cause" narrative. Many fans (known as Browncoats) and scholars have come to see the rebellious behavior of Mal and his crew as perhaps too close a metaphor for the Civil War. As a "Lost Cause-er," Mal is, essentially, deemed to be fighting for the Confederacy against a corrupt, overweening Union. Many anti-government, Tea Party, and alt-right individuals have taken to the series as apparently possessing kindred views, whereas Joss Whedon's political views are nowhere, actually, in that ballpark. The Confederacy was a haven for racism and white supremacy, and these are not qualities or beliefs one would associate with Mal Reynolds, so the metaphor is not complete. But for some, the Alliance/Union vs. Independents/ Confederates makes a modern watch of the series uncomfortable, to say the least.

Knowing that Whedon fashioned *Firefly* after reading Michael Shaara's Civil War novel *The Killer Angels* may not help one overcome the feeling that the series romanticizes the Confederacy and its way of life, to its own detriment. Many episodes make a point of dismissing slavery ("Shindig") and revealing Mal's antipathy towards it, but in today's hyper-partisan world, that may not be enough for some viewers. There are those forces, today, who view the United States government as an intruding, totalitarian nanny state, and stand-in for the Alliance. Yet the Confederacy in the Civil War remains a racist, treasonous anti-diversity state that fell, at least in part, from its own hubris and unwillingness to compromise. To ask viewers to adopt Mal's viewpoint is to ask them to adopt the viewpoint of the Confederacy in the Civil War, against the Union. Although some fans may lament the fact that politics plays such an important role in an appreciation for *Firefly*, it's impossible to ignore. The series was created that way to provide a thematic context of a futuristic outer-space Western.

15

What Are the Five-Best Episodes of *Firefly*?

Ranked from fifth to first in this chapter are this author's selections for the top five episodes of Joss Whedon's late, lamented Fox series, *Firefly*. The following episodes were selected on the basis of world-building, character-building and the overall "Whedonesque" tone, or atmosphere. Also, as in other chapters with "top five" episodes, it is not necessary that Whedon write or direct the choices. As the overriding presence behind the series, his stamp is on every episode.

#5. "The Train Job" Written by Joss Whedon and Tim Minear. Directed by Joss Whedon. Airdate: September 20, 2002

"The Train Job" is *Firefly*'s second episode, and the installment directly following the events of the pilot, "Serenity." Oddly, however, "The Train Job" was actually the first episode aired by Fox back in 2002. This out-of-order airing is believed by to have had a severe impact on the series' success with general audiences, and some fans.

Regardless of the famous scheduling hiccup, "The Train Job" is a stand-out segment that continues to build on the post-Civil War-in-space leitmotif of the overall series at the same time that it develops more fully, the mythos, characters, and story-arc. In "The Train Job," Mal Reynolds (Nathan Fillion) and his crew—still desperate for cold, hard cash—seek work from a local crime lord, Niska (Michael Fairman), a man known for utterly destroying those who cross or disappoint him. Niska tasks Mal and his group with stealing a shipment of Alliance cargo on a hover-train bound for the city of Paradiso. To Zoe's (Gina Torres) chagrin, however, that cargo is guarded by a squad of heavily armed Alliance soldiers. Nonetheless, thanks to Mal's ingenuity, the cargo is successfully "liberated" by the group of bandits on *Serenity*.

A new problem emerges, however, when Mal discovers that the cargo contains medicine desperately needed by the miners of Paradiso, who are suffering from a degenerative illness called Bowden's disease. Now Mal must make an unenviable choice. Should he return the medicine and help the town, only to face Niska's violent wrath? Or should he take the money and run, with poor families suffering as a direct result of his actions?

"The Train Job" opens on the anniversary of Unification Day some six years after the Battle of *Serenity* ended the war against the Alliance. Unification Day is thus a celebration of the fact that the Alliance defeated the Independents, and a remembrance of the very day that Mal's way of life came to an end. As "The Train Job" commences, Mal initiates a saloon fight over the topic of Unification Day, and thus re-establishes the series' overarching context: an examination of post–Civil War mores and situations . . . transposed to space, and the future. Mal explicitly attributes the Independent defeat to the fact that the Alliance had "superior numbers." His explanation mirrors historical reality. General Robert E. Lee, in his letter to Confederate troops on April 10, 1865, noted the "overwhelming numbers and resources" of the North as a cause for the Confederacy's defeat.

Historian Richard Current has likewise noted that "God was on the side of the heaviest battalions," meaning the North, or the Union. In *Firefly*, viewers are meant to conclude the same facts about the Alliance (our Union surrogate) and the Independents (our Confederacy surrogate). The Alliance used its overwhelming resources to crush the Independents. Intriguingly, Mal's discussion of the defeat—blaming his side's loss on the superior numbers of the Alliance—could also be parsed as sour grapes; as an acknowledgment of his belief that the Independents had better fighters and a more just cause than the Alliance, but lost only because of overwhelming force. Similarly, for some folks in the South, the Civil War has never really ended, and is constantly being re-fought in "what if" scenarios. It's much easier for those folks to blame the Confederacy's loss on a gargantuan enemy than on their side's failed strategy, or overwhelming issues of morality. There's a little bit of that same quality in Mal's griping, to be certain. He's fighting a war that is long-ended and which, in some context, is irrelevant to his present situation, except that he is governed, broadly speaking, by his "enemy."

"The Train Job" also features Mal making the argument that "I'm thinking we will rise again," re-parsing the famous "The South will rise again" battle cry of many post–Civil War Southerners. What makes the comment so much fun in this setting, however, is that Mal's remark

Warrior Woman: Mal's chief lieutenant, Zoe (Gina Torres).   *John Muir Photo Archive*

coincides with the literal rising of *Serenity* over a mountain peak, to back him up following the saloon brawl. For many, the visual joke defuses the politics of the moment as Mal's ship literally hovers behind his position. For others, the joke may be a signifier that *Firefly* is taking on lost-cause revisionism, or libertarianism as a political cause, merely transplanted to the future.

The entire Unification Day angle as explored by "The Train Job" is fascinating because it establishes some points worth debating about the Alliance. First, the Alliance commemorates its defeat of Independents, thus literally, *independence*. And secondly, one must wonder about the Alliance's use of Orwellian language. Is *unification* really something that can be forced on someone, or won through a war? Being *united* suggests a shared purpose, and clearly—at least in terms of Mal—that "unity" doesn't yet exist. It is may be more accurate to say that the Alliance conquered the Independents, and forced submission. But that doesn't have the politically correct ring of Unification, does it?

One amusing aspect of the episode's opening fight sequence involves a very clichéd visual composition made fresh by the futuristic setting. In Western movies since time immemorial, combative cowboys have been violently tossed out of saloon windows by their enemies, only to land hard on the street outside. Here, Mal endures the same fate, but he doesn't crash through glass . . . he goes through a hologram, or force-field. This moment seems to be a deliberate announcement by the creative team that not only is *Firefly* recreating the post–Civil War/beginning of the Frontier era context in space (or "the black"), but in doing so with a sense of fun and ingenuity to boot.

The very setup of "The Train Job" suggests a kind of familiar caper or heist Western, wherein either a train or a stagecoach is robbed by merry bandits. Recently, a very similar scenario was featured in *Solo: A Star Wars Story* (2018), a franchise film set in a world of spaceships, and with a lead character, Han Solo, who is often compared to Mal Reynolds. The moral problem for Mal in terms of this particular heist, however, is that he learns he isn't only stealing from the Alliance. Instead, he's stealing from poor families who won't thrive without much-needed medicine. River explicitly reminds the audience in "The Train Job" that Mal's name means "bad" in Latin, and so the question becomes: Is Mal a bad guy? Is everything (even his anti-Alliance feelings) a hint of his corrupt, quarrelsome nature? "The Train Job" answers that question quite definitively, since Mal risks jail-time to deliver the needed medicine to Paradiso. He may play at being a bandit, or not caring about people, but he clearly possesses a moral compass. He wants everyone to think he has "checked out" of the 'Verse, and is pursuing only his self-interest. This is one episode that rips that "scoundrel" veneer from the character, and reveals Mal's true nature.

Ironically, what does go uncommented on in "The Train Job" is the fact that the Alliance—the real bad guys of the series—was actually doing a good deed when Mal interfered with it! The Alliance was delivering medicine to the sick. In fact, they even placed armed guards alongside that medicine to assure that it would get to its destination unmolested. This fact is a reminder that the universe of *Firefly* is not a black-and-white one, and that sometimes Mal's assumptions and biases are not correct, even if his heart is in the right place. In "The Train Job," he makes a terrible mistake, and then must risk his crew and ship to set it right. He is a complex and human character, and it is rewarding that Whedon and Minear allow him to make, and then address, his mistakes. There is always a danger when one hates something so vehemently (like Mal hates the Alliance), that one ends up allying oneself with a force much, much worse (like Niska). In a sentence, that's the predicament Mal faces in "The Train Job."

In terms of other episodes details, "The Train Job" picks up on the plotthreads initiated in "Serenity," namely Shepherd Book's familiarity with the milieu of the criminal underworld, and the ongoing debate between Inara and Mal over her controversial vocation as a companion. Is Inara actually a therapist and healer, or merely a prostitute? Is she a feminist icon who makes her own choices, or has her society only duped her into believing that while she serves their needs? In "The Train Job," Inara notes that she selects her clients, not vice-versa, and that companions only choose lovers who "share the same kind of energy." Again, this appears, at least on the surface, to suggest an empowering profession, and we see in a later episode, called "Shindig," how Inara leverages her power against a noble man and wins.

"The Train Job" is also the first episode to feature River's nightmarish flashbacks of her time in Alliance custody. Furthermore, the story introduces the two Alliance agents with blue hands, who re-appear throughout the story. In addition to this plot thread, Niska's storyline continues throughout the series, so "The Train Job" sets up some important narrative elements. Niska's hardcore way of doing business comes back to haunt Mal in "War Stories." *Firefly* is often compared to *Star Wars* (1977), and Mal directly to Han Solo. This Niska subplot, from a certain perspective, is not unlike Solo's encounter with Jabba the Hutt. In both cases, working for a crime boss turns out very badly when the smuggler/criminal disappoints his employer.

As the complexity "The Train Job" confirms, *Firefly*, in its second episode, already lays down its outline for the season (or half-season, as it were), and assiduously constructs its character/story-arc. The episode moves with such speed, grace, and assurance, and also features some dynamic, feature-film-quality visual effects, of the hover-train in motion, and *Serenity* flying nearby. Finally, "The Train Job" successfully illuminates Mal's moral center. The overall strong quality of the episode doesn't mean it should have aired instead of the pilot episode. That's a mistake, no question. But it's a strong episode of the series, nonetheless.

#4. "Serenity." Written and directed by Joss Whedon. Airdate: December 20, 2002

Six years after the hopeless battle of *Serenity*, former Independent Mal Reynolds (Nathan Fillion) commands a small Firefly class ship, *Serenity*. With a crew of misfits, he ekes out a minimal existence by taking on small-time, occasionally illegal jobs. After a space-salvage operation for a gangster named Badger (Mark Sheppard) goes south, Mal realizes he needs to pick up passengers to pay for more fuel. A young doctor, Simon Tam (Sean Maher); a man of God with a mysterious past, Shepherd Book (Ron Glass); and a stranger named Lawrence Dobson (Carlos Jacott) board the craft at the Persephone docks, before Mal tries to make a deal on distant Whitehall with a former client who once took shots at him.

On final approach to Whitehall, *Serenity* encounters a Reaver ship, but manages to evade the monstrosity for a time. Soon, a mole on the ship threatens the crew's safety, and Simon is forced to reveal a secret. His sister, River (Summer Glau), has been brought aboard *Serenity* in secret. She's a fugitive from the Alliance, and one that the government very much wishes to see returned. Now Mal must deal with fugitives from the law, a tricky, untrustworthy client, and the return of the deranged Reavers.

"Serenity," the inaugural episode of Joss Whedon's *Firefly* (2002), begins to diagram a compelling series-long tension between the passionate, colorful nature of man, and the largely uncaring nature of the 'Verse (the series' term for outer space). The episode visually balances the intimacy and urgency of human, mortal life with the remote, fearsome, and de-humanizing aspects of survival in space. Although its visual flourishes were appropriated wholesale by the re-imagination of *Battlestar Galactica* (2003–2008), *Firefly* spearheads a very distinctive visual style. It is one which abundantly reflects the adventure's core theme: man's struggle to remain free in a "system" of life that no longer recognizes the individual as valuable.

Accordingly, "Serenity" premieres with footage of the Battle of *Serenity*, a campaign set six years before the primary action of the series. The unsteady, hand-held camerawork provokes an instant sense of immediacy and closeness to the action. This scene represents not only a reasonable facsimile of modern documentary war footage, but a boots-on-the-ground perspective of mankind's last stab at freedom before the huge Alliance sweeps in and enforces cosmic "unity."

To put it another way, this preamble, set in Serenity Valley, is all fire and heat in terms of its inspirational dialogue from Captain Mal about "holding the line," in terms of the herky-jerky camera-work, and also in terms of the battlefield itself, where plumes of fire sporadically and violently dot the war-torn landscape. Almost immediately after this preamble, the episode cuts six years to the future, and all that fire and heat is gone, replaced determinedly by ice and cold. The camerawork now lands the viewer in the vacuum of space. No explosions detonate, no inspirational speeches are uttered as we see suited figures moving about in slow silence during a deep-space salvage operation.

Importantly, there is no sound in space, and *Firefly* is one of the few programs to observe that scientific fact. But in terms of dramatic impact, to transition from the hot, loud, messy war for independence to the frozen, remoteness of quiet space after the conflict is thematically vital. For in this unpleasant present, the voice of independence, of mankind's very nature, has been defeated and squelched by Alliance rule. In fact, individuality and liberty—as represented by the free-ranging *Serenity*—is hard to locate in this realm. The camera seeks it out in extreme long-shot, and must finds its focus in the process. The ship is not immediately or easily visible. Throughout the series, then, *Serenity* and her colorful crew are visual signifiers of the Battle of *Serenity*'s noble ideals. The ship and crew represent humanity: sensual, and passionate. The setting outside the ship, in the solar system at large, is representative of the opposite set of values, and therefore dehumanizing and remote.

In a further attempt to promote a sense of closeness with the characters and their ideals, the premiere episode eliminates the typical TV sense of decorum. For example, the viewer actually gets to see a toilet in Mal's quarters. It might be the first onscreen toilet in more than fifty years of TV space adventuring. Later, the camera lingers on Inara washing up with a cloth and a basin of water, partially disrobed, and once more, the approach is passionate, or sensuous. How often, in outer-space drama, do we witness characters bathing or using the bathroom? During this montage of Inara washing, the footage both briefly pauses—or freezes—and jump-cuts to other angles, as though time itself has skipped a track. The point of such unconventional techniques is to visually mimic human imperfection or emotional intimacy. A moment can't actually be extended, but it can *feel* like it is extended when we fully experience it. Overall, part of film's magic as an art form is that it boasts the capacity to express that idea through the manipulation of time and image. It's as though the viewer witnesses a stolen moment of vulnerability.

At one point in the opening episode, *Serenity* encounters the Reavers: a group of humans who have (apparently) reacted badly, nay psychotically, to the dangers and remoteness of space. The message is plain and fits in neatly with the series' philosophy. The Reavers have surrendered their humanity in this inhuman realm, and embraced the bleakness, emptiness, and danger. They are murderers and rapists, pushing out further every year, responding to the Alliance's regime of order not with passionate humanity, but with nihilistic chaos. There is a difference, after all, between a committed "opposition" dedicated to its belief system, and a kamikaze run. The *Serenity* represents the former; the Reavers, the latter.

In terms of outer space's remoteness and lack of intimacy or individuality, Mal notes that its signifier, the Alliance, is known not for helping people, but rather explicitly "getting in a man's way." So the philosophy

Mystery woman wrapped in Enigma: River (Summer Glau).   *John Muir Photo Archive*

here, as it is throughout, is anti-state, to be certain. But more than that, it is pro-individuality in bent. Consider that the series concerns a group of very different characters working together, despite those differences, to survive. Each one of the characters views the universe differently but seems to agree on only one point: the Alliance infringes too much on mankind's right to dictate his own path. The crew of *Serenity* may be "lost in the woods," as per the episode's dialogue, but "the woods" is nonetheless where it wants to be. Outside the woods, the Alliance has usurped liberty and freedom. The Alliance doesn't recognize its citizens as individuals with rights and protections, but only as "precious commodities" who should be subjected to the government's whims. The Alliance, the audience learns, has "played with" River's brain, to unknown ends, a fact which precipitated Simon's rescue.

"Serenity" sets up many of *Firefly*'s thematic precepts, but also introduces the dramatis personae, both in terms of the ship's crew members, and its new passengers, Simon, River, and Shepherd Book. Like the others, each of these non-crew characters possesses his own sometimes secret reasons for wishing to remain in the "woods." Much of the joy in watching the series comes from learning more about these characters, and their mysterious pasts. Most notably, Mal is presented strongly in "Serenity" as a "man of honor among thieves," to use Badger's words. Delightfully, he's also a man full of contradictions. For example, Mal deplores the Alliance for getting in a man's way, but can just as easily face down a crew member and tell them that his ship is a dictatorship, not a democracy. "We don't vote on my ship," he declares. Isn't the very thing he hates about the Alliance the idea that it doesn't hear or acknowledge his voice? He recreates that dynamic on a small scale on his ship, but is often blind to that fact. The viewer also learns in "Serenity" that Mal is both anti-religion in general, based on his interplay with Book, and incapable of viewing Inara's role as respected companion as something that empowers her. A bit of a traditionalist, Mal is uncomfortable with the idea that a woman can be strong, good, and also highly sexual.

In terms of technology and tactics, "Serenity" introduces much of the series lingo and information, which explains why it, not "The Train Job," should have aired on Fox first. Viewers learn about *Serenity*'s typical escape ploy: a "crybaby" satellite that can be deployed to emit a distress signal and misdirect Alliance cruisers. They also begin to get a feel for the ship's capabilities, including "hard burns" "full burns," and a "crazy Ivan." In short, "Serenity" is a well-thought-out, cerebral introduction to the characters and world of *Firefly*. More significantly, the premiere episode introduces the visual conceits of this outer-space adventure, and its thematic perspective to boot. It's hard to believe that Fox decided not to air this feature-film-quality introduction to the 'Verse as the series premiere episode. What was the Alliance, er, network, thinking?

3. "Shindig." Written by Jane Espenson. Directed by Vern Gillum. Airdate: November 1, 2002

There's a quirky little joke in the introductory scene of "Shindig," a highly entertaining and romantic episode. It opens in a seedy bar on some backwater planet, and the unsteady, hand-held camera prowls across the room to Captain Mal Reynolds (Nathan Fillion) and his muscle, Jayne (Adam Baldwin), as they play a friendly game of pool with some rough-looking customers. Lo and behold, the pool balls suddenly blink out of existence during a power fluctuation before just as quickly re-materializing. The customers let out a collective whine of dissatisfaction until the camera draws audience attention to a sign on the wall that reads: "Management Not Responsible for Ball Failure."

Make no mistake: the words "Ball Failure" possess a double meaning in "Shindig," an episode penned by Jane Espenson. For the episode *really* concerns the cocksure attitude of Captain Reynolds and his sense of, well, *testicular fortitude* as he risks his life in a "duel to the death" over the honor of Inara (Morena Baccarin), a companion and the apple of Mal's eye. No Ball Failure here, thank you, ma'am. *Brain failure*, perhaps. But not Ball Failure.

"Shindig" occurs mostly on the planet Persephone, as Captain Reynolds attempts to drum up work from a *"psychotic low-life"* business associate named Badger, a character introduced in the pilot. Meanwhile, Inara has arranged to meet with a high-class and totally insufferable client named Atherton Wing for a high-profile dance, the planet's *"social event of the season."* By an odd set of circumstances, Mal ends up attending the dance too, with Kaylee as his date. He's there in an effort to talk up a prospective customer (Larry Drake), a man who may be looking to move some property off-world. Intensely jealous of the wealthy, handsome Wing, Mal ends up decking Inara's date before the night is over. As Kaylee observes: *"Up until the punching, it was a real nice party . . ."*

Of course, Mal's headstrong and violent action spur a challenge *according to the customs and laws of Persephone.* Atherton Wing, an expert swordsman, will duel him. Mal, typically klutzy with a sword, is outmatched and outclassed. And at sunrise, he could be a dead man.

During the course of "Shindig," Mal tells Inara that he is uncomfortable in her "high-class" world, but she replies that Mal always breaks the rules, no matter with which society he happens to be interfacing. This is a keen insight into the character, and is reminiscent of the famous joke Woody Allen made in *Annie Hall* (1977). Mal, like Woody Allen's character in that film, wouldn't be part of any club that would have him as a member. In less comedic terms, Mal is a man who stomachs no authority but his own, and who is so impulsive when challenged, or even when he *perceives* a challenge, that he becomes self-destructive. That insight is also the very advice, perhaps, that allows for Mal's ultimate victory. With Atherton, Mal doesn't play by the rules, and he's most certainly not a gentleman. Mal escapes by the skin of his teeth in "Shindig," but it's intriguing that the very quality that makes Mal a great man (his reliance on his instincts and thinking outside of society's norms) also repeatedly endangers him and his crew, and vexes the woman who obviously loves him.

The Mal/Inara relationship dominates "Shindig," and rightly so, since Espenson's story examines the stubbornness and class roles of both characters. Mal refuses to fit in with his society, and works hard, in fact, *not* to fit in. Inara is so desperate to belong, perhaps, that she is willing to accept a career in sex work that many non-practitioners view as ignoble. They are perfect together. Mal won't join any club, and Inara is willing to do anything to join *any* club.

Even while these two characters nab the lion's share of the action in "Shindig," the rest of *Serenity's* crew also gets some good moments in the episode. Kaylee holds court at the dance after some mean girls rudely insult her. And Wash and Zoe share an intimate bedroom scene aboard *Serenity* that on first blush is funny and intimate, but given the events of the *Firefly* movie, now resonates in an entirely different and tragic fashion. This episode reveals the intimacy and love they share.

Once more, *Firefly*'s camerawork must be noted. For the most part, the camera here is hand-held, thereby provoking immediacy, but when the episode settles down in high society on Persephone, the camerawork adjusts abruptly and suddenly turns formal. The viewer's perspective changes from empathy-encouraging, almost casual close-shots to majestic long shots. There's a fair amount of spinning and tipping too, as if the camera itself has joined the ritzy dance. This shift in visual technique helps the viewer visually comprehend the spirit and atmosphere of this high-falutin' Alliance world.

Firefly universally features droll dialogue, and "Shindig" is certainly no exception, offering some whip-smart banter between Mal and Inara. The episode also shows off Mal at his rogue-ish best (or worst, depending on one's perspective) and even finds time to serve as a variation on the oft-used "Arena" genre convention of science-fiction TV: *the hero's duel to the death with a superior opponent.* This trope goes back to a short story by Fredric Brown about a contest between alien races, and virtually every sci-fi series has depicted some variation of it. Kirk battles a Gorn in *Star Trek*. John Koenig battles three alien killers in *Space: 1999*'s "Rules of Luton," and Buck Rogers enters a contest with an opponent called the Traybor in "Buck's Duel to the Death." In "Shindig," Mal doesn't battle a lizard-man or Gorn, but rather a guy, Atherton Wing, who is clearly reptilian, anyway.

"Shindig" is a beloved episode for Mal/Inara shippers, but its other distinct value is in its revelation of how those two characters interact with the larger culture. On the ship, they can spar and be equals. In polite company, Mal and Inara reveal a new set of insecurities.

#2. "Our Miss Reynolds." Written by Joss Whedon. Directed by Vondie Curtis-Hall. Airdate: October 4, 2002

Captain Reynolds and the crew of *Serenity* stop a group of bandits on a backwater planet and later celebrate their victory with the happy locals.

When the ship returns to space, however, Mal discovers a lovely stowaway aboard named Saffron (Christina Hendricks). Saffron reveals that, by her laws, she and Mal were wed the night before. But Mal, who was drunk at the time, refuses to accept the custom of the Triumph Settlers. Instead, he promises to start Saffron on a new life on another world.

In the meantime, Saffron cooks Mal a meal, offers to wash his feet, and even suggests sharing a marital bed with him. Her willingness to "serve" Mal rankles Zoe (Gina Torres), and compels Jayne to make Mal an offer for her. At Shepherd Book's urging, however, Mal remains a gentleman. But when Saffron shows up in his quarters and attempts a seduction, Mal succumbs to just one kiss.

That kiss, as it turns out, comes from narcotic lipstick, and Saffron finally reveals her true colors. She's actually working with a group of nearby space pirates, and plans to lure the *Serenity* into a trap, a giant electric net that will kill the crew while keeping the vessel intact for salvage.

"Our Mrs. Reynolds" is the *Firefly* episode that really cements the magic of this particular Joss Whedon series. The narrative is extremely simple, involving a visitor who turns out to be a treacherous turncoat. But the overwhelming sense of fun and joy emerges from the established crew's interaction with that "guest" character, and with each other. In this case, Christina Hendricks (*Mad Men* [2008–2016]) proves an absolute show-stealer as Saffron, creating a character who, single-handedly, manages to fool just about the entirety of *Serenity*'s crew.

Saffron is a charismatic, compelling character, and one who approaches each established personality on *Serenity* where they are the weakest. As such, and in a universe that also includes the Alliance and Reavers, this individual makes for the most fascinating and watchable villain thus far. In a very real sense, she is the anti-Mal. Like Reynolds, she is fiercely independent, cunning, and brilliant. But quite unlike Mal, she appears to possess no moral code.

In fact, while watching "Our Mrs. Reynolds," this author was reminded of one of the reasons he carries such an abiding love for the original *Star Trek* (1966–1969). The stories were often great on that series, it is true, but the non-great stories were often carried by incredibly amusing and emotional moments between Kirk, Spock, and McCoy. In some way, this observation may be true of all series that become pop-culture phenomena, whether *Trek*, or *The X-Files*. There are going to be weak stories, eventually, but watching good actors play compelling characters lifts those stories. "Our Miss Reynolds" is straight-forward, and mercilessly exposes the characters, their fantasies, and their weaknesses. For instance, Jayne is willing to give up Vera—his beloved gun—for Saffron. Zoe and Wash face tension over Saffron's cooking, and coddling of Mal. Shepherd Book gets to play the scold. Even the wise and insightful Inara is nearly taken in, before realizing the depths of Saffron's capacity to trick. The story here is fine, but the performances lift the tale to another plateau.

Indeed, Saffron succeeds as much as she does because each character sees in her something that he or she needs or desires. Book wants to protect an innocent, to be the good, upright man. Wash longs for a more "traditional" wife, and Mal desires—deeply—a woman who can see his nobility of spirit. Saffron is able to, moment-to-moment, satisfy each of those fantasies, and pull the wool over each man's eyes.

Another aspect of this episode worth noting: There is no overt nudity or sex in "Our Mrs. Reynolds," but damn if this isn't a really sexy episode, as Saffron executes her seduction of Mal. The key to getting him to kiss her, it turns out, isn't physical, but mental. Saffron "plays" on the captain's need to be seen as good and righteous. That's the turn-on that he can't refuse.

The episode's final, delightful joke is that Mal believes that Inara kissed Saffron, thereby incapacitating her, when in fact the companion kissed him when he was unconscious. For all his wheeling-and-dealing and speech-making, Mal remains, in the end, his own worst enemy.

The formula for "Our Mrs. Reynolds" is repeated, in some ways, in this author's selection for the greatest episode of *Firefly*: "Objects in Space." In both stories, a charismatic outsider comes in to test the main characters, with unpredictable results, and a great sense of humor.

#1. "Objects in Space." Written and Directed by Joss Whedon. Airdate: December 13, 2002

In "Objects in Space," the crew of *Serenity* runs afoul of a unique and dangerous bounty hunter: Jubal Early (Richard Brooks). Early has been secretly shadowing the ship for some time, and plans to acquire River and return her to the Alliance for a big pay day. Early sandbags much of the crew in short order, including Captain Reynolds, but finds that River isn't

Big Dumb Brute with Guns: Jayne Cobb (Adam Baldwin). *John Muir Photo Archive*

the easy mark she appears to be. In fact, River unnerves Early by claiming to be "one" with *Serenity*, and revealing personal secrets about him that she couldn't possibly know. But Early only grows more dangerous as River grows craftier.

A strong argument can be made that "Objects in Space," written and directed by Joss Whedon, is the most complex, and also the very best, episode of *Firefly* (2002), as well as a perfect distillation of the series' overall aesthetic qualities. The episode's central villain, Jubal Early, is named for a Confederate general in the Civil War, and thus revives the series' exploration of that milieu, although in a futuristic/outer-space setting. The real Jubal Early (1816–1894) was a man who served General Robert E. Lee and Stonewall Jackson in the Civil War, but not before making known his point-of-view that secession and war were the wrong courses of action.

In some way, the bounty hunter Early seems similarly conflicted. The man boasts a singular intelligence, and a unique manner of expressing himself, yet he also seems captive to his baser instincts, to his sadistic side. It seems like anyone as smart as Early should know better, and it is clear that he has come to deceive himself about why he acts as he does ("It's my job," he notes). But River cuts through the lies. She "sees" Early for what he really is: a monster.

There's a great and totally oddball Jubal Early moment midway through the show, in which Simon (Sean Maher) asks the bounty hunter if he is working for "the Alliance." Jubal mishears the term, and thinks that Simon has asked him if he is "a lion." This description gives Early reason to pause and reflect, and he actually contemplates if he is, in fact, symbolically "a lion." It's a crazy, weird, inventive, out-of-the-norm moment, but it exposes crucial aspects of Early's psychological gestalt. The first thing to consider is that he is a vainglorious narcissist. The second is that, as base and monstrous as he is, Early is wicked smart, and a philosopher even. The question of whether or not Early is "a lion" adheres to the overall approach to the hour, which stresses existentialism, and the idea that we are "just floating in space," and thus objects without meaning . . . at least until we imbue ourselves with meaning. The episode intimates that we all could be lions, or even a spaceship, as River notes of her one-ness with *Serenity*, if that is how we choose to regard ourselves.

Jubal Early stops to consider if, metaphorically, he could be considered "a lion" (a fierce and cunning animal), and that odd reckoning emerges from his ability to philosophize and rationalize away "meaning" in his own life. He hurts, maims, and kills people for a living, but Early contextualizes those acts as merely being part of a "job." Similarly, River wishes to vanish from existence itself, to become one with *Serenity* because she feels unloved and unwanted by the crew. What *is* River? A danger to the crew? A sister? A crazy woman? A psychic "reader?" Is she something with independent, objective meaning, or is River actually only the "thing" that others view her as?

River grapples with this idea, perhaps, because of her mental aberrations. At one point during the episode, she holds up a gun, but importantly, she views it as a tree branch. Again, we asked to consider the meaning of this "object in space." A gun is designed expressly for killing. Contrarily, a branch is a stick or part of a tree that grows out from a central bough or trunk. It is an extension of something, an outgrowth from a hearth. In grabbing hold of the branch, is River actually contextualizing herself (and the gun) as an outgrowth of *Serenity* (presumably the tree in this metaphor)? Is her act of holding the gun in fact the action of protecting the hearth, or reaching out to the others?

What's important, perhaps, is the "boundary transgression" River undergoes in this particular episode, at least according to scholar Karin Beeler in her essay "The Transformation of River Tam." Beeler notes (in *Seers, Witches and Psychics on Screen*; 2008, page 47) that "Objects in Space" showcases River's essential other-ness by transitioning from being human to being part of the machine (as part of *Serenity*, during her ruse). Then she becomes human once again, and, finally, another machine, in the form of Early's spaceship. As J. P. Telotte notes in *The Essential Science Fiction Television Reader*, River comes to identify herself "more closely with the inert technology of the ship than the crew." On a more basic level, River is able to put herself into the "experience" of reading and sympathizing with others. She takes over the sheltering/protective duties of *Serenity*, and also sits in Early's chair, and comes to see him as he really is.

"People don't appreciate the substance of things," Jubal Early says in "Objects in Space," and perhaps that phraseology is a way of noting that the crew can't appreciate the substance of River because she is so different from the other humans. Ironically, Early is guilty of the same transgression. He doesn't see—until it is far too late—the substance of River. His misreading of her—his misinterpretation of the "substance" of River—is what leads to his downfall. Early and River are both dangerous, and both cunning, but River can "become" something else, something outside her psyche so that she can see and appreciate the substance of things. Early can't escape his ego and narcissism enough to see that perspective.

This episode is very cleverly constructed and brilliantly executed, but ultimately, one need not ponder any of this material to enjoy "Objects in Space." The episode is tense, the conflict is direct and urgent, and Early is an unforgettable villain. Joss Whedon's writing is heavy on symbolic underscore, and it is fascinating the way his teleplay and direction balance a predator (a lion) against a force of nature (a river/River Tam). Accordingly, *Firefly* ends its TV run on a high note, and in this author's reckoning, the highest note of the series.

16

Serenity (2005)

Cast

Nathan Fillion:	Captain Malcolm "Mal" Reynolds
Gina Torres:	Zoe
Alan Tudyk:	Wash
Morena Baccarin:	Inara
Adam Baldwin:	Jayne
Jewel Staite:	Kaylee
Sean Maher:	Dr. Simon Tam
Summer Glau:	River Tam
Ron Glass:	Shepherd Book
Chiwetel Ejiofor:	The Operative
David Krumholz:	Mr. Universe
Michael Hitchcock:	Dr. Mathias
Sarah Paulson:	Dr. Caron
Rafael Feldman:	Fanty
Yan Feldman:	Mingo
Tamara Taylor:	Teacher

Crew

20th Century Fox Presents a Karzui Enterprises/Sand Dollar Production

Casting:	Anya Colloff, Amy McIntyre Britt
Music:	David Newman
Film Editor:	Lisa Lassek
Production Designer:	Barry Chusid

Director of Photography: Jack Green
Written by: Joss Whedon
Produced by: Barry Mendel
Directed by: Joss Whedon
M.P.A.A. Rating: PG-13
Running time: 119 minutes

Even as *Firefly* left TV screens, thanks to its fickle host network, Fox, series creator Joss Whedon schemed to bring the beloved characters back for an encore. When the series DVD sets were released, sales went through the roof, proving that an audience existed for more adventures in the *Firefly* universe, and Whedon approached Universal about shooting a feature film. The studio heads proved interested and acquired the film rights from Fox.

The newest chapter in the *Firefly* saga was to be a low-budget motion picture called *Serenity*. It was made for under $40 million and shot in 2004, in just fifty days. Not only did Whedon helm his first feature, but every member of the original cast returned for the film. And when *Serenity* opened in theaters in September of 2005, it opened at number two at the box office, and an impressive $25 million take.

Reviews were also uniformly positive. *Chicago Reader* critic Andrea Grovnall called it a "rousing feature directing debut" for Whedon, while *The AV Club*'s Tasha Robinson described it as "taut, immersive, and alternately hilarious and heart-breaking." At *Orlando Weekly*, critic Steve Schneider stated: "In the context of an action cinema driven by false hope, misogyny and sadism, *Serenity* is an inspiring respite."

Negative reviews were snarky, and mostly about the fact that the property originated on television. Chris Hewitt, at the *St. Paul Pioneer Press*, lamented that viewing *Serenity* was "like watching the sequel to a movie I missed." And Kyle Smith, of the *New York Post*, commented that watching *Serenity* was so much like watching a TV show that it "ought to come with a clicker" so viewers can switch "to the next movie at the multiplex."

Despite the overwhelmingly positive reviews, and glee of *Firefly* fans, *Serenity*'s winning streak at the box office did not continue long, and the film ultimately did not make back even the cost of its budget, rendering it a commercial failure, and calling into question the future of the franchise. It was a devastating blow, and even in 2019, *Serenity* fans were awaiting the next live-action chapter in this space-Western saga. Perhaps the most difficult thing to accept about the film's failure is the fact that it is so well made, so entertaining, and so smart. By all rights, *Serenity* is a brilliant film, and perhaps Whedon's best to date. One can only wish it met with more mainstream success.

I aim to misbehave.

In terms of its narrative, *Serenity* continues the story of Mal Reynolds, his crew, and his ship, the Firefly class vessel *Serenity*. The film opens with a history lesson (courtesy of a teacher and her classroom) about how "Earth could no longer sustain" the population, and the human race was forced

On the bridge: the gathered crew of Serenity gazes out into the 'Verse in the feature film follow-up to *Firefly*.   *John Muir Photo Archive*

to move to a solar system housing many habitable planets. The inhospitable worlds were terraformed, and the Alliance, "a beacon of civilization," was born. Independents resisted the rise of this "benevolent" government, and a civil war was fought. The Alliance won.

After this visually appealing history lesson, the film picks up with the origin story of River Tam, the star pupil of an Alliance scientist. "A living weapon," Tam is held against her will and experimented on until she is rescued by her brother, Simon, a once-promising physician who gave up his career to save his sister. Notably, these scenes precede the events of the TV series (and seem to tell a slightly different tale). Then, audiences meet an operative (Ejiofor) tasked with finding and recovering Tam for the Alliance.

The story then moves to the *Serenity*, with Mal planning his latest heist, the robbery of an Alliance payroll in an outlying world. He plans to use River on the mission for the first time, as he wants her to use her psychic powers to help him get the loot. Simon objects to Mal's plan, but is

Hiding on the ceiling. River (Glau) escapes from the Alliance in unique fashion in *Serenity* (2006).
John Muir Photo Archive

overruled. The plan goes awry, however, when a raiding party of Reavers also attacks the planet.

Later, River is "activated" by the Alliance, using a transmission that reaches her on the planet Beaumont. The transmission turns Tam into a powerful, and near-invincible, hand-to-hand combatant. In solving the mystery of River's programming, the *Serenity* crew seeks the help of a hacker, Mr. Universe (Krumholz), and inadvertently uncovers the origin of the Reavers, on a mysterious world known as Miranda. There, Mal sees the ultimate extension of the Alliance's policy to "improve" people, a fact that he must share with the universe. With the operative in pursuit, however, there are casualties among Mal's crew.

Watch how I soar.

Serenity is a cinematic masterpiece about rogue adventurers in "the black" (outer space), which deftly blends the heart, pace, and swashbuckling excitement of the best *Star Wars* films with the characters, thrills, pathos, and social commentary of the best *Star Trek* films. In this case, the film concerns current events as much as the future. The film was produced in the first years of George W. Bush's War on Terrorism after 9/11, which brought a terrorist surveillance program and wireless surveillance into public knowledge. In order to protect the country, making its citizenry safe and secure, the government initiated these programs to monitor citizens' communication.

In *Serenity*, of course, the Alliance is able to find River via its constant surveillance of all planets under its jurisdiction. Mr. Universe seems the futuristic equivalent of WikiLeaks: a person able to expose illegal surveillance and secrets of the state, via his technology. It's intriguing to note that 2005 was also around the time of one of the first social networks, Myspace, a site in which citizens provided their own information about their lives, and eschewed privacy. It was the start of an age in which secrets were in plain sight, and the government might have eyes and ears anywhere. Of course, as *Serenity* notes, the power can travel both ways in this future. Once a signal is transmitted, the "signal" can't be stopped.

This seems a paean to the transformative power of the internet at the start of the Web 2.0 era.

When one views the work of Joss Whedon, one can't help but be impressed by the artist's capacity to surprise audiences, and guide the whole enterprise to shocking destinations. This film is no exception. In *Serenity*—somewhere in the middle—a main character from the TV series dies. It's a sad, but noble, death, one that drives the action forward and helps to establish the real power and reach of the villain. It's a necessary death, not unlike Obi-Wan Kenobi's in *Star Wars*, or even Spock's in *The Wrath of Khan* (1982). "Good," you can almost hear the audience mutter after the sad scene is finished, "we're sorry to lose this great character, but at least that's out of the way. We're safe."

But then Whedon does something truly innovative and rather nasty. He kills *another* of his main characters.

Senselessly. Brutally. Unexpectedly.

And this shocking murder occurs right before the film's biggest battle. Fans will complain, because the character is so beloved. But the fact of the matter is this: never in a sci-fi movie has there been a more brilliantly timed "murder" of a beloved character. When this character dies, the audience freezes, emotionally walloped.

Joss Whedon's message is simply this: *No one is safe. All bets are off.*

Consequently, the film's finale is about a hundred times more effective than it would have been without the diversion of the first death and the surprise of the second. When the *Serenity* crew subsequently stands and fights in the climax—hopelessly outnumbered before hordes of Reavers—and the remainder of the beloved crew members begin dropping like flies, the movie kicks into high gear. People in the theater gasped during this scene, at least in the theater where I watched the film. When Zoe took a hit to the back, my wife literally *shrieked*. "Is *everybody* going to die?" she whispered to me.

This is the most intense, heart-wrenching climax of any sci-fi movie franchise since 1986's *Aliens* (when we lost great characters like Hudson and Vasquez), and certainly doubly so for a TV-turned-movie franchise. By contrast, consider Data's death in *Star Trek: Nemesis* (2002). Yes, it was sad, but the producers didn't want audiences to feel bad when leaving the theater, so the filmmakers had a replacement named B-4 all lined up. In other words, audiences knew everything would be okay.

Not so in *Serenity*, and Whedon is a clever, if sadistic, genius for the timing and effect of this second death. Alfred Hitchcock used to state that he enjoyed playing audiences "like a piano," and Joss Whedon has mastered that talent as well. We all mourn the deaths of these characters, but they serve the movie incredibly well. They rocket the finale into white-knuckle territory. Because of the deaths, the film stops being a "TV-show-turned movie" and it ascends to another level, a riveting cinematic experience.

The specifics of the death are extremely important too. The character who dies, this well-liked "leaf on the wind," is, importantly, Whedon's voice in the series. The character speaks in Whedon's contemporary, ironic tone, puncturing any possibility of pretension. To lose this character is to lose Whedon's voice in the drama, and that is simply devastating. So much of Whedon's work is about communication. Wash is not only Whedon's voice of acerbic intelligence, he is the voice of the audience.

Serenity also reveals that Joss Whedon is a strong visual stylist. People always complain about TV directors and their transition to movies, but Whedon is not hindered at all by his small-screen beginnings. On the contrary, he understands how to use the frame and how to compose beautiful and meaningful shots. The opening sequence, which moves from outer space to *Serenity*'s bridge, through the hall, down a flight of stairs, into the cargo bay and then up onto a ledge, is practically worthy of Brian De Palma. It's an unbroken shot with tons of snappy dialogue, and both Whedon and the cast bring it off brilliantly. It's an important early shot too, because it flawlessly establishes the reality, or rather physicality, of the ship *Serenity*. The audience feels as though it is aboard the craft, having walked the length of it. One couldn't achieve this sense of reality with lots of cuts; it would feel stagey.

The film's physical confrontations are also gorgeously rendered. When this author interviewed Whedon in 2004, he was in the midst of shooting *Serenity*'s fight sequences, and we discussed, among other things, how fight sequences resemble dance. And for Whedon, he made it clear it was important to him to see *the entire body* of a fighter or dancer in an action/musical scene. So it was with great delight that one can watch

Serenity and detect how well Whedon directs the fight scenes with River, particularly the first fight in the bar, when River becomes activated by the Alliance signal.

Whedon lets the camera stand back, so viewers can see the full breadth of the choreography, so audiences can see River (Summer Glau) fully engaged in lethal motion. There are few cuts in the fight, and consequently the scene boasts an unusually strong rhythm. It was the right choice to perch the camera at a distance, because the notion of River as a "living weapon" is transmitted beautifully. We see for ourselves, without insert shots of kicks or punches, what she is capable of achieving. Much like the opening shot, Whedon's decision to limit cuts and reveal bodies in full form reflects its narrative.

Story-wise, Joss Whedon is long established as a maestro, and his 2005 tale features a terrific surprise in the last act, one that puts the entire universe of *Firefly* in a new light. The monsters of this universe, it

Paint job: Inara (Morena Baccarin) restores Serenity to her former glory.   *John Muir Photo Archive*

is learned, are man-made. The Reavers are not just people who went to the edge of space and went crazy by the infinity they witnessed. Instead, the Alliance created these monsters by attempting to pacify the population of Miranda with a gas called PAX. They believed they could improve people, and did the exact opposite. They destroyed people, and destroyed lives. Since this may be the last live-action iteration of the Firefly universe, it is appropriate and rewarding that Whedon decided to explain the mystery behind the monstrous and terrifying Reavers.

Beyond the spaceships and the fight scenes, *Serenity* is really a film about love. Simon loves his sister, River. Mal loves his crew. And Mal delivers a great speech at the close of the film about how love keeps his ship flying. It is in that beautifully directed-and-performed climactic moment that one realizes Whedon has given the genre a great film about another "found family," and more to the point, a classic character in Mal Reynolds. He truly rivals other space captains, ones with names like Solo or Kirk. He's a pragmatic sort, but also one of essential decency. And he likes to fight battles he can't win. The only way Mal does win, actually, is through the loyalty he inspires in his crew. He'd be nothing without them, and he knows that. More than ever, Mal reminds this author of Rick in *Casablanca*, a comparison other writers have also suggested. Both men have strong morals, but they try to cloak that morality by hiding far from the action. They have abandoned their fights until called upon to return to them.

Serenity may not have succeeded in theaters during its run more than a decade ago, but lest it is forgotten, *Blade Runner* was not a success in its original theatrical run either. In fact, it was a critical and box-office bomb. *Serenity* received better reviews. But beyond that comparison, perhaps it will, like the Ridley Scott film, continue to age well. Audiences may discover—*better late than never*—that this is one of the genre greats.

17

Did Joss Whedon create a Web Series?

Dr. Horrible's Sing-a-Long Blog (2008)

Cast

Neil Patrick Harris:	Billy/Dr. Horrible
Felicia Day:	Penny
Nathan Fillion:	Captain Hammer
Simon Helberg:	Moist
Nick Towne:	Bad Horse Chorus #1
Jed Whedon:	Bad Horse Chorus #2
Rob Reinis:	Bad Horse Chorus #3

Crew

Mutant Enemy Presents *Dr. Horrible's Sing-a-Long Blog*

Music:	Jed Whedon
Director of Photography:	Ryan Green
Film Editor:	Lisa Lassek
Written by:	Maurissa Tancharoen, Jed Whedon, Joss Whedon, Zack Whedon
Produced by:	Michael Boetz, David M. Burns, Joss Whedon
Directed by:	Joss Whedon

Home is where the heart is. So the real home is in your chest.

Billy—a.k.a. Dr. Horrible (Neil Patrick Harris)—records the latest video for his fans, reading their email, and providing information about his latest plan to "destroy the status quo," by taking over the planet, and bending it to his will. Though Billy is the villainous Dr. Horrible, he is also a lonely man who pines for a woman named Penny (Felicia Day), whom he knows from their mutual laundry days at a local laundromat. Penny is a genuinely good person, working for good causes, including a local homeless shelter.

As Billy makes in-roads in a relationship with Penny, he is usurped by his arch-nemesis, the pompous superhero and champion of the city: Captain Hammer (Nathan Fillion). Hammer knows that Billy is Dr. Horrible, and that he is interested in Penny. Hammer steps in to take the girl for himself.

This act makes the "evil inside" Billy rise and he hatches a plan to use a freeze ray, and humiliate and defeat Captain Hammer. Unfortunately, Penny dies in the final confrontation, giving Billy his "cred" as a villain, but destroying his life in the process.

Now Billy truly is a super-villain.

It's not enough to bash in heads. You have to bash in minds.

Dr. Horrible's Sing-Along Blog is a musical superhero comedy for the web, and structured in three acts. The roughly $200,000 production was self-funded by Joss Whedon, and shot in Los Angeles with a cast and crew working for free. Whedon co-wrote this online production along with his half-brothers Zack and Jed Whedon, and Maurissa Tancharoen. He produced it during the 2007–2008 writers' strike.

That strike stretched from November of 2007 to February of 2008, and was the result of writers attempting to improve their remuneration for studio projects. At issue was the level established as the MBA (Minimum

Basic Agreement), and the fourteen-week strike cost the city of Los Angeles approximately $1.5 billion, according to National Public Radio.

Dr. Horrible's Sing-A-Long Blog premiered over three nights, July 15, 17, and 19, 2008, and "aired" on streaming platforms including Hulu and Netflix. The CW aired *Dr. Horrible's Sing-a-Long Blog* (with some editing) on October 9, 2012. The film ultimately made a profit, grossing roughly $3 million, which was more than enough to compensate the cast and crew for the efforts. The film was also an award winner and was selected as "Favorite Online Sensation," for the People's Choice Awards. The web series won seven Streamy Awards at the first Streamy ceremony.

Critics were effusive in their praise as well. Writing for the *New York Times*, critic Mike Hale wrote "[A]s you would expect from Mr. Whedon, the show is funny, in an elliptical, sardonic way, especially in the song lyrics." Upon the release of the mini-series on DVD, *Collider*'s critic-in-residence, Nico, opined: "The only good thing to come out of the Writer's Strike is *Dr. Horrible's Sing-Along Blog*. If you enjoy creativity, performance, singing, or America, you will enjoy this fine work."

In terms of artistry, *Dr. Horrible's Sing-a-Long Blog* is perhaps the most Whedonesque of all Whedon films. While the musical threatens at times to succumb to all-out camp, it instead goes the opposite way, proving genuinely affecting, especially in its third act. Throughout the production, the story feels like a light satire of superhero tropes, only with toe-tapping tunes, and then the director pulls the rug out from under the viewer. After so many jokes and laughs, *Dr. Horrible's Sing-a-Long Blog* ends in tears with the tragic death of Penny. This is an eventuality no fan saw coming, and changes the nature of the whole piece.

Robert Lloyd, the critic for the *Los Angeles Times*, picked up on this tonal sadness. "It is a sweet, rather sad piece that—like the songs, by Whedon and his brother Jed, which are at once mock-heroic and actually heroic, mock-moving and moving in fact—works both as parody and as a drama. It also works as comedy, from line to line and moment to moment, but it is not, really, a comedy. It kept me quite unsettled, seeing it for the first time—and subsequent times, for that matter."

Indeed, at first blush, Billy appears to be a harmless, awkward kid playing at being a villain (or super-villain). He hangs out with lame sidekicks, must practice his villainous cackle, is uncomfortable around women, and is, all around, socially inept more than "evil." At Penny's death, however, that all changes. Now the costs of his behavior are high, and Billy is no longer harmless. He has become what he wanted to be: a monster. But the price of being that monster, the death of Penny, is never something he could imagine himself paying. His complete victory over Captain Hammer is spoiled by the side-effect of his evil plan, the death of the only person who cared about him at all.

Oddly, *Dr. Horrible's Sing-a-Long Blog* seems more timely ten years after its premiere than it did, necessarily, in 2008, when it was on the frontier of online productions. Today, the web-series seems like an oddly prophetic view of what fandom has become in 2018 and 2019: toxic and destructive. Vitriolic and out-of-proportion fan responses to *Star Trek: Discovery* (2017–), *Star Wars: The Last Jedi* (2017), and even *The X-Files* Season 11 (2018), have proven that seemingly harmless geeks are obsessed with villainy in their own way, much like Billy, pushing racism and sexism, and lodging attacks against any agenda they deem to be the product of "SJWs" (social justice warriors).

Nerds were once thought of as being brilliant but socially inept, much in the mold of Billy, but like Billy many have now crossed the line into disturbing, even monstrous behavior, that is a total rejection of the franchise's ethos they ostensibly worship (or worshipped). *Dr. Horrible's Sing-a-Long Blog* thus plays like a twisted mirror, projecting the future of popular fandoms. Those who are lonely and inept, the production reveals, can fall to the "dark side," and lose their inherent goodness. At the end of the web-series, Billy notes that he does not feel a thing, anymore. He is numb from what he has done, and in that damaged state will be able to launch undreamed-of horrors.

Dr. Horrible's Sing-a-Long Blog also captures the fickle nature of fans. They all love Captain Hammer, until they don't; until he is defeated by Dr. Horrible. What holds their fan attention is passing, ephemeral; until something shinier or newer arrives to usurp the old favorite. Even the adoration of Captain Hammer raises questions about fan discourse (and perhaps, even, politics) in our nation. How can people follow this guy? How can they see this braggadocio and bully as someone to worship, or aspire to be like? He's smug, narcissistic, and cruel.

The same question might be asked of Billy. Why do people gravitate towards villains? Is it just raw power? In raising these sorts of questions, *Dr. Horrible's Sing-A-Long Blog* lives up to Whedon's legacy of dissecting the superhero or fantasy genre in which he often works. Can heroes be villains? Can villains be heroes? Are heroes and villains at opposite ends of the spectrum, or are they all just people, labeled for our convenience, but possessing, essentially, the same characteristics and foibles? Captain Hammer is a bully for justice; and Billy fancies himself a disruptor, someone who must destroy the Old Order, so a new, better one can stand in its place.

What are we to make of each character?

If the climax of *Dr. Horrible's Sing-a-Long Blog* proves both haunting and prophetic about Web 2.0 Age fandom, then the remainder of the film earns the title of Whedonesque through the director's particular penchant for pairing fantasy with the concrete details of reality, or daily life. In other words, the film assumes both a universe of superheroes and supervillains, and then suggests the infrastructure to support them. The juxtaposition of the fantastic with the bureaucratic, the pedantic, is the thing that makes the film stand out from other productions.

For example, as noted above, Billy employs a voice coach to improve his evil laugh (because . . . standards). Similarly, he wants to join the Evil League of Evil, a guild that seems to possess a number of bureaucratic rules about what it takes to be a villain. Billy must jump through a lot of gatekeeper hoops to qualify as a member. One thing the league insists upon: he must kill someone which, ominously, Billy notes, is not his style. Those words come back to haunt him, after Penny's death.

Similarly, the notion of a supervillain doing his own laundry at a cheap coin wash, or a superhero confidentially noting that his hammer is actually his penis, are funny touches that bridge the gap between the genre's greatest flights of fancy, and the most basic of human truths about day-to-day life. Everyone in the film, even Captain Hammer, seems to be lonely, in search of happiness. Penny is the only one, however, who seems to derive that happiness from helping others, by doing something for the community, instead of just hurting people. This is perhaps the most powerful critique of the superhero genre, and an apt one in the age of "Dark Knight"–styled adventures.

Inevitably, Batman movies become about opposing forces battling each other. But these forces are two sides of the same coin. They argue over "*You* made *me*? *I* made *you!*" A place like Gotham City becomes the battleground for these opposing characters, such as Batman and the Joker, to duke it out, and work out their personal issues. Forgotten in this equation, but very much restored in the brilliant MCU films, is the notion that superheroes exist not to battle villains, not to kill their opposite number, but to help people; to rescue a community in need.

In *Dr. Horrible's Sing-A-Long Blog*, Penny is the only main character not affiliated with a costume, or a fantasy identity. And yet, one might rightly argue that she is the film's only actual superhero. Why? Because she cares for others, whether it be Billy, Hammer, or the homeless. It isn't even about the caring, per se (deeds, not words, after all, to quote *Megaforce* [1982]). Rather, Penny is the only one who acts to save the community, to do something for someone else. Hammer is concerned only with his self-aggrandizement (and the humiliation of Billy) and Billy just wants to join Bad Horse and the Evil League of Evil. What does it say about our world that Penny is collateral damage in the battle between Hammer and Evil? That the only person who cares for others is the victim in this titanic clash?

At *Den of Geek*, writer Sarah Dobbs expressed disappointment, in the article titled "Why Penny Matters," with the blasé way in which Penny is dispatched. Dobbs doesn't see the character of Penny as having much agency, or even insight, since she dies thinking Captain Hammer will save her . . . and he's a coward and a jerk. The author sees Penny's death as the revival of an old trope: the death of the hero's girlfriend.

However, Whedon subverts that trope here by making Penny literally the only person in the entire production who could rightly be called a good person, or more aptly, a superhero. Her death, therefore, becomes not a cliché designed merely to impact the future of the hero, Billy. Rather, Penny's death signifies in some way the death of altruism, or community, in a superhero's universe. Without the presence of someone decent or good, a crusader, the world is left with extremists like Billy and Hammer endlessly fighting one another, trying to gain an advantage. Her death, therefore, is doubly poignant, and meaningful. It pushes Billy to the edge of despair and makes him the villain he only played at being. Simultaneously, her death removes hope, and real goodness, from the world, a world ostensibly of superheroes, but really one of villains on all sides.

With Dr. *Horrible's Sing-a-Long Blog*, Whedon repeats, successfully, the peculiar alchemy of *Buffy the Vampire Slayer* TV series, or *Firefly*. He creates a work of art that appears light and bubbly, and escapist, all the while subtly and persistently offering social criticism about the form he has adopted. The musical is a film genre that is about yearning, need, and, truly, communication: the ability for the audience to hear, in song, the thoughts and desires of a protagonist or antagonist. Musicals were most popular in the 1930s, when Americans sought an escape from the Great Depression, and the storm of Fascism driving across Europe. Here, the escapist format of the musical allows Whedon to expose superheroes and supervillains alike as needy, self-serving, and corrupt. We are privy to their thoughts and dreams and learn that they are not paragons of darkness or light, but people just like the rest of us, conflicted, and driven by pettiness and, in terms of Billy and Hammer, a deep emptiness inside.

Although *Dr. Horrible's Sing-A-Long Blog* is a low-budget production, it is a high-minded one, showcasing again Whedon's ability to see "underneath" pop-culture formats and structures. In a way, it is perfect that this production ended up on the internet first, as that has become, over the decades, the perennial home of fans, for better or worse.

The internet was, first, the great promise of freedom and democracy, a platform where everyone would have an equal voice, and the best idea in the marketplace would be the one to thrive. Very soon after its inception, however, people began to see how on the internet commentary and responsibility could be separated through anonymous comments. This uncoupling of these two elements would turn people into laptop supervillains, spewing hatred and bullying on a scale never before possible (see: The *Star Wars* Kid, or the treatment of Kelly Marie Tran.) Not all fans use the internet for this purpose, of course, but *Dr. Horrible's Sing-a-Long Blog* not only predicts the rise of YouTube personalities or vloggers with dedicated followings or subscribers, it predicts the idea that on the internet, even the best people may choose to follow someone who identifies as a villain, or who lies to them, or who bullies others, simply because he or she possesses the power to do so.

Dr. Horrible's Sing-a-Long Blog is something of a minor miracle. Ironically, the film is itself proof of what the internet could be: a place where independent art thrives, and passion projects come to life. It's too bad that so many fans did not pick up Joss Whedon's challenge here, and begin to create original internet programming. They chose, by and large, instead, to make *Star Wars* and *Star Trek* fan films, thus living in someone else's universe instead of developing their own artistic energies and visions. But Whedon provided a model of what could be done: a genre-blending, laugh-a-minute, toe-tapping entertainment with an embedded critique of the superhero genre, and even, modern fans.

18

Dollhouse (2009–2010)

Cast

Eliza Dushku:	Echo
Harry Lennix:	Boyd Langton
Fran Kranz:	Topher Brink
Tahmoh Penikett:	Paul Ballard
Enver Gjokaj:	Victor
Dichen Lachman:	Sierra
Olivia Williams:	Adelle De Witt
Reed Diamond:	Laurence Dominic (Season 1)

Crew

20th Century Fox Television, Boston Diva Productions

Created by:	Joss Whedon
Casting:	Anya Colloff, Amy McIntyre Britt, Michael V. Nicolo
Production Designers:	Stuart Blatt, Camerone Birnie
Costume Designer:	Shawna Trpcic
Music:	Mychael Danna, Rob Simonsen
Directors of Photography:	Lisa Wiegand, Ross Berryman
Film Editors:	Peter Basinki, Paul Trejo, Elena Maganini
Executive Producer:	Joss Whedon
Producers:	Eliza Dushku, Kelly A. Manners

Would you like a treatment?

In 2009, the first new Joss Whedon–created TV series in seven years, *Dollhouse* (2009–2010), premiered on the same network that had canceled his last, and perhaps most beloved series, *Firefly*. The new series aired Fridays at 9:00 p.m., and was heavily promoted by the network. As if to correct a previous and grievous wrong, Fox also demonstrated a strong sense of patience with the new Whedon series. The Powers-That-Be didn't cancel the series after a relatively low-rated first season, but brought *Dollhouse* back for a second season, and then, finally, permitted for closure with a series finale. Whedon had originally planned out a five-season story-arc for *Dollhouse*, but the series was resolved in its two seasons (and twenty-seven episodes) instead, a fact which resulted in some complex time-jumps, and a dramatic (and not always successful) acceleration of narrative and character arcs. Still, those twin "Epitaph" episodes, which serve as a coda for the series, are among the best in the canon in terms of scope and heartbreaking twists.

Did I fall asleep?

Dollhouse is the story of an optimistic activist named Caroline Farrell, played by Eliza Dushku, who runs afoul of the powerful Rossum Corporation, which owns the mysterious locations known as *dollhouses*. There are twenty dollhouses around the world, including one in Los Angeles. Although, to the naked eye, they look like high-end spas, health clubs, or even, perhaps, "escort services," they are actually places where clients can "buy" people, male or female, and live out their fantasies, dark or not, with them.

Under legal duress, Caroline must sign a five-year contract to lend her body and mind to the dollhouse in L.A. to make up for her infraction against Rossum. Caroline's original personality and identity are thus "wiped" from her mind and stored on a cartridge-like hard-drive at the dollhouse. Then, new identities—those meeting client needs and desires—are uploaded into her brain for each excursion.

Those who undergo this process of becoming a different person are termed *actives* and the "missions" they go on with clients are called *engagements*. After each engagement, actives such as Caroline—who now goes by the codename *Echo*—have their minds wiped, going to what they think is a "treatment." When they awake, they know they have been asleep, but theoretically should not possess any memory of their uploaded and wiped identity. Echo, however, begins to develop a kind of "core" memory that survives each new personality upload, and each deletion.

Running the Los Angeles dollhouse is a strong, secretive woman named Adelle De Witt (Olivia Williams), who serves rich clients and sometimes even avails herself to encounters with the dolls, a fact which belies her isolation and loneliness. She is an ambiguous figure for much of the series, until confirmed to be an ally near the close of the series.

De Witt's associate is Topher Brink (Fran Kanz), the young genius who invented the "active architecture," the technology used to wipe and upload, and then again wipe human minds. An arrogant genius, Topher comes to see, over the course of the series, how his technology is misused by Rossum. The actives are "blank slates," and innocents, rendered "empty" and asexual, in defiance of human nature. Topher comes to see that, in a way, his technology has enslaved people, and made them toys, or "dolls," for the rich and powerful.

One episode of *Dollhouse*, "True Believer," shows a male doll experience a so-called "*man reaction*" (read: erection) while in proximity to a woman in the communal shower. This is troublesome because in the "doll" state, actives are supposed to be total innocents. This "man reaction" is an early indicator in the series that the "wiping" procedure isn't as complete as Topher believes it to be, and that human nature is not so easily subverted or rewritten.

Another regular character in the series is Boyd Langton (Harry Lennix), Echo's handler and bodyguard, who sees to Echo's safety during her many engagements. Also stationed in the Dollhouse is Reed Diamond's Laurence Dominic, a seemingly sinister NSA agent whose loyalties and motives are not immediately apparent. He later becomes a protagonist, or at least an anti-hero in the series, fighting alongside Echo, near the end of season one.

In the Dollhouse itself, Echo is not alone. There are other actives who go on missions, including Sierra (Dichen Lachman) and Victor (Enver Gjokaj), who despite their constant programming and deprogramming develop a powerful love for each other. Again, there's an idea here of a core memory or identity, one that survives the active programming.

Over the course of the series, Echo's sense of original self grows dramatically. Despite lacking her original identity as Caroline, she begins to become cognizant of her enslavement, and starts to see Rossum as her true enemy. Unfortunately, Echo's unusual nature puts her in constant danger. Other actives who have remembered their engagements have gone mad from the experience, and sent to "The Attic," a terrifying prison for malfunctioning "dolls" at the top level of the dollhouse. One active, called Alpha (Alan Tudyk), has become a mad schizophrenic from his memories of forty-eight separate personalities, and has broken free of the dollhouse. One episode sees his return, and his plan to get close to Echo.

On the outside, a dedicated and dogged FBI agent, Paul Ballard (Tahmoh Penikett), investigates the existence of the Los Angeles dollhouse, and is mocked by his colleagues for pursuing what they believe is a myth. As the series unwinds, Ballard sees photos and videotapes of Caroline Farrell, and falls in love with her. This affection is his ulterior motive for discovering, definitively, the existence of the dollhouse. Unbeknown to him, a doll is pretending to be his neighbor, and actually spying on him and his progress, all along.

If this premise sounds complicated, then it has been reflected accurately in the writing above. *Dollhouse* involves the nature of identity and memory, and even the idea that gender is, ultimately, not tied to the physical body. Throughout the series, people "hide" inside those of other genders and ages, cloaking their true selves. The series finale suggests, even, that lovers of different genders can share one mind, and continue their relationship . . . in one body. According to scholar Genie Nicole Giamo, this Whedon series explores "the dangerous potentialities of neurological memory modification, including women without bodily autonomy, men severed from corporeal reality, governments in shambles, mass amnesia, slavery, and 'mind death.' These case studies combine to suggest that, when memory is manipulated or otherwise modified by external agents, concepts like free will, identity, and labor are co-opted to serve the interests of the powerful and rich." It's daring, cutting-edge material.

Or perhaps I should have written that it could have been so, had *Dollhouse* survived for the intended five years. The first several episodes of season one move at a slow place, as the audience follows Echo on one engagement after the next, in what seems an episodic series, with only touches of inter-episode continuity and storytelling. Instead, the series feels, at least at first, like a demo tape to show off Eliza Dushku's versatility as a performer. One week she's a hostage negotiator, the next a rock star, the next a survivalist, and so forth.

Then, however, matters suddenly accelerate, and the episodes start to develop at light speed, eschewing the "engagement of the week" format and going full-bore into the series' deep mythology. In essence, the series at one end is too episodic to be all that intriguing, and too complex at the other end to allow for deep engagement from casual viewers. It's an imperfect formula, one that damages the sense that *Dollhouse* is a consistent series.

Some episodes capture a fragile balance. For instance, the first-season entry "The Target" commences with a full head of steam, depicting a flashback that delves into the dollhouse's mysterious history. In particular, the audience witnesses in washed-out, over-exposed tones, a catastrophic *"composite event"* that occurred three months earlier. This violent incident saw an active named Alpha—suddenly in possession of his memory after casting off his state of *tabula rosa*—go postal and murder several armed guards and at least two fellow actives. Alpha was eventually put down, after cutting up Dr. Saunders (Amy Acker) . . . *or so we've been told*. Oddly, the knife-wielding psychopath spared Echo.

Meanwhile, in the episode's present, Echo has been imprinted with the personality of a rough-and-tumble outdoorsy woman, one who can go toe-to-toe with a rugged client, played by Matt Keeslar. This muscular, thick-necked client wants a mate who can white-water raft, climb mountains, and match him in every way imaginable (including in the bedroom). *Or so it seems.* After sexual intercourse with Echo, the macho client quickly demonstrates he's a psychopath, one who hunts her down in the isolated woods to prove that she is "worthy of living."

This description makes "The Target" sound utterly ridiculous, yet in true Whedonesque fashion, the episode brims with surprises, unexpected twists, and narrative U-turns, especially in the connection between the flashback and the present scenario, and the resulting narrative is an energetic, imaginative and hyper forty-five minutes. With strong action, good pacing, and a tantalizing glimpse of the past, "The Target" satisfies viewer curiosity both about Echo in the present, and her history at the Dollhouse.

Specifically, one can see how the mythology of the series is building here, with Echo beginning to remember bits of her previous life and personalities, and even holding onto a piece of this particular imprint (particularly one gesture demonstrated by Keeslar's character). The audience is also introduced—*in very enigmatic, spare terms*—to the season's apparent villain or Big Bad: Alpha. Audiences learn in "The Target" that

The created family of *Dollhouse* (2009 – 2010): Left to right: Ballard (Tahmoh Penikett), Victor (Enver Gjokaj), Echo (Eliza Dushku), Sierra (Dichen Lachman), Topher (Fran Kranz), Adelle DeWitt (Olivia Williams) and Langton (Harry Lennix).   *John Muir Photo Archive*

Alpha's mystery ultimately *"leads back to Echo,"* and it is a tantalizing revelation.

Another first-season episode also effectively mixes stand-alone action with mythology. Echo goes on an "engagement" imprinted as a master thief in "Gray Hour." The job involves stolen art, and a secret vault rendered penetrable for a brief span by a security update *gray hour.* Unfortunately for Echo and her fellow thieves, a mysterious cellphone transmission from Alpha—*a remote wipe*—transforms her back into innocent, skill-less Echo in mid-assignment. Which means that Topher, De Witt, and Sierra at the dollhouse facility must scramble to rescue Echo from the locked vault before security guards capture her. The technology of a remote wipe becomes a key factor in the series finale's apocalyptic setting.

But in her "blank slate" persona, Echo is understandably confused to find herself far from the safety of the dollhouse womb, and Topher reports that she might undergo *"extreme sensory overload,"* meaning Echo could become either passive or *"Carrie at the prom."* Unfortunately, Echo doesn't really go either way, and the episode—to adopt the lingo of the writers themselves—becomes *"one giant anticlimax."* "Gray Hour" features a terrific plot device (an active wiped in mid-assignment), hints again at the capabilities of the season's "big bad," Alpha (who has apparently developed technology far beyond even Topher's genius level), and offers some vital background information about the actives, particularly that—even wiped of memories—they possess *"instinctual survival tools,"* meaning that the strong will flock to the strong, and so forth. In this way, the series seems to suggest that whether or not we have our memories, some aspect of identity remains in the mind. Even if a person is overwritten with new programming, the original programming continues to exist. We are who we are supposed to be; who we are wired to be, despite technological overlays. It's a fascinating meditation on personhood and self-concept, and when and where identity arises in the brain.

There are many such good concepts at work on this series—and even underscoring this very episode of *Dollhouse*—and yet the series is not nearly as successful or as coherent as Whedon's other TV work. Nor has it developed the same level of devoted fan following. The question, of course, is why this would be the case.

Perhaps the answer rests with the *dramatis personae*: the characters, usually Joss Whedon's strong suit. Here, Paul Ballard (Penikett) feels like a cliché—the dogged and dedicated cop with a soft spot for a beautiful face and a tragic story. De Witt (Williams) is a cold fish, and, if not a villain for most of the series, she plays her cards so close to the vest that viewers can't read her or invest in her. And Topher (Kranz) is glib, arrogant, irritating, and over-the-top.

However—*most critically*—in terms of Sierra and Echo, it is extremely difficult to sympathize or identify with someone who is, at least primarily, a blank slate. Dushku is a good actress, perhaps even a remarkable one. To the extent that she manages to exude shades of Echo's "core" personality from week-to-week while "imprinted" with different characters is a testament to her presence and talent. But it's simply not enough to make a viewing of *Dollhouse* feel *intimate*. Instead, the series feels distancing, not inviting, which makes it the exact opposite of *Firefly* or *Buffy the Vampire Slayer*.

As there are no compelling characters with whom to undertake this journey, there's some kind of emotional void marring many episodes of *Dollhouse*. That void often gets filled with action scenes that aren't that well-staged, quips that aren't that funny, or philosophy that is tantalizing . . . but also maddening, since it is tossed out in the form of minuscule bread crumbs in the stand-alone style episodes.

You ever try to clear an actual slate? You always see what was on it before.

The episodes "Epitaph One" and "Epitaph Two: Return" attempt to address these series shortcomings. Sierra and Victor become real people instead of just ciphers, with a relationship to care about (not to mention a child to raise). Echo grows to become a dedicated fighter/rebel and charismatic individual. De Witt reveals that she is against Rossum's plans for world domination. Topher goes insane with guilt and regret, and even Ballard grows to become that familiar Whedon character, the "Sacrificial Lamb," the character (much like Doyle in *Angel*, or Spike in *Buffy the Vampire Slayer*) whose death gives new meaning to the hero or heroine's fight.

The problem with the series is, to restate it, that all this information gets revealed in two action-packed, fast-moving, thematically dense episodes, instead of over the course of a five-year series, so the balance feels wrong. The series move at a snail's pace, and then rockets, wildly, toward a deep conclusion. In the final analysis, *Dollhouse* is at first too slow and formulaic, and then, in the end, so complex that the audience doesn't feel the emotional resonance it should when the characters reach their final destinations.

With *Dollhouse*, Joss Whedon was given a "blank slate" to create a new cult-TV series masterpiece and fan favorite, and he even had the network on his side this time, at least for the most part. And yet, in the most positive environment he had encountered since *Buffy the Vampire Slayer*, the result was a series that is probably the least favored among his die-hard fans. The series' cancellation was announced by the Associated Press on November 11, 2009, and the final episode of the series ("Epitaph Two: Return") aired on January 22, 2010.

19

What Are the Five-Best Episodes of *Dollhouse*?

Alone among Joss Whedon's series, there aren't that many great episodes of *Dollhouse*. Instead, some demonstrate real potential, while others feel like time-wasters separated from an overarching myth-arc. Therefore, it is difficult to select five great episodes out of the twenty-seven. There is general consensus among fans about the quality of an episode such as "The Attic," and many fans agree with this author that the "Epitaph" episodes are strong ones. However, some fans feel, not entirely wrongly, that the "Epitaphs" feel like an entirely different series. With the understanding that mileage may vary, here are the author's choices for the best five episodes of *Dollhouse*.

5. "Ghost." Written and Directed by Joss Whedon. Airdate: February 13, 2009

Ever meet someone who seems too perfect? Too beautiful? Too smart? Too witty? Who says all the right things in every situation? Who is—in a phrase—*too good to be true?* Well, maybe that person *is* too good to be true; maybe he or she is actually an "active" on a mission, a resident of Joss Whedon's *Dollhouse*.

It's tempting to comment about the myriad ways, historically speaking, in which pilots don't necessarily reflect the quality of the series that follow them. That pilots suffer under the weight of having a great deal to accomplish: both introducing a slew of characters and vetting a new, fresh, self-contained story. It's not an easy task crafting a good one, let alone a great one. *Dollhouse*'s opening episode should have been a slam dunk, but wasn't.

This pilot episode ("Ghost") was crafted after several episodes of the series were already in the can. Creator Joss Whedon famously went back and devised a new pilot, one that would more accurately reflect the narrative and arc of *Dollhouse* as a whole. Given that rare and valuable opportunity, it's a little baffling why "Ghost"—strong as it may be in parts—isn't more involving, dynamic, and focused. It's clear here that the larger premise is better than this episode's execution; that the overall "ideas" are more engaging than the particular story.

To the specifics now. *Dollhouse*, as introduced in "Ghost," is the tale of a secret, highly illegal facility called, you guessed it, The Dollhouse. There, secretive Adele De Witt (Olivia Williams) oversees a cadre of agents called *actives*. Under her direction, these actives go out on missions called *engagements*. The actives, however, aren't simply secret operatives: they are "*clean slates.*" Their original personalities have been removed ("*wiped*")

Promotional shot of *Dollhouse*'s season two cast: Left to right: Sierra (Lachman), Topher (Kranz), Victor (Gjokaj), DeWitt (Williams), Echo (Dushku), Ballard (Penikett) and Langton (Lennix).

John Muir Photo Archive

and for each new mission, they are *"imprinted"* with new personalities (and, therefore, new skills) that fit the mission. In "Ghost," for example, a young active named Echo (series star Eliza Dushku) is outfitted with the memories of an expert negotiator (or *several* negotiators, actually) to bring quick closure to a high-profile kidnapping.

Managing the programming and mental wiping is nerdy young scientist Topher Brink (Fran Kranz). Serving as handler to Echo is a veteran ex-cop, Boyd Langton (Harry Lennix), and acting as physician to the stable of physically fit actives is Dr. Claire Saunders (Amy Acker), a recurring character. Meanwhile, a resourceful cop, Paul Ballard (Tahmoh Penikett), attempts to find and expose the secret Dollhouse, to the dismay of his superiors and cohorts in the bureau. Paul believes that wiping out a human personality is the same thing as murder, and desires to bring those at the Dollhouse to justice for human trafficking.

Living placid, memory-less lives in the gilded cage of the Dollhouse, the actives are innocent, naïve, and truth be told, a little dumb. They seem like dim bulbs. One may be unpleasantly reminded, at least in "Ghost," alas, of the clone farm in *Parts: The Clonus Horror* (1979). There, all the physically fit young clones dwell in a Garden of Eden of ignorance until one curious clone tastes an apple from the tree of knowledge (or rather, a beer can from Milwaukee). On *Dollhouse*, Echo is destined for the same journey: one of discovery and self-discovery outside the protective walls of her prison/home. Because Joss Whedon is the personality behind *Dollhouse*, Echo's odyssey proves an intriguing, thought-provoking ride. One can detect the seeds of greatness in the *Dollhouse* pilot, even if little of the potential is realized.

For example, the actives—when taking on the personalities of other people—also adopt their weaknesses. That's an interesting notion, a sort of hidden brand of "kryptonite" that could pop up and impact an "engagement" unexpectedly. Here, Caroline is gifted not just with a skill to negotiate, but with post-traumatic stress disorder from an event in her model's life when she was actually kidnapped as a child. Similarly, in taking on the characteristics of this real-life negotiator, Echo also sacrifices her perfect eyesight, and must wear glasses.

"Ghost" also introduces the distinctive moral overtones of this series: *Can a wrong ("wiping" and "imprinting") ever make a right (helping people in need*)? There's something affecting and deeply sad about watching Echo talk about meeting the "right guy" only to, moments later, undergo a wipe and forget all about him. How can the people around her stand by and let this happen? How can they justify what they do? Dig a little deeper, and more questions are raised. Was this *really* the right guy for Echo, or just the right guy for the personality with which she was imprinted? Would the real Caroline have given this guy the time of day?

Ultimately then, one must ask two important questions in regards to *Dollhouse*. First, does the pilot provide an adequate framework for Joss Whedon to present his trademark social commentary on women, society at large, and pop culture? And second, do fans want to watch Eliza Dushku make this journey of discovery for a few seasons? The answer in both cases is a resounding affirmative.

On the former front, "Ghost" suggests the ultimate subjugation of women in the culture. This is a world where they can be "rewritten" to be willing lovers for men who might not otherwise merit their attention or love. Here, money can literally buy a woman, body and soul. In real life, there may be reasons, financial or psychological, for a woman to be involved in a bad relationship. Here, the software uploads make the woman actually love the man who uses her. It's a quantum leap forward for slavery and patriarchy, and a huge step backward for women' rights. The epilogue of "Ghost" already points to a compelling feminist story point and direction for the series. There, we see a pre-Dollhouse Echo in a high school video, discussing her aspirations.

Were those aspirations fulfilled by involvement in the Dollhouse? Or cut off?

Even from the pilot episode, the audience knows the answer. The patriarchy enslaves Echo, forcing her to submit her body and mind to external corporate control, not for the purposes of her own agency, but for the purpose of the corporation itself.

One might be tempted to view the whole storyline as absurd, or far-fetched, but consider that, in 2019, some people in the U.S. government have had serious discussions about re-distributing women as sex objects to angry, socially awkward men called "incels" (meaning involuntary celibates). The idea underlining this is that men, even awful men, deserve access to women's bodies, and government should step in to make certain they have it. In many ways, this is the idea of *Dollhouse* brought to reality. What the women want is immaterial, and they have no agency. They are just commodities to be used and controlled by men.

4. "A Spy in the House of Love." Written by Andrew Chambliss, Maurissa Tancharoen, and Jed Whedon. Directed by David Solomon. Airdate: April 10, 2009

"A Spy in the House of Love," a strong first-season entry for *Dollhouse*, involves Topher's surprising discovery of a spy inside the Dollhouse, one who can tap into his high-tech imprints and alter them without his knowledge. The NSA is suspected to be behind the secret mole, and one fast-paced portion of the episode concerns an *Alias*-like infiltration of that national agency by a disguised Sierra. But actually, the episode is structured cleverly to follow the series' four primary actives as they go out on individual engagements. These dolls are Echo, Victor, November, and Sierra, and each mini-adventure adds to the narrative of the main story at the same time that it builds strong character touches.

In an act of self-preservation, Echo volunteers, for instance, to be imprinted as an expert interrogator, one who eventually brings down the spy. As mentioned above, Sierra goes on a dangerous assignment at the NSA. November, meanwhile, unwittingly carries information for the spy inside the Dollhouse to a bewildered Ballard (Penikett). Finally, Victor's semi-regular, "a lonely heart," turns out to be De Witt (Olivia Williams), the very woman running the entire show.

For the first time in the series, "A Spy in the House of Love" permits the audience to see the cracks in De Witt's shield: her loneliness, her isolation, and her moral qualms about the Dollhouse and its mission. *Everybody knows the truism that it's lonely at the top, right*? Well, De Witt has been living that truth for a long time, and secretly seeking companionship and solace with a doll. The important thing is that this aspect of her personality gives viewers another layer with which *to contemplate and sympathize*. De Witt is so consumed by her work that she doesn't have time to create a real relationship with another human being. Instead, she must program that relationship. Second, she is not above utilizing the technology that she hates to seek personal satisfaction. De Witt may have qualms about the Dollhouse and its technology, but she has already surrendered to it by making personal use of it.

The identity of the spy is revealed before the episode's denouement, and the revelation is quite the shocker. This "mole" character and Echo launch into a brilliantly orchestrated physical re-match (their first tussle was in "True Believer"); and the much-discussed "attic" came into play during the finale. Like Echo herself, *Dollhouse* proves itself as a truly evolving series with this particular stand-out episode. With Echo's dawning awareness, and the presence of several competing agendas and characters boasting hidden—and conflicting—loyalties, this Whedon series ascends to a commendably complex, and even addictive level of storytelling.

3. "The Attic." By Maurissa Tancharoen and Jed Whedon. Directed by John Cassaday. Airdate December 18, 2009

From its very inception, *Dollhouse* teased of a terrifying place known as "The Attic," a realm where bad dolls went to be punished . . . and were never seen again. This second-season episode makes that land of fear a real place, and in the process delivers one of its finest installments.

In "The Attic," Echo has been covered in what looks like plastic shrink-wrap and wheeled into the Attic, where she appears to flat-line. While she is examined, she breaks out of her restraints, kills two technicians, and searches for her friends, Victor and Eric, who have also been taken there. Every time she nearly makes a rescue and escape, however, she finds herself back in restraints, reliving the same events. Echo soon learns that those dolls relegated to the Attic are kept in a "fear-induced, adrenaline-fueled overdrive state," while their brains are experimented upon. In short, they have entered a nightmare world from which no one can return.

Soon, Echo begins to travel through different realms of this Matrix-like mind-world, including a wintry wonderland, where she encounters her young self. Sierra and Victor are trapped in their own nightmare worlds of rape and trauma-inducing war scenarios in the Middle East, respectively. Echo soon realizes that everyone who goes to the Attic is not only trapped in a nightmare, but being hunted by a madman called Arcane, who is trying to take out Rossum's mainframe computer. Echo teams up with her friends, as well as Laurence Dominic, who was sent to the attic in "A Spy in the House of Love." Basically, they must all work together, since their minds are linked, to escape from the Attic and forestall an apocalypse, an "end of civilization" brought on by the Dollhouse tech. This episode is about their efforts, but is also a prophecy of coming events as the series writes its final chapters.

A remarkable mind-trip, "The Attic" seems ahead of its time in many ways, which makes it a powerful entry in the series. In the 2016 *Black Mirror* episode "San Junipero," the series creators imagined a world where human minds are linked/stored in a computer to live a life of fantasy/ desires. The Attic here is the antithesis of that, the hell to San Junipero's heaven. Here, individual torments, such as Sierra's rape, are relived ad infinitum as characters become trapped in their own worst nightmares and memories. The episode portrays traumas arising not just from sexual abuse, but in wartime, and also in childhood. At the same time, it lays down bread crumbs about the apocalypse featured in the series' climactic episodes "Epitaph One," and "Epitaph Two: Return." Echo's fear embodied in this episode seems to be that she can't save anybody, neither Victor nor Sienna, nor even Paul, who, in the real world, is dealing with a fried brain, necessitating his *transformation* into a doll himself.

The nightmares featured in "The Attic," are diverse, and lensed in cold, desaturated, dehumanizing shades of blue in some instances and yet, despite the individual terrors, the characters are connected to one another through it all, a metaphor for our world. All humans must face their nightmares, but other people are there to help them confront these demons. The episode also revives the old *Nightmare on Elm Street* (1984) aesthetic that if you die in your dream (in the Attic), then you die in real life. Inventively, the answer to escaping this digital world of torment is just that: to die in real life, and be revived in consensus reality, once unhooked from the Attic.

"The Attic" also proves surprising because Arcane's worst nightmare is an apocalypse which actually comes about. And, as the audience learns, Arcane (really a man named Clyde battling the Rossum Corporation) is not the real monster. He was one of the founders of Rossum, but has since changed alliances and is attempting to discover the central hub where all realities are connected. Like Echo, he wants Rossum destroyed.

"The Attic" succeeds because it predicts, in some ways, one side of the future called "The Singularity," the idea that human existence will continue in cyberspace, or in computers. Death will be conquered, not by the soul, but a storage device that houses lingering consciousness. This idea makes sense given the series' premise: minds uploaded and wiped, and saved in cartridges. Bodies are not the only receptacles for identities, *Dollhouse* suggests. Life can also exist inside the computer.

The problem revealed by this idea is that technology doesn't create an immortality of any inherent worth, instead, creating a literal hell of an afterlife, a place of unrelenting and eternal torment for its denizens. Although there are resonances here of *The Matrix* trilogy, as well as Cronenberg's *Existenz* (1999), *Dollhouse* breaks into new territory with its story of a corrupt corporation's attempt to monopolize freedom and life, for its "own" board members. Everyone else on the planet is merely raw material for corrupt plutocrats to take over and exploit, a literalization of the idea that the 1 percent has taken over the wealth, leaving 99 percent without it. Although the series predates, at least a little, the Occupy Wall Street Movement of the Early 2010s, it was clearly picking up on the same vibe; the idea that "corporations are people." In *Dollhouse*, the rich have already absorbed most of the country's material wealth, but now they are taking over the bodies of the people as well. This is *Dollhouse*'s unexpected endgame, and one that proves incredibly timely given the social movements developing in its era.

2. "Epitaph One." Story by Joss Whedon. Written by Maurissa Tancharoen and Jed Whedon. Directed by: David Solomon. Airdate: August 11, 2009

The final—and perhaps best—two episodes of *Dollhouse* occur after a dramatic time-jump. "Epitaph One" and "Epitaph Two: Return" occur in a post-apocalyptic world in which the Dollhouse technology—the ability to wipe and upload new minds—has gone mobile, and spread across the globe like wildfire. In this world, satellites can wipe out identities on a huge scale, without requiring any hardware whatsoever, like the chair seen in Topher's lab in the L.A. Dollhouse. Now, people with impure motives can turn others into slaves, soldiers, cannon fodder—*anything*, and from vast distances. And people have no effective defense against this technology.

As the episode begins, Felicia Day (of *Dr. Horrible* fame) plays Mag, a new character. She is a survivor who flees pandemonium on the L.A. streets and ends up with a small band of survivors inside the Dollhouse establishment. These refugees learn of a rural sanctuary called "Safe Haven," and must deal with a mole in their midst. The episode juxtaposes this post-apocalyptic world with a storyline from the past. There, we learn more about Ballard and Echo, and even see Topher's first day at the *Dollhouse*. We learn that he has gone mad with guilt in this future, but is attempting to determine a defense against remote imprints.

Eliza Dushku, the series star, gets very limited screen time in this episode, and yet "Epitaph One" succeeds because it explores the ultimate destination of technology like the Dollhouse's. Society has collapsed into strange factions. People who are not imprinted are called *actuals*, and they tattoo their bodies with their names as a defense against being imprinted. This way, they will remember who they really are. There are also *tech heads*, people who fight while embracing the new technology, and *dumb shows*, those who don't seem to know who they are. Meanwhile, the board members of Rossum have achieved immortality, switching bodies via download and living without fear of death. When one body dies, its personality is simply downloaded into another.

The weakness of this episode is that it introduces many characters in the post-apocalyptic setting, and there is not much personal connection with them, though Day registers strongly. It is hard to muster interest for these fresh characters, when audiences would rather learn more about Echo, Victor, Sierra, and Adele. Some of the action in the (abandoned) Dollhouse in Los Angeles is also hard to follow, in addition to being impenetrable. But the merit of this episode is obvious: it sets up the parameters of the apocalypse. The audience learns what Dollhouse technology has caused, who caused it, and how the populace of 2019 must live to attempt to stay safe (and with memories and identities intact).

Thus, this episode is all about diagramming the nature of this particular post-apocalyptic world. The next episode—and the last of the series—"Epitaph Two: Return"—succeeds by revisiting the familiar characters, and revealing the final steps in their journey. Their final destinations would not be comprehensible without this penultimate show.

1. "Epitaph Two: Return." Written by Andrew Chambliss, Maura Tancharoen, and Jed Whedon. Directed by David Solomon. Airdate: January 29, 2010

This is the ending that loyal fans of *Dollhouse* surely wanted. In the post-apocalyptic world of 2019, viewers see the main protagonists of the two-season series fight to restore society to normal, and come to see the final chapters in their journeys.

For some characters, the end is not exactly happy. Topher, who has gone mad from guilt and shame at the creation of the Dollhouse technology, finds redemption. He believes he can "bring back the world" by using a "pulse bomb" to restore everyone's actual identity. He manages to do so, but must activate the pulse manually, and is killed when he activates the device.

More genuinely upsetting, perhaps, Paul Ballard, Echo's confidante, dies during a street fight, seemingly a casualty of random violence. The impact of this sudden murder is shocking, and devastates Echo. She has kept Paul at arm's length, thinking there would be time, after the battle, to have a real, romantic relationship with him. Instead, she is left alone, and the haunting last moments of the series find Echo uploading Paul's mind and identity into her own consciousness.

Now, she will never be without him.

This solution is the positive yin to the negative yang regarding Dollhouse technology. Yes, said technology can create slaves of people. It can provide immortality for the wealthy "have and have mores." But it can also provide a different kind of immortality. Now, when a loved one dies, a piece of them can remain behind, continuing to exist.

Victor and Sierra get an interesting final act too. They have separated into different factions. Victor is now a tech head, while Sierra eschews all technology. Together, however, they have a child, and they overcome their different viewpoints about Dollhouse technology to raise that child as a family. This seems a realistic, practical ending for the characters that balances the negative (the apocalypse) and the positive (the ability to connect with another's mind) of the technology. Eventually, the series suggests, all new technology becomes a source of compromise for families, as they look toward the future. People will have different opinions about it, but put down those opinions to do the things that humans have always done: fall in love, marry, and raise a family together.

Watching "Epitaph Two: Return," one may wonder if the writers moved, finally, beyond the audience's ability to keep up. At one point, Echo shares scenes with a little girl who is housing Caroline's personality. So Echo is part-Caroline, and the girl is part-Caroline. Yet the little girl does not look or sound like Caroline. The complex nature of this story about identity nearly requires note-cards so audiences can remember whose identity is housed where. One must constantly recall that the same character can be conversing with him/herself from a different body. It's bizarre, it's edgy, and it can be, frankly, confusing too.

Although "Epitaph Two: Return" loses Echo's story for a while, it ends on her final choice, to incorporate Paul's identity into her own personality. This is a meaningful gesture, and one all about individual agency. In the first episode of the series, viewers learn that Caroline had to give up her body and soul to Rossum Corporation. She gave up her right to choose in this endeavor, becoming (for a contracted time of five years) the person others wanted her to be.

But in "Epitaph Two: Return," the Dollhouse technology is still in play, and it is Echo, finally, who makes the choice about whom she "uploads" to her consciousness. She chooses for herself, and for her own reasons, to join with Paul, proving that it is not the technology of the series itself that it is evil, but the anti-freedom, anti-person, anti-choice agendas for which it has been used. This seems a very Whedonesque touch; the notation that people, not machines, are good or evil. The technology is dangerous only in that it is misused, and the last moments of the series prove how it can be used in a pro-human, agency-preserving situation.

In the end, "Epitaph One" and "Epitaph Two: Return" reveal that *Dollhouse* could have been an incredibly thoughtful, timely, and provocative series. The problem is, of course, that it didn't get the five years to grow, a piece at a time, toward the stunning finale seen here. And that fact mitigates the success of this last chapter. "Epitaph Two: Return" is largely satisfying and inventive, but every now and then it can feel to the viewer that he has skipped a chapter.

20

Agents of S.H.I.E.L.D. (2013–)

Cast

Clark Gregg: Phil Coulson
Ming-Na Wen: Melinda May
Brett Dalton: Grant Ward/Hive
Chloe Bennet: Daisy Johnson/Skye/Quake
Ian De Caestecker: Leo Fitz
Elizabeth Henstridge: Jemma Simmons

Crew

ABC Studios, Marvel Television, Mutant Enemy Productions
Casting: Sarah Finn, Hannah Cooper, Tamara Hunter
Music: Bear McCreary
Production Designer: Gregory S. Melton
Cinematographers: Felix Parnell, Allan Westbrooke, Jeffrey C. Mygatt
Executive Producers: Stan Lee, Jeph Loeb, Maurissa Tancharoen, Jed Whedon, Joss Whedon, Jeffrey Bell, Alan Fine, Joe Quesada, Brent Fletcher, Jim Chory

We're the line between the world and the much weirder world.

In the early 2010s, the MCU, or Marvel Cinematic Universe, had achieved pop-culture escape velocity. After its summer 2012 release, Joss Whedon's *The Avengers* became the number-three top-grossing film of all time (behind only *Avatar* [2009], and *Titanic* [1997]). And in the summer of 2013, *Iron Man 3* also proved a giant hit, even if purists complained about the screenplay's rewrite of the Mandarin character, changing the villain's nature from his Marvel's comics origin. As the MCU grew, the TV arm of the franchise was in development, and Joss Whedon was at the vanguard.

In particular, Whedon planned to bring Agent Phil Coulson back from the dead and perch him at the head of the organization known as S.H.I.E.L.D. (Strategic Homeland Intervention, Enforcement and Logistics Division) as well as the TV series *S.H.I.E.L.D.* ABC commissioned it, and Whedon associates from *Dollhouse*, Jed Whedon and Maurissa Tancharoen, became the show-runners while Joss Whedon planned for *Avengers 2: Age of Ultron* (2015). The new TV series would surround Clark Gregg's miraculously alive Coulson with a colorful and diverse cast of characters including Melinda May (Ming-Na Wen), an experienced pilot and soldier; the hacker (and later inhuman and Coulson's surrogate daughter), Daisy "Skye" Wilson (Chloe Bennet); plus a couple of scientists: engineer Leo Fitz (Ian De Caestecker) and biologist Jemma Simmons (Elizabeth Henstridge). A mole in the group, Grant Ward (Brett Dalton), was also part of the main ensemble cast.

With great fanfare and tremendous ratings, *Agents of S.H.I.E.L.D.* premiered in September of 2013. More than twelve million viewers watched the first series, making it the highest rated prime-time premiere since the debut of the rebooted *V* in 2009. The reviews were not positive, however, with some critics considering it a second-string series, one that would forever stand in the shadow of the MCU. Writing in *Slate*, critic Willa Paskin opined: "The shame is that a series about a band of heroes trying to hunt down more potential heroes could be the perfect antidote to TV's own overly dark cliché: the anti-hero. But instead, it resists the call, too self-serious to be really goofy, and yet too fan-boyish to rescue even one hour of television from mediocrity."

The *New York Times* also found problems with the premiere episode. Reviewer Mike Hale noted that "the first week's adventure feels perfunctory . . . even given the restraint of introducing characters and backstory, and most of the team members are strictly two-dimensional." The *New York Post*'s Dan Greenfield agreed, stating that the opener's script "is a mite too pleased with itself."

Others, like Tim Goodman at *The Hollywood Reporter*, noted that the pilot for *Agents of S.H.I.E.L.D.* is "one of those good-not-great propositions," an opinion shared by the *Washington Post*'s Hank Stuever, who wrote that the show could feel "exclusionary, and frankly, a little too cornball and cutesy about its own geekiness."

As of this writing, the series continues to run on ABC, and will remain at least six seasons before leaving the air. Each season features an arc (or mini-arcs, as in the case of some later seasons), and attempts to highlight distinctive and memorable connections with the MCU, and the Marvel universe in general. For instance, *Agents of S.H.I.E.L.D.* has managed, during its time, to work in shout-outs to Extremis, Ghost Rider, the Kree, Inhumans, and other key tech, personalities, and gadgets from its source material. However, on the other side of the equation, not a single Avenger has yet to appear in the series, and no character originated on the series (like Quake, for instance), has migrated to the big screen.

This lack of meaningful crossover with the big characters of *The Avengers* has often made *Agents of S.H.I.E.L.D.* feel separate from the franchise films. Another problem the series faces is that even while movie characters seem to studiously avoid appearances on the program, it must nonetheless work its way into the continuity of the films, a difficult proposition. The 2014 film *Captain America: The Winter Soldier*, for instance, revealed that Hydra had infiltrated and subverted S.H.I.E.L.D. The film ended, essentially, with the destruction of S.H.I.E.L.D., and so the TV series had to respond and deal with that plot development. Similarly, *Avengers: Infinity War* (2018) ended with half the universe's population being disintegrated, and the biggest question for fans involved the TV series. Would Thanos's finger-snapping destruction, using the Infinity

Gauntlet, extend to the ABC series' cast? The answer was negative, but again, there was the perception of a disconnect with the MCU proper, or the series having to work, at the very least, around the big-budget movie plan.

Joss Whedon has commented on the tension between the movies and TV arm of the Marvel world himself, noting that the TV show (*S.H.I.E.L.D.*) gets "leftovers," but that it can't really be any other way, given the budgets and profit expectations for the films.

And *expectations* is an important word to add to this discussion. *Agents of S.H.I.E.L.D.* premiered with huge expectations in the aftermath of *The Avengers*, as well as high ratings, but it was Netflix, not ABC, that has become the custodian of the MCU on TV. After the negative reviews and the sometimes convoluted storytelling of the first season, ratings dropped significantly, and each season the series ended up on the bubble, not even guaranteed a renewal.

Yet, ironically, the series grew more confident in its second season, so the quality of the program improved . . . just as ratings dropped. By the third season, fewer than three million were watching the series regularly, even as hard-core fan devotion increased, indicating clear approval of the creative changes.

Series star Chloe Bennet is apparently displeased with the lack of synergy between the MCU and the ABC series. In 2016, she had the following to say at the Wizard World convention in Des Moines, Iowa (and her words were reported in *Uproxx*): "People who make movies for Marvel, why don't you acknowledge what happens on our show?" Addressing the fans directly, she asked, "Why don't you guys go ask them that? Because they don't seem to care! . . . The Marvel Cinematic Universe loves to pretend that everything is connected, but then they don't acknowledge our show at all. So, I would love to [appear in a Marvel movie], but they don't seem too keen on that idea"

The actor has a valid point. All the Avengers needn't appear on *Agents of S.H.I.E.L.D.*, but not even one character has done so, in five years. What a boost to the fans, and the series, such an appearance would be! Even more damningly, it seems like a no-brainer, given S.H.I.E.L.D's presence in *Captain America: Civil War* (2016), to have one series character, whether Melinda, Skye, or someone else, flying a Quinn Jet, or appear in a cameo. The showrunners have done a great job of incorporating the plot-twists of the films into their story-arcs, but there seems to be an invisible wall, or embargo, against cross-populating TV and film casts. Even Coulson did not appear in an MCU film again until 2019's *Captain Marvel*, and then only in scenes set in the 1990's, preceding the character's death in *The Avengers*.

At its core, *Agents of S.H.I.E.L.D.* is about the same concept as all other series (or films) sponsored by Joss Whedon: an ad-hoc dysfunctional family coming together and triumphing over "Big Bads" who either

Left to right: Daisy (Chloe Bennet), Joss Whedon, and Agent Coulson (Clark Gregg).
John Muir Photo Archive

want to destroy the world, or the members of that family. In S.H.I.E.L.D., Coulson must grapple with the mystery of his own resurrection following his murder at Loki's hands in *The Avengers*. The answer to his resurrection lies with a secret initiative called T.A.H.I.T.I., and one that is only fully uncovered after a long story-arc.

Meanwhile, Melinda "The Cavalry" May comes from a tragic past involving her biological family, and her daughter, and as the series unfolds, she must grow back her humanity and connection to humanity, to an extent. As noted above, "Skye" becomes Coulson's surrogate daughter, finding herself, her powers, and her role in the scheme of things as seasons develop. Fitz and Simmons, meanwhile, share an adversarial, would-be romantic relationship that eventually comes to fruition. All these individuals are different, burdened by their pasts, their pathologies, and even their experiences. But they become whole, ironically, only within the S.H.I.E.L.D. family. This dynamic makes the series a reflection of the dynamic in *The Avengers*.

In terms of science fiction or superhero storytelling, *Agents of S.H.I.E.L.D.* does not break much new ground in the Whedonverse. Rather, it invokes many of the same story tropes seen throughout *Buffy the Vampire Slayer* and *Angel* in the 1990s and early 2000s. What makes the series different is that these old stories are brought to life in more fully serialized storytelling and under the Marvel umbrella, which means characters and concepts from comics (and the MCU) can appear regularly. But the series involves common genre concepts such as amnesia (in regards to Coulson's resurrection), a trope which goes back to *Adventure of Superman* in the 1950s and a 1953 episode "Panic in the Sky." The amnesia idea was revived in *Buffy the Vampire Slayer* ("Tabula Rosa") and brought into *S.H.I.E.L.D.* as a multi-episode-arc. Other tropes involve the notion of a villain trying to convince a hero that reality is a dream, and so forth. Although Whedon is not the showrunner for this series, his obsessions with certain types of stories and characters is apparent.

Agents of S.H.I.E.L.D. was widely expected to end after the 2018–2019 season, for an abbreviated span of thirteen, rather than twenty-one, installments, but as this book was being written, there was some discussion that the series would continue on ABC beyond that date termination date, and Season 7 is scheduled to air mid-2020. Some in the industry read the possibility of a revival as a result of the failure of another Marvel series, *The Inhumans*, and Marvel's determination to keep its TV arm running on network television.

Regardless, *Agents of S.H.I.E.L.D.* had already taken an intriguing journey through more than 100 episodes. It went from heir to an Empire and appointment television, to badly reviewed mishmash, to resurrected cult-favorite. With the possibility of a seventh season, *Agents of S.H.I.E.L.D.* may yet shapeshift to another fascinating iteration.

21

What Are the Five-Best Episodes of *Agents of S.H.I.E.L.D.?*

Although it may seem difficult to believe, *Agents of S.H.I.E.L.D.* will soon have been on the air nearly as long as *Buffy the Vampire Slayer*'s record seven seasons. In this considerable span, the Marvel series has demonstrated its versatility and storytelling chops, and grown from a mediocre "hype"-driven series to a genuinely addicting and high-quality genre program. Below is a list of stand-out episodes from seasons one through five of *Agents of S.H.I.E.L.D.* The sixth season had not yet aired when this book went to press.

#5. "Pilot." Written by Joss Whedon, Jed Whedon, and Maurissa Tancharoen. Airdate: September 23, 2013

"There are heroes among us, and monsters. It's a world of wonder."

With those prophetic words, *Agents of S.H.I.E.L.D.*, the TV arm of the MCU, opens its inaugural chapter. In this pilot episode, which drew a whopping twelve million viewers on its premiere, Agent Phil Coulson (Clark Gregg) is revealed to be alive, if not well. In fact, this tale establishes a mystery about precisely the way he survived Loki's attack in 2012's *The Avengers*. That mystery involves a top-secret operation called *T.A.H.I.T.I.* that proves a key aspect of the serial-storytelling through at least the third season, and has some repercussions through the fifth. Coulson, viewers learn, apparently believes he faked his own death to motivate the world's mightiest heroes to work together. The truth is somewhat more sinister and upsetting.

The series pilot also introduces a key character named Skye (Chloe Bennet), who is part of the hacker freedom group called "Rising Tide," and who becomes enmeshed in the business of S.H.I.E.L.D., the secretive organization which she describes as involving "scary men in dark suits." Skye grows into a popular character in the series, and is revealed to be a "gifted" person, or *inhuman*. In later episodes, Skye (whose character's real name is Daisy Johnson) is also the superhero Quake. This heroine made her first appearance under the auspices of Brian Michael Bendis and artist Gabriele Dell'Otto in *Secret War 2*, which was published in July of 2004.

In terms of settings, this episode follows the MCU timeline closely after *Iron Man 3* (2013), and thus involves the "Extremis" plotline from that film, at least tangentially. That concept of human bombs is carried on here, and the audience also learns of "Project Centipede," which involves an arm implant (that resembles a centipede) and utilizes gamma rays to enhance strength and power. A familiar face to the Whedonverse, *Angel*'s J. August Richard, shows up at the very start of the series as an "unregistered gifted" person who is attempting to keep his nature and gifts secret, though Skye tags him "The Hooded Hero," and the character recurs throughout the series. His character here has a pedigree in Marvel Comics too, as Deathlok, who first appeared in 1974, in *Astonishing Tales*, and is referred to as "Deathlok the Demolisher."

As one might expect, *Agent of S.H.I.E.L.D.*'s pilot arrives steeped in two Joss Whedon signature touches: allusions to associated canon, and the knowing or ironic humor about said canon. Here, there is Coulson's connection to *The Avengers*, the guest appearance of Agent Maria Hill, played by Cobie Smulders, and the aforementioned notation about Extremis. Similarly, Ron Glass, from *Firefly* and *Serenity*, makes an appearance as a physician tending to Coulson.

In terms of the latter element, the dialogue is knowingly smart about this superhero universe. "With great powers comes a ton of crap you are not prepared to deal with," notes one character, cleverly making a commentary on the famous "with great power comes great responsibility" construction from the Spider-Man mythos. Later, another character quips that something is "a disaster," and is met with the rejoinder, "No, it's an origin story." This reference alludes to the beginning of a journey as a superhero, but also the fact that this episode itself is something of an origin story, at least for the TV-iteration of S.H.I.E.L.D. Finally, it is fair to note that this pilot is obsessed with a familiar Whedon belief about storytelling, namely that a character who is resurrected from the dead must earn that resurrection, lest viewers no longer take death seriously, and nothing matters. Coulson does return from the grave in this pilot, but there is a cost to this resurrection that he must discover, and cope with, throughout the series' run.

While there are certainly more entertaining and affecting episodes of *Agents of S.H.I.E.L.D.*, the pilot's inclusion on this list is necessary, as this is the story that sets up everything, and begins to explore the way the characters will deal with one another. It's the jump-off point for everything that follows, and on those grounds provides dramatic, funny, and complex elements. The pieces all get set up here, so they can fall into place later.

#4. "Writing on the Wall." Written by Craig Titley. Directed by Vincent Misiano. Airdate: November 11, 2014

The "T.A.H.I.T.I." plotline is largely resolved in this second-season episode, and it couldn't come at a better time. In the continuity, Coulson has been slowly going mad, carving elaborate and indecipherable symbols on a wall with a knife. While Skye attempts to learn the meaning behind these symbols ("a map to nowhere"), Coulson's grip on sanity loosens.

At the same time Coulson seems to be going mad (and growing dangerous), a killer is at large, carving similar symbols into the bodies of victims. Is this Coulson's destiny, too: to become a murderous madman?

As S.H.I.E.L.D. investigates, Coulson learns of a project involving GH325, an alien compound that could bring agents back to life, and was initially designed "to revive a fallen Avenger." Unfortunately, the compound is "unstable" and has been triggering odd behavior in the agents brought back to life, those who have lost their memories and are living new lives. Coulson learns all this information by putting himself through a kind of torture machine that will probe his dormant memories.

In the end, the pieces for this long-simmering plotline come together, "beginning to take shape," and Coulson confronts the killer. After doing so, Coulson's compulsion regarding the alien symbols disappears, and the agents realize how to interpret the alien map he was incoherently inscribing.

"The Writing on the Wall" proves a satisfying resolution to Coulson's two-season "resurrection subplot," earning the character's revival, essentially, by making him suffer until the truth is revealed about what really happened to him after he died in *The Avengers*. At the end of the story, the Agents of S.H.I.E.L.D. learn that the map involves a blueprint of a strange city, and leads seamlessly into the next series subplot, or arc. The story succeeds because it takes Coulson's plight seriously, and reveals to what lengths the character is willing to go to learn the truth about his past. The episode is part gruesome serial-killer story and part "amnesia" story (a staple of the superhero format), but a satisfying end to a long-standing puzzle.

So many TV series (see: *Lost* [2004–2011]) are superb about setting up great and wonderful mysteries, and yet very few are able to resolve them in a way that doesn't leave fans disenchanted, or divided (see: *Battlestar Galactica* [2005–2008] "Daybreak"). "The Writing on the Wall" attends to all the loose plot threads involved in Coulson's character-arc, and moves the series forward at the same time.

#3. "Spacetime." Written by Jed Whedon and Maurissa Tancharoen. Directed by: Devin Tancharoen

In this third-season episode, Skye/Daisy begins to experience a prophetic vision of doom, and decides, with the help of Coulson and her colleagues, to "reverse-engineer" the vision to prevent it from occurring. In particular, she sees in her vision a confrontation involving her S.H.I.E.L.D. friends and also the death of a homeless man who is experiencing the visions. She is sure that she can save them all.

The brief synopsis above may not sound particularly promising, and yet "Spacetime" is one of the most involving and relentless episodes of *Agents of S.H.I.E.L.D.* as it deals with a near-constant in the Whedonverse, prophecies, and also contends with the so-called Cassandra Syndrome in relation to Skye's obsession.

What is the Cassandra Syndrome or Complex? Stated simply, once a prophet knows about the future, is it possible to convince others of that knowledge? Or does the prophet's knowledge actually make the future happen, perhaps because of his or her interference? In other words, the Cassandra Complex meditates on the notion of whether the future itself is fixed, despite any person's particular knowledge of it. "The Cassandra Complex" originates in Homeric legend. Cassandra, the daughter of Troy's King Priam, is a seer cursed by the god Apollo. She knows the future, yet is cursed never to be believed or her warnings heeded. Instead, she is cursed to see what will come, and know she is powerless to change it, no matter how much she protests or interferes. This idea is adjusted a bit for superhero-dom in *Agents of S.H.I.E.L.D.* Instead, the notion is that a gifted or super-heroic person may possess the most incredible and inhuman powers imaginable, but that doesn't mean that he or she is invincible, or can change their fate, the fate of their friends, or anyone for that matter.

An added level of responsibility comes into play because a character such as Skye believes she holds so much power and responsibility to wield, yet she is actually powerless before the forces of fate. She lives to help others, to do right, and yet the prophecy is paralyzing. How is one to deal with knowledge of future events? Throughout one climactic scene in the episode, the action occurs under a billboard on which is emblazoned the legend: "Moving You Ahead." This legend seems to suggest the manner in which human beings travel through linear time: always moving ahead; always moving into the future. But what if humans were to know the destination ahead of the trip? Would they change that trip?

"Spacetime" is not the first instance in the Whedonverse of characters attempting to navigate the puzzle of a prophecy. In *Buffy the Vampire*

Ming-Na Wen as Melinda May, taking out an assailant in *Agents of S.H.I.E.L.D.*
John Muir Photo Archive

Slayer, for example, Buffy is often gifted with prophecies of doom and gloom. In one early episode, "Prophecy Girl," Giles learns from an ancient tome that Buffy is to die in her battle with the Master, and therefore all her friends attempt to circumvent the prophecy. But Buffy's (temporary) death actually proves a necessary precursor to the Big Bad's defeat, and therefore a crucial stop on the road to the future. In this case, knowing the future doesn't help and can actively do harm. The Shansu prophecy does much the same thing to Angel, and makes the brooding vampire (and would-be-champion) all the more diffident.

The upshot seems to be the notion that knowing the future is not an answer to a problem, but merely another problem. Prophecies appear to be shortcuts, but more often than not are psychological and intellectual traps, ones that make people second-guess their choices. In "Spacetime," burdened by her sense of responsibility, Skye's prophecy involves, very much, the same dynamic. Even though the idea has been vetted before on television, in time-loop-type episodes of *The X-Files* ("Monday") or *Star Trek: The Next Generation* ("Cause and Effect"), the prophecy, or "doomed future" aspect of "Spacetime," renders it highly compelling.

#2. "4,722 Hours." Written by Craig Titley. Directed by: Jesse Bochco. Airdate: October 27, 2015

A visually dazzling stand-alone episode of *Agents of S.H.I.E.L.D.*, "4,722 Hours" plays more like a full-fledged, big-budget motion picture than a serialized tale in a twenty-hour visual novel. In this remarkable story, S.H.I.E.L.D. scientist Jemma (Elizabeth Henstridge) gets pulled into another reality through a dimensional portal. She goes through a gateway and ends up in a barren world where two moons hang in the sky. Although the gravity is close to that of Earth, the day/night cycle is off, and Jemma endures something like seventy hours without sunlight.

By hour eighty-seven, she is talking to herself.

Matters go from bad to worse as a sandstorm roils the surface, and Jemma must find food and water in order to survive. She must grapple with a tentacled monster in a pond to get the sustenance she needs. And frighteningly, there seems to be some monster hiding in the storms.

While her friends in S.H.I.E.L.D. back on Earth try desperately to save Jemma from her isolation on a distant alien world, the stranded woman realizes that she is not alone. Will Daniels, an astronaut from a mission some years back, is stranded there too, and after some initial distrust, they develop a friendship, and more. Will reveals to her that this planet doesn't have rules, "it has moods." But they are stronger together than apart, and some of the planet begins to seem less maddening when the challenges are shared. But when the portal to home opens again during a storm, only one of the stranded individuals can go home.

The ultimate *Robinson Crusoe* story, "4,722 Hours" offers a terrific creative conceit, with hours being marked by Jemma's long time of being marooned on an alien planet. At 752 hours, she falls into a cave and is held in a cage by the possibly mad Will. At 855 hours, she is working on a map to get to the portal by the time it re-opens. At 3,010 hours, Will and Jemma make their move to the no-fly zone to reach the portal, and on and on. These periodic reminders of elapsed time put the characters' relationship, and plight, into perspective.

Similarly, the lack of opening theme and standard introduction make this episode seem like a unique piece, and somehow more consequential than the typical "arc" episode of the series. As the story unfolds, viewers learn that Will has been stranded since 2001, and the time on year on Earth is now 2014. He has been stuck in this monstrous, chaotic terrain for something like half his life. And even though he finds Jemma, and by 4,720 hours they are together (sharing a bottle of wine that has turned to vinegar), they are not home, and he knows it. Or as the episode's dialogue notes: "This isn't our home. This is hell."

Jemma's relationship with Will, forged in this nightmarish place, and via the battle for survival in such chaotic terrain, throws up a solid soap-opera impediment to her developing romantic relationship with Fitz. Far away, on another planet, he is working to save her, but to survive each day, Jemma and Will are the ones who grow close. So there is an underlying purpose here, beyond toughening up the Jemma character. This episode, with its monsters and de-saturated night sky, threatens the order of the Jemma/Fitz relationship, and calls it into question.

Visually, "4,722 Hours" is gorgeous, and unlike any other episode of *Agents of S.H.I.E.L.D.* Also, there is no team dynamic at work here, and instead, one individual, Jemma, takes center stage. Every TV series ever made features an established format, some kind of formula that repeats every week. In a way, that is a good quality, as audiences know what to expect when they tune in. On the other hand, familiarity breeds contempt, and an episode such as "4,722 Hours" testifies to the elasticity of this series format or approach to storytelling. *Agents of S.H.I.E.L.D.* can still step outside expectations to deliver a stunning surprise like this remarkable one-of-a-kind installment.

#1. "The Real Deal." Written by Jed Whedon, Jeffrey Bell, and Maurissa Tancharoen.
Airdate: March 9, 2018

The series' 100th episode aired in 2018, and may just be the best install-ment yet produced. The episode, "The Real Deal," involves a frequently seen Whedon trope—a monster that can physically manifest fear—yet at the same time is a crowd-pleasing story that explores Coulson's journey throughout the first five seasons, and also caps the romantic relationship between Fitz and Jemma.

In "The Real Deal," another dimension begins bleeding into our con-sensus reality. Fitz realizes it is a "Fear Dimension" that bring everyone's deepest phobias to life and "manifests them physically." He employs a device to stop the Fear Dimension from continuing to spread, but it must be deployed manually. Coulson, who is physically dying anyway, volun-teers to be the one to do the deadly job, but the revelation of his condition spawns anger from his team, especially Skye. No one wants to lose him, and everyone is disturbed to learn that he is dying.

When he attempts to close the spreading Fear Rift, however, Coulson is faced with an apparition who tells him that his entire life since Loki mortally wounded him (in *The Avengers*) is but a delusion. Right now, this manifestation of fear tells Coulson he is dying on an operating table after being lanced by Loki's scepter. Coulson tries not to waver in his grip on reality, but his fears grow stronger, until his team comes through for him. After the Rift is sealed, Coulson officiates at the wedding of Fitz and Jemma, and the ceremony is attended by a very special visitor.

"The Real Deal" is a perfect representation of its era. Although vil-lains have, before in the Whedonverse, attempted to convince heroes that their lives are a dream (see: *Buffy the Vampire Slayer*, "Normal Again") or manifested fear (*Buffy*, "Fear Itself"), this story carries an extra psychic weight because of its emotional character interaction, and because of the references to earlier seasons, and even the original *Avengers* film. In particular, Coulson delivers a remarkable speech in this episode in which he notes: "People need things to believe in, especially now," and even "Institutions are important." These remarks seem very much on-point in the Trump era, when institutions are being led by people who want to destroy government departments, or are derided or under attack by the president and his Twitter account. Many Americans feel a sense of loss about the direction the country has taken, and about the fall of pillars. Since Trump's election in November 2016, many upset people have opined that it feels as though we are all living in an alternate dimension, and one of "fear" at that. "The Real Deal" posits a similar type of invasion, as a dark dimension bleeds into our own, and threatens the very fabric of reality.

The episode also features affecting dialogue about the value of S.H.I.E.L.D. itself. It is noted that the organization is an "idea, a symbol that must continue, no matter what." Those are Coulson's words to Skye/ Daisy, and they are absolutely valid. An organization has to be bigger than one person. Again, consider the Trump era, when a sitting president has attacked the Justice Department, the F.B.I., the Intelligence Community, and other institutions. These are symbols of law and order that must continue if America is to be free, and outlast the current occupant in the White House. It's as though, in "The Real Deal," Coulson speaks not only of his reality, but ours as well.

The episode also expertly provides an alternative viewpoint. S.H.I.E.L.D. is "more than a team," and Coulson is the face of that idea. He is part and parcel of that symbol, and even though he may die, his group is not ready to lose him yet. He may not trust them completely, and they may feel resentful that he did not tell them the truth about his condition, but they all come together to beat back the Fear Dimension.

Agents of S.H.I.E.L.D., having endured for five season of this writing, has featured highs and lows, and suffered from the belief that it is the less-important arm of the MCU, but episodes such as its 100th, "The Real Deal," make a point of reminding viewers of the great journey the series' characters have taken, and will continue to take. In this episode, Coulson notes at one point that his "threshold for preposterous is way out of whack," again, likely a sideways critique of the Trump era, but the same cannot be said of the series. Five seasons in, and frequently airing episodes such as "The Real Deal," this Marvel series remains grounded in good storytelling, and excellent characterizations.

Part IV

The Superhero Whisperer

22

The Avengers (2012)

Cast

Robert Downey Jr.:	Tony Stark/Iron Man
Chris Evans:	Steve Rogers/Captain America
Scarlett Johansson:	Natasha Romanoff/Black Widow
Chris Hemsworth:	Thor, God of Thunder
Mark Ruffalo:	Dr. Bruce Banner/The Hulk
Jeremy Renner:	Clint Barton/Hawkeye
Tom Hiddleston:	Loki, God of Mischief
Clark Gregg:	Agent Phil Coulson
Cobie Smulders:	Agent Maria Hill
Stellan Skarsgard:	Selvig
Samuel L. Jackson:	Nick Fury
Gwyneth Paltrow:	Pepper Potts
Paul Bettany:	Voice of Jarvis
Alexis Denisof:	The Other

Crew

Marvel Studios and Paramount Pictures present *The Avengers*

Casting:	Sara Finn, Randi Hiller
Costume Designer:	Alexandra Byrne
Production Designer:	James Chinlund
Music:	Alan Silvestri
Director of Photography:	Seamus McGarvey
Film Editors:	Jeffrey Ford, Lissa Lassek

Producer:	Kevin Feige
Executive Producers:	Victoria Alonso, Louis D'Esposito, Jon Favreau, Alan Fine, Jeremy Latcham, Stan Lee, Patricia Whitcher
Story by:	Zak Penn, Joss Whedon
Written by:	Joss Whedon
Directed by:	Joss Whedon
M.P.A.A.	Rating: PG-13
Running time:	143 minutes

We're sort of like a team.

In Joss Whedon's *The Avengers*, agents for S.H.I.E.L.D. under the direction of Nick Fury (Jackson), toil in secret on an alien device called the Tesseract, which had been recovered from Red Skull decades earlier by Captain America. Loki, God of Mischief (Hiddleston) and brother of Thor, however, appears and steals the device, brainwashing Clint Barton/Hawkweye (Renner) and a scientist, Selvig (Skarsgard) in the process.

Nick Fury realizes that the Tesseract is so powerful an energy source that the Earth could be in serious jeopardy. Accordingly, and over the objections of his superiors, he assembles a team of unique individuals to battle the threat. These individuals include the ingenious inventor/millionaire Tony Stark/Iron Man (Robert Downey Jr.); the bored but true-hearted Captain America (Chris Evans); brilliant scientist and green rage monster Bruce Banner (Mark Ruffalo); and undercover agent extraordinaire, Natasha Romanoff/Black Widow (Scarlett Johansson). The team gathers on S.H.I.E.L.D.'s flying heli-carrier and, almost immediately, serious frissons develop among this unusual and diverse team.

After Loki is captured by Iron Man and Captain America, his brother Thor (Hemsworth) also appears on Earth, and after a battle in which Loki is captured, returns to join the Avengers with the others. Unfortunately, it has been Loki's plan all along to be captured. He manages to escape and disable the heli-carrier, killing Agent Coulson (Clark Gregg) in the

Iron Man (Downey Jr.) and Cap (Evans) attempt to apprehend Loki, not pictured, in *The Avengers* (2012).   *John Muir Photo Archive*

process. He then sets loose the Hulk, an act which divides and distracts the Avengers.

With his enemies in shambles, Loki brings an army of alien soldiers, the Chitauri, through a space portal in order to attack Manhattan. Now the Avengers must come together as a team, and repel Loki's alien invasion.

You may not be a threat, but you'd better stop pretending to be a hero.

Earth's mightiest heroes come together on the big screen for the first time in the 2012 film that catapulted its writer/director Joss Whedon to the superhero and Hollywood director "A" lists, and ultimately came to gross more than $1.5 billion. Indeed, *The Avengers* remains, to this day, ensconced on the list of highest-grossing films of all time. As of this writing, it is number three on this list, behind two James Cameron films.

But before *The Avengers* was produced, there had never been a superhero film like it, one where multiple heroes, hailing from different comicbooks, appeared together. Certainly, on TV, Lou Ferrigno's Incredible Hulk had appeared alongside Daredevil and Thor in a series of late-1980s TV movies, but never before had something like *The Avengers* been attempted on such a colossal scale, and with such resources behind it, namely more than $200 million.

The plan to create a team superhero film came at the end of Marvel's so-called "Phase One." The films so far in the MCU canon were: *Iron Man* (2008), *The Incredible Hulk* (2008), *Iron Man 2* (2010), *Thor* (2011), and *Captain America: The First Avenger* (2011). The team-up would be the icing on the cake, or the punctuation to the shared universe's first stage of development.

Joss Whedon came to the *Avengers* franchise when a script by Zak Penn was already in place. Whedon quickly discarded the majority of this draft and undertook a rewrite himself, or actually a series of rewrites as there was a duration when it appeared that Scarlett Johansson would be out as Black Widow, and the Wasp (a hero later introduced in *Ant Man and the Wasp* [2018], played by Evangeline Lilly), would be a member of the team. Eventually, Black Widow returned to the fold, and Whedon penned his screenplay about a diverse, quarrelsome group of individuals forced to work together. Whedon noted at a Comic-Con panel in 2010 (as reported by Ryan Dowray of *MTV News*): "[T]hese people shouldn't be in the same room, let alone on the same team . . . and that is the definition of family."

Shooting on the film began in the spring of 2011, and principal photography occurred in New Mexico, Pennsylvania, and Manhattan. After extensive post-production special effects work, the film was ready for its May 2012 premiere. It immediately won accolades, as well as earning a fortune at the box office. For the first time in his career Whedon had written and directed a project that was both loved by cult-fans and critics, and a major winner in terms of commerce. He was also left exhausted by the lengthy conception and preparation.

Critic Amy Biancolli, writing for the *San Francisco Chronicle*, stated that the film includes "moments of genuine pathos, genuine humor, genuine surprise. As much as the film adheres to the strictures of the standard comic-book movie, it also pops with a knowing, loving, Whedon-world jokiness that keeps everything barreling along." Kevin Phipps, of *The A.V. Club*, went even further in his praise, noting that "Whedon checks off all the boxes, then sets about creating new expectations for what a big screen superhero movie ought to be."

Arizona Republic's Billy Goodykoontz singled out the film's director by opining that the "real hero here is Joss Whedon, who directs the film with a fanboy's enthusiasm and a thorough knowledge of the genre."

The Avengers was—and remains—widely heralded as Whedon's masterpiece, and the film that opened the floodgates for efforts such as *Batman vs. Superman: Dawn of Justice* (2015), and *Justice League* (2017). There were, however, some longtime Whedon fans and critics who felt like there was less of the creator's personality apparent in the film than any other of his celebrated works of art; a concession, they felt, to the necessity of building a tentpole film and franchise in the MCU. The *Globe and Mail*'s Rick Groen lamented the film's "sterile opulence, or if you prefer, a magnificent emptiness." A. O. Scott, of the *New York Times*, similarly detected what he felt was a "grinding, hectic emptiness, the bloated cynicism that is less a shortcoming of this particular film than a feature of the genre."

Those who felt disappointment with the amount (or, specifically, the lack) of "Whedon-ness" in *The Avengers* have a valid point, but should also remember that a TV series offers multiple hours to depict characters, over many years. A film, by the medium's very nature, is a different beast. A film must address plot, theme, and character in a mostly complete fashion in no longer than two-and-a-half hours, generally. The *Buffy* or *Firefly* fans who wanted more Whedon in *The Avengers* can't be blamed for hoping to reconnect more fully with their favorite creator's worldview, and yet, by the same token, it is an expectation that largely cannot be met.

Given the limitations of a feature film, it is not impossible to register how Whedon adapted his long-standing creative aesthetic to this blockbuster. *The Avengers* contends very much with a quarrelsome "found" family, but a family nonetheless. Each of the film's main characters grapples with some personal issue or crisis, but manages to overcome it by working in the team. Samuel L. Jackson is Nick Fury, the "Bad Father," figure that the other heroes must learn to reject, to succeed as a team. Although Fury is not in any sense a villain, the "Bad Father" archetype is one familiar from Whedon efforts such as *Buffy the Vampire Slayer*. There, Giles loved Buffy dearly, but also made some poor decisions as part of the Watcher's Council. Eventually, he even left Buffy to return to England, when she was at her weakest and most vulnerable, in season six. Here, Fury's main flaw seems to be his ambition, his desire to create weapons from the Tesseract. The revelation of his plan renders him less than trustworthy to the Avengers.

The "created" family in the *Avengers* is quite quarrelsome indeed. Cap and Iron Man never see eye to eye, nor do Banner and Stark. The conflicts between these and other characters play out in verbal fireworks, but also in stunning action sequences. Fans have always wondered who might win in a fight: Thor or Captain America? Thor or Iron Man? And for the first

Nick Fury (Samuel L. Jackson) takes matters into his own hands, or weaponry, in the climax of *The Avengers*.   *John Muir Photo Archive*

time on film, that kind of contest is mounted, and engaged, resulting in what can only be termed fan-gasms.

What makes the film special, and feel like Whedon's work, is the way the writer focuses in, laser-like, on the characters' flaws. Iron Man, for instance, constantly battles against the idea that he is in the hero game only for his self-glorification. Captain America constantly needles him, telling him, "You're not the guy to make a sacrifice play" and that "sometimes there isn't a way out." He even tells him he isn't really a hero, and that he should stop playing at being one. These comments ring in Tony's ear until he must make his own choice, in the film's epic battle over Manhattan, precisely what kind of hero he wishes to be. Ironically, Tony

Leader of the Avengers: Iron Man.   *John Muir Photo Archive*

Tony Stark (Robert Downey Jr) sans armor.   *John Muir Photo Archive*

is the one who must make the sacrifice play, taking a nuclear missile out of New York, and carrying it through a portal to the Chitauri, in space. If the portal closes while he is away from Earth, he dies. If the bomb detonates when he is nearby, he dies. If the Chitauri fleet engages him, he dies. But Tony makes the "sacrifice" call, and proves his worth in the end. Captain America's needling, one might argue, allowed Tony to see a part of himself he had not seen before, or recognize that he is, actually, the hero Captain America seems to believe he is not.

Similarly, Captain America grapples in *The Avengers* with his feelings that he is old and useless in the new, high-tech world of the 21st century. A product of the early twentieth century, he is not certain what he can bring to the table in the modern era. The woman he loved is old, time having passed her by. The world he loved when he was a boy, of friendship and innocence, is also long gone. The great cause of his life, defending America from the Nazis, is also past. His war, for all intents and purposes, is over.

But there is a path forward for Captain America. Agent Coulson tells him, in no uncertain terms, "Everything that is happening . . . people might just need a little old-fashioned" heroism. There is comfort and familiarity in being old-fashioned. And "old fashioned" doesn't have to mean "obsolete." In the final battle in Manhattan, Captain America realizes that his ability to lead others, learned in a simpler time, and in a different war, is still a skill of value in this new technological age. As the

Steve Rogers (Chris Evans), or Captain America, shirtless, in *Captain America: First Avenger* (2011).   *John Muir Photo Archive*

Chitauri attack, Captain America uses time-tested knowledge of tactics and strategies to rally his fellow Avengers and organize the police.

The other team members in this created family also have personal crises to overcome, though they are not diagrammed as carefully and confidently as those of Stark or Rogers. Thor knows he must defeat Loki, and yet Loki remains his brother, despite all his villainy. Thor knows the right thing to do, but an Asgardian Hamlet, in some sense, is not always ready to act accordingly. Loki, an Asgardian and a brother, is a weak spot for him, and he knows it.

The Hulk, meanwhile, continues to grapple with his rage, revealing in a rousing, crowd-pleasing sequence, that his act of heroism is not his form of control, but rather his letting go of his control; surrendering to the monster inside. His secret is that he is always angry. Loki thought that freeing the Hulk would be the thing to tear the Avengers apart. Instead, freeing the Hulk is what makes the team unstoppable in the face of daunting odds.

All these welcome character touches result in a superhero film of considerable depth. An important quality to understand about Whedon's script and direction is that he doesn't view depth, necessarily, as meaning angst, or brooding. This is where his geek credentials are so vitally important to his approach to art. Whedon understands that comic-book–inspired stories can be serious, but fun, and don't have to revel in "darkest night" to be taken seriously. He paints on a canvas other than black. Directors not so fully steeped in the comics try so hard to impose gritty reality, or change uniform colors from the comic, or dwell in darkness to bring what they believe is verisimilitude to superheroes. It's all largely unnecessary, and it is impossible to deny that The Avengers helps bring superheroes out of the "Dark Age," where everything is utterly realistic, but doom-laden as well. Nolan's Batman trilogy pops to mind in this regard. The superheroes of Whedon's Avengers face crises, setbacks, defeats, and challenges, and yet the film retains a jaunty, upbeat atmosphere throughout.

Indeed, it is largely the failure of the sequel, 2015's Age of Ultron, to re-conjure the joie de vivre and high spirits of The Avengers that prevents, perhaps, more people from enjoying it. Something about the DNA of The Avengers just feels right, as Whedon marshals humor, pathos, and thrills in just the right quantities and combination to present a thinking-man's blockbuster. The film is nearly three hours in duration, and yet does not feel ponderous, and somehow manages, contrarily, to seem upbeat and bright. Even the film's lengthy climactic battle over Manhattan moves quickly and adeptly, and doesn't grow repetitive from all the smashing and fighting.

Again, this is not something that can be said of the lookalike sequence at the end of *Man of Steel* (2013), which ultimately succumbs to a feeling of sensory numbness as city blocks are decimated, before viewers' eyes . . . for long spells. Here, the fight in the city is not about the destruction, but about teamwork, and the heroics of each team member.

Intriguingly, the precise story structure is one that has been aped often since the film's release. In the narrative, Loki arranges for his own capture so he can psychologically separate and devastate his opponents. He lets himself be taken because his plan (to set free the Hulk)

Earth's mightiest heroes (and one villain), out of uniform. Left to right: Jeremy Renner, Chris Hemsworth, Scarlett Johansson, Robert Downey Jr., Chris Ruffalo, and Tom Hiddleston.

requires him to be detained in the hero's key facility. This idea of a villain facilitating his or her capture so as to execute a sinister plan is one that has since appeared in films as diverse as *Skyfall* (2012), wherein James Bond captures Silva and holds him in a cell at M16, and with Benedict Cumberbatch's Khan Noonien Singh in *Star Trek: Into Darkness* (2013), aboard the U.S.S. *Enterprise*. It is nearly a foregone conclusion now in blockbusters that a villain's capture is all "part of the plan." While it's no doubt true that there are older examples of this trope, such as Hannibal Lecter's escape from custody in *The Silence of the Lambs* (1991), *The Avengers* seems to have brought the plot device back to the forefront of Hollywood's imagination.

Also, *The Avengers* is the film that really pulled together the MCU in a powerful way. The big-screen teaming of the many heroes, uniquely, brought about renewed attention to the characters' individual movies and film projects, and lent a new excitement to them. Joe Johnston's *Captain America: The First Avenger* (2011) proved one of the lower-grossing films of Phase One, and lacks the razzle-dazzle and humor of something like the first *Iron Man*. After Captain America's turn with the team in *The Avengers*, his follow-up sequels, *Captain America: Winter Soldier* (2014) and *Captain America: Civil War* (2016), were undisputed box-office goliaths.

Similarly, *The Avengers* unified the MCU in a powerful way, beginning with this film the long and impressive journey to the saga's biggest story yet: *Infinity War* (2018). But many mainstream audiences probably cared less about the details, and more about the fact that in 2012 Joss Whedon had assembled the greatest team of cinematic superheroes ever, and did so with large dollops of humor and heart.

23

The Avengers: Age of Ultron (2015)

Cast

Robert Downey Jr.:	Tony Stark/Iron Man
Chris Evans:	Steve Rogers/Captain America
Scarlett Johansson:	Natasha Romanoff/Black Widow
Chris Hemsworth:	Thor
Mark Ruffalo:	Dr. Bruce Banner/The Hulk
Jeremy Renner:	Clint Barton/Hawkeye
Cobie Smulders:	Agent Maria Hill
Stellan Skarsgard:	Selvig
Samuel L. Jackson:	Nick Fury
Paul Bettany:	Jarvis/Vision
James Spader:	Ultron
Don Cheadle:	James Rhodes/War Machine
Aaron Taylor-Johnson:	Pietro Maximoff/Quicksilver
Elizabeth Olsen:	Wanda Maximoff/Scarlett Witch
Anthony Mackie:	Sam Wilson/Falcon
Idris Elba:	Heimdall
Hayley Atwell:	Peggy Carter
Linda Cardellini:	Laura Barton
Thomas Kretschmann:	Strucker
Andy Serkis:	Ulysses Klaue
Julie Delpy:	Madame B

Crew

Marvel Studios and Walt Disney Pictures

Casting:	Sara Finn, Reg Poerscout-Edgerton
Costume Designer:	Alexandra Byrne
Production Designer:	Charles Wood
Music:	Danny Elfman, Brian Taylor
Director of Photography:	Ben Davis
Film Editors:	Jeffrey Ford, Lissa Lassek
Producer:	Kevin Feige
Executive Producers:	Victoria Alonso, Louis D'Esposito, Jon Favreau, Alan Fine, Jeremy Latcham, Stan Lee, Patricia Whitcher
Written by:	Joss Whedon
Directed by:	Joss Whedon
M.P.A.A. Rating:	PG-13
Running time:	141 minutes

I suppose we're both disappointments.

The Avengers—Iron Man (Robert Downey Jr.), Captain America (Chris Evans), Thor (Chris Hemsworth), Black Widow (Scarlett Johansson), The Hulk (Mark Ruffalo), and Hawkeye (Jeremy Renner)—launch a daring and violent raid on the European HQ of Hydra's Baron Von Strucker (Thomas Kretchsmann) in Sokovia, a poor country on "the way to everywhere." The battle is won by the heroes, but there are some new and dangerous players in the game: Inhumans Wanda Maximoff, or Scarlet Witch (Elizabeth Olsen), and her brother, Pietro, or Quicksilver (Aaron Taylor-Johnson). Pietro's power is remarkable speed and agility, while Scarlet Witch possesses fearsome psychic and telekinetic abilities.

After the battle, Stark and Banner work on Stark's plan for world peace, which for the playboy millionaire involves wrapping a "suit of armor around the world." Specifically, they use the alien AI they discover in Loki's scepter, and couple it with Stark's friendly AI, Jarvis (Paul Bettany).

In the process, the scientists develop a being called Ultron (James Spader). Alas, the newborn Ultron sees world peace only as a possibility with the destruction of the Avengers, and the extinction of the human race.

While Scarlet Witch imposes terrifying and possibly prophetic visions on each of the Avengers, showing them each what they fear most, Ultron goes about upgrading his physical form, while distracting the Avengers with the Hulk, who runs amok in a modern city. Ultron then launches his most devastating attack yet, in Sokovia. The Avengers must save the entire country, which has been ripped from the ground, and lifted high into the atmosphere. If this huge chunk of land crashes to Earth, it could destroy all life on the planet. Joining the Avengers in the final battle is the physical form of Jarvis, who survived Ultron's creation, and is now known as Vision (Paul Bettany).

I wanted to take this time to explain my evil plan.

With the global, smashing success of 2012's *The Avengers*, a sequel was not only in the offing, but the subject of incredibly high expectations from moviegoers and critics alike. Joss Whedon was back at the helm for the film, but, if anything, the resulting sequel only proved how difficult it is to create a film like this, juggling a large cast, action set-pieces, and still featuring that ineffable, difficult-to-conjure feeling of "heart." *The Avengers* seems to have come together almost effortlessly in that regard. The filmmakers, including Whedon, made it look easy, when surely the opposite was true. *Age of Ultron* feels, in honor of its villain perhaps, far more mechanical.

Ultron himself is a well-established character in Marvel Comics' canon, having first appeared in an issue of *The Avengers* in 1968. In that reality, Ultron was built by Hank Pym, Ant-Man, and based on the hero's brain-wave patterns. In the film of 2015, he is the Frankenstein Monster–like child of Tony Stark, primarily, since at this juncture Ant Man had not been introduced to the MCU. In the comics, Ultron went on to menace the Avengers many times, and the Fantastic Four, as well. For his screen debut, Ultron's plan for world domination had a budget of $250 million, and the film opened in nearly 4,500 theaters nationwide.

There is only one path to peace: your extinction.

The reviews for the new Whedon superhero team film on its release in the spring of 2015 were, perhaps not surprisingly, mixed. The *San Francisco Chronicle*'s Mick LaSalle wrote in his review that the film is "supercharged and lifeless, frenetic and stone-cold dead, a barrage of action scenes that look fake, yet make you wonder if fake is the new real." *New York Magazine*'s critic David Edelstein noted that the film is a "mess by all conventional narrative standards," yet a "fascinating case study in the rules of 'universe' storytelling. Chief among them is that a film must not be self-contained."

The *Boston Globe*'s Ty Burr took aim at the film's villain. "Ultron's goals never make much sense beyond the basic-kill-the-Avengers-and-destroy-the-Earth checklist," he wrote, "nor does he develop as a character over the long haul. He's just a static baddie, fun to look at and handy with a quip, but ultimately as dull as unpolished chrome."

Critics may not have liked the film, but *The Avengers: Age of Ultron* nonetheless made over $1.4 billion at the box office, counting both domestic and foreign receipts, and that was good news for its director, and Marvel Studios. The bad news, perhaps, is that this second entry in the franchise remains also the lowest grossing of the three *Avengers* films made thus far. Worse, *Jurassic World* (2015) opened the same summer as *Age of Ultron*. It cost $100 million less to produce, and grossed $1.6 billion worldwide. Earth's mightiest heroes had come in second to a pack of dinosaurs at a theme park.

No matter who wins or who loses, trouble always come around.

Age of Ultron most assuredly does not recapture the high-flying spirit or easy charm of its predecessor. Watching it is, largely, a chore, and long stretches feel dull, or overly dark, without apparent value. Although the film features common Whedon obsessions such as dark dreams or prophecies that threaten to rip apart "created" families, there seems to be no sense of joy in the film, except in a few noteworthy moments.

Scarlet Witch (Elizabeth Olsen): Villain-turned-Avenger in *Age of Ultron* (2015).
John Muir Photo Archive

One such moment of pure, giddy fun occurs in the scene during which the Avengers party together after the successful Sokovia raid, and attempt to prove they are each worthy by lifting Thor's hammer. No one can do it, with the possible exception of Captain America. This character-based scene is funny and captures beautifully the group dynamic of the world's mightiest superheroes. The moment provides depth for the characters, specifically, by playing on Thor's insecurity when he sees Cap move the hammer, and Iron Man's dependence on technology when he uses one of his metal hands to attempt to lift the hammer.

This fun moment is undercut, appropriately, by the birth of Ultron, who opines that *none* of the heroes are worthy. "How could you be worthy? You're all killers," he declares, turning team-building into team-destruction. Moments such as these are sharp and effective, and sell the story effectively.

Alas, moments like that are few and far between in this mostly lugubrious 2015 sequel. More to the point, one feels that its central conceit—that the Avengers are all "monsters"—does not work quite as intended. The underlying leitmotif of the sequel seems to be that *everyone* is a monster, but that monsters need love too. The word "monster" is repeated so often that the conceit feels a little over-stretched, or even preachy. "We're mad scientists, we're monsters, we've got to own it," Stark notes at one point. Later, Vision notes "Perhaps I am a monster." And in the lead-up to the film's final battle over Sokovia, the inspirational speech from Tony goes: "Ultron thinks we're monsters . . . it's about whether he's right."

Controversially, Black Widow also refers to herself as a monster, in the film's most divisive scene. The monster references go deep and far in the film, from Black Widow and the Hulk playing a variation of *Beauty and the Beast* together, to Tony Stark playing Dr. Victor Frankenstein to his monstrous child, Ultron. The idea is good, but the reliance on the "monster" leitmotif is not always well thought out. One would be hard pressed to figure out how the true-hearted Captain America is a monster, or sees himself as a monster, even if he was made from a bottle, as Stark likes to remind him. "What kind of monster would let a German scientist experiment on them in order to protect their country?" Tony shoots back.

Black Widow's admission that she considers herself a monster is, as noted above, controversial with audiences and critics. Basically, her admission arrives in a scene in which she reveals to Banner that as a trained Russian assassin, she was sterilized, and therefore rendered incapable of bearing children. Some audiences criticized the scene, and felt that it was stating that an inability to bear children makes a woman a monster, thereby generalizing Black Widow's admission to all people of the female persuasion. However, the remark is absolutely less offensive than this reading suggests. Black Widow's description of herself as a monster comes at the end of a long monologue in which she explains how she is basically a killing machine, born, bred, and trained to do one thing: murder. That is the thing that makes her, in her own words, monstrous. She's talking about the upbringing that robbed her of her ability to be more than a killer. But at the end of that dialogue is the discussion of her sterility, and so some people have made the mistake of reading into only one part of the monologue.

Lest anyone accuse the author of being an apologist, the fact of the matter is that it seems abundantly plain that Black Widow's remarks

Does she look like a monster to you? Black Widow (Scarlett Johannson), in action, from *Iron Man 2* (2010).   *John Muir Photo Archive*

take into account her whole story, her whole "journey," and do not refer specifically to motherhood as a qualifying factor for human-ness. Still, it is fair to note that Joss Whedon may have made the perception of sexism worse by comments he made on Twitter in spring of 2015. As noted above, *Avengers: Age of Ultron*'s big competition for the summer of 2015 was the Colin Treverrow movie *Jurassic World*. After a trailer dropped for the dino-sequel, Whedon went to Twitter and reported that he found it "seventies sexist."

Specifically, Whedon noted of the Claire/Owen dynamic: "She's a stiff, he's a life-force—really? Still?" The comment was construed by many readers as hypocritical, given what they saw as the sexist nature of Black Widow's admission that she is a monster, presumably because of her inability to bear children. Worse, the comment actually seems petty, as though Whedon was just looking to take a swipe at the film that would prove to be his sequel's biggest competitor. It caused quite the bruhaha, and since most of the criticism of Whedon came from those who already shared his point of view on politics and feminism, it was also a harbinger for the public-relations nightmare he would find himself in during the summer of 2017. Call it an unforced error.

Avengers: Age of Ultron is also marked as a Whedon film by its inclusion of a familiar trope: the prophetic vision. Scarlet Witch possesses the capability in the film to "warp" the minds of the superheroes, and uses that skill again and again to plant seeds of doubt about the future (as seen in Infinity War), but also splinter the team just as it needs cohesion. Thor's vision concerns the destruction of Asgard, an image that becomes reality in *Thor: Ragnarok* (2017), while Tony Stark's vision shows him surviving a battle, while all the other Avengers die. The latter vision works on two levels. First, it makes him question his decision to lead the team, and indeed, Stark eventually leaves it rather than do so. And secondly, it sets up the horrors of *Infinity War*'s finale (and the revealed horrors of 2019's *Endgame*) in which heroes are killed. Black Widow's vision concerns her upbringing, a facet of the character which may be featured in the upcoming stand-alone. But again, as described elsewhere in this text, avoiding (or making true) a prophecy is a key Whedon plot-point.

Why else does *Age of Ultron* feel stale and a bit overlong? There are some discernible reasons. *Ultron*'s plot to divide the Avengers is fine, but it depends on the release of the Hulk, and that, coincidentally, is also Loki's plot in *The Avengers*. So, for two movies in a row, the villains view Hulk as the team's weak point, and single him out. Set him free, and the Avengers are divided!

Second, Sokovia is sort of, well, Suckovia. Sorry for the alliteration, but it's true. Whedon doesn't manage to generate much empathy for the denizens of this country (which is well established in the comics), and yet much screen time is spent on one family being threatened by Ultron's plan. It's probably not a nice thing to write, but in a film featuring Captain America, Thor, The Hulk, Vision, Iron Man, Scarlet Witch, Nick Fury, Hawkeye, Ultron, Scarlet Witch, and Quicksilver, it seems a pity to spend so much screen time on a kind of basic nuclear family in which the audience has no prior investment. It's clear why the family is present in the drama, so that the stakes feel not just colossal and impersonal, but close by and intimate, human. The idea is that the audience should empathize with these characters in the middle of a war zone because they represent us, the every-family. Sadly, the family just comes off as more people in need of rescuing, and feels more like a cliché or off-the-shelf types than legitimate characters. For once in a Joss Whedon work, a conceit simply does not seem valid. And yet, there it is again, the same types of characters—an imperiled every-family—in *Justice League* (2017).

There just doesn't seem to be a lot of or passion evident in this film, onscreen, by the director. Even the "hero shots" seem derivative. In *The Avengers*, there is a great shot staged by Whedon in which all the primary heroes land in Manhattan, in close proximity, and the camera circles them in one triumphant shot. It's the beauty shot of the team, and its composition and execution are gorgeous. There are two attempts to generate a similar moment in *Age of Ultron*. In the opening raid on Hydra, the heroes all "break the line" of the enemy at the same time, and we see each Marvel hero, together in the same shot, in profile. It is composed well, but seems like a throwaway, positioned as it is in the midst of the film's first, kinetic action scene. Then, in the climax, there's a scene of the heroes standing again in close proximity, back-to-back, fighting off an army of Ultron clones. It too fails to deliver the kind of psychic frisson or vibration of the hero shot in *The Avengers*. Both shots more look like an attempt to recapture an old glory, rather than diagram a new, glorious path for these wonderful heroes.

Ultimately, *The Avengers: Age of Ultron* is a disappointment. It boasts a few spiky moments, but mostly feels lifeless, like Joss Whedon was simply too exhausted to bring Earth's mightiest heroes to life a second time. Making a movie like this takes a toll on its creators, and an aura of fatigue just hangs over this sequel, the least-satisfying Avengers movie thus far.

24

Justice League (2017)

Cast

Ben Affleck:	Bruce Wayne/Batman
Henry Cavill:	Clark Kent/Superman
Gal Gadot:	Diana Prince/Wonder Woman
Jason Mamoa:	Arthur Curry/Aquaman
Ezra Miller:	Barry Allen/The Flash
Ray Fisher:	Victor Stone/Cyborg
Amy Adams:	Lois Lane
Ciarin Hinds:	Steppenwolf
Diane Lane:	Martha Kent
Jeremy Irons:	Alfred
Amber Heard:	Mera
J. K. Simmonds:	Commissioner Gordon

Crew

Entertainment, Cruel and Unusual Films, DC Comics, DC Entertainment, RatPac-Dune Entertainment LLC, Lensbern Productions and Warner Bros. Present a Zack Snyder Film

Costume Designer:	Michael Wilkenson
Music:	Danny Elfman
Written by: .	Chris Terrio and Joss Whedon

Produced by:	Charles Roven, Deborah Snyder, Jon Berg, Geoff Johns
Directed by:	Zack Snyder
M.P.A.A. Rating:	PG-13
Running time:	120 Minutes

This world will fall like all the others.

Although DC Comics, Julius Schwartz, and Gardner Fox introduced the Justice League of America way back in the year 1960, this superhero team has taken a long and circuitous route to live-action production. In 1973, for instance, ABC-TV brought the Justice League to television in an animated format with the child-friendly *The Super Friends*, a veritable mainstay of 1970s and 1980s Saturday morning TV programming. Produced by Hanna-Barbera, the series focused on popular heroes Superman, Batman, Robin, Wonder Woman, and Aquaman. Lesser-known heroes were not commonly featured, though Green Lantern and The Flash were added to the stable over the years. Instead of featuring Martian Manhunter or Black Canary, the series created kid-friendly heroes like Wendy and Marvin, the Wonder Twins, and even a Wonder Dog. D.C. fans were not impressed, at least for the most part.

The greatest indignity for this superhero team, however, arrived in 1979 with an NBC live-action series that ran for just two episodes ("The Challenge" and "The Roast,") and which was titled *Legend of the Superheroes*. Woefully under-budgeted, and written with a cloying, condescending brand of humor, this series is an insult to the characters it features, and a significant reminder of the bad old days of the 1970s when comic-book characters were sometimes treated as jokes instead of respect-worthy individuals from a consistent and fascinating universe.

In "The Challenge," the Legion of Doom convenes. After the Riddler (Frank Gorshin) calls roll, Dr. Sivana (Howard Morris) introduces to the membership to his "doomsday machine," a bomb that will detonate in one hour and destroy the world's population. Meanwhile, at the Hall of Heroes, Batman (Adam West), Robin (Burt Ward), and the other members of the Justice League (including the Flash, Green Lantern, Hawkman,

Captain Marvel, the Huntress, and Black Canary) catch wind of Sivana's plan while honoring Retired Man (William Schallert), an aging superhero. The League leaps into action to find the bomb. They search for it at a gas station, at a used-car lot, and in a park. Unfortunately, after drinking poisoned lemonade made by the Legion of Doom, the heroes lose their powers. Now they must find the bomb (at Hidden Island Lake) without benefit of their remarkable abilities.

Right down to its final chase on jet-skis, *Legends of the Superheroes*: "The Challenge" resembles nothing so much as a stage attraction designed to be performed at Sea World. There are only two main studio sets here—the Legion of the Doom and the Hall of Heroes—and they are filmed in a totally underwhelming fashion. Basically, the scenes set at these locations are filmed as if this production is a stage play, with a camera perched well back from the action, filming everything under the proscenium arch in long shot, and then featuring cut-ins of mid-range shots (probably gleaned in a second take). The script is pretty bad and unfunny anyway, but by filming in such long-shots so often, the humor quotient is reduced considerably. This is a TV show that's about as funny as a heart attack.

The episode's exterior sets are not much to write home about, either. They are (in order of appearance): a gas station, a used-car lot, a park, and a lake with a pier. Yes, all the greatest superheroes and superhero villains in the DC universe have gathered at these mundane settings, but never actually really fight in any of them. Instead, they run around, interrupt picnics, and frequent lemonade stands. The final battle happens back at the Legion of Doom HQ, on the stage setting. Thus the production values of this series—politely speaking—stink. The special visual effects are similarly weak, dependent entirely on old-fashioned chroma-key tricks. Those could still pass muster in the seventies on Saturday morning programs, but this series was meant for prime-time. And the teleplay? Well, if this gives you any idea, it begins with a toast to a hero called, jokingly, Retired Man, features a line about the 1978 Warren Beatty movie *Heaven Can Wait*, and culminates with the superheroes losing their powers because they all stopped—one by one, apparently—at the same suspicious lemonade stand and got a drink there.

Of course, for Batman and Robin this shouldn't be a problem, since they don't possess any powers. to begin with. The element that transmits most powerfully, really, is the total, rampant disrespect for the DC comic characters and their universe.

The original *Batman* TV series was campy, it's true, but the production values were good enough to qualify it for fame as some brand of sixties "pop art." This 1970s show, shot on cheap videotape, looks as though it were made by producers taking a vacation in and around their resort home. Every detail of the show is miserable. This result is all the sadder because *Legend of the Superheroes: "The Challenge"* is one of the few opportunities that fans have had to see such DC characters as Solomon Grundy, Giganta, Sinestro, The Huntress, Hawkman, and Black Canary in live action.

The episode titled "The Roast" was likely even worse. As the title suggests, the episode is structured as a "Friar's Roast" type event. It's a roast of the superheroes in their underground headquarters as they are "honored" by arch villains. Ed McMahon is the host of the proceedings. How could DC Comics—or Hanna-Barbera, for that matter—ever have agreed to treat the Justice League so shabbily? The variety-style program is not just embarrassingly bad, like *The Star Wars Holiday Special* of 1978, but actually racist, sexist, and ageist in execution. Let's go to Ghetto Man first, to explore the racist angle. He is an African-American man in a costume that screams "pimp," who is a walking stereotype of seventies "black" jokes. His shtick is terrible ("Hawkman in Harlem" would be "Kentucky Fried" chicken, he says), even if somewhere in "Ghetto Man's" presentation is the (correct) idea that minority characters were largely under-represented in the superhero Valhalla. Unfortunately, the valid point is lost in the racially charged and largely offensive monologue.

Scarlet Cyclone, another subject roasted onstage, proves that this series doesn't like old people, either. The senior citizen hero falls asleep in the middle of a story, can't remember his next line, and is the butt of a lot of bad jokes. The jokes here, following those of "Ghetto Man," make "The Roast" seem awfully mean-spirited.

This quality is also seen with Aunt Minerva an old, diminutive women who wants to bed the terrified Captain Marvel. When the sex-obsessed old maid transforms and becomes a lovely young woman, however, Captain Marvel changes his tune. If that sounds a bit kinky and adult, consider the sequence here in which a Barbara Walters–like reporter—named Rhoda Rooter—jokes about Atom and Giganta's sex life. He's tiny, and she's huge. It's all skin-crawlingly inappropriate, and a total coarsening and cheapening of characters who have been beloved for generations.

The twenty-first century saw a return to animation for the Justice League, and perhaps its best, most faithful iteration yet with an animated series that ran for two years on the Cartoon Network. Again, however, assembling a live-action version of the team proved difficult. At the time of Christopher Nolan's success with the re-booted cinematic *Batman* saga, circa 2007, *Mad Max* director George Miller was hired to direct a JLA film from a script by Kieran and Michelle Mulroney. Jessica Biel was named Wonder Woman at one point, and Adrien Brody was reported to have been cast as The Flash. By 2008, neither actor was officially contracted for either role. Then, a writer's strike scuttled the project.

This left the WB series *Smallville* (2001–2011) to assemble the Justice League, for an episode titled "Justice," and featuring Superman, Aquaman, the Green Arrow, Cyborg, and the Flash.

But DC fans still sought an honest-to-goodness Justice League movie, and not long after the 2012 success of Whedon's *Avengers*, plans were made for a DCEU (DC Cinematic Extended Universe) that would not only feature stand-alone superhero films, but a JLA team film as well. The universe premiered with *Man of Steel* (2013), a dark and disturbing retelling of Superman's origin story. Then, the series moved to a "versus" type spectacle, *Batman vs. Superman: Dawn of Justice* (2016). Both films were directed by Zack Snyder, a highly visual artist who had given the world films including the remake of *Dawn of the Dead* (2004), and *300* (2007), based on the Frank Miller graphic novel. The biggest DCEU hit, however, came in the summer of 2017: Patty Jenkins's *Wonder Woman*.

The pump seemed set for a cinematic universe that would rival Marvel's, and in its own unique, if controversial, fashion. To wit, *Man of Steel* and *Dawn of Justice* seem darker in tone than other superhero films, eschewing the camaraderie and esprit-de-corps of the MCU. It was a valid choice to differentiate the DCEU, and Snyder seemed like the very talent who could pull it off, in large part because he is known as a dazzling visual artist. If Joss Whedon's strength is character and dialogue, Zack Snyder's strength is composition.

Justice League was announced for late 2017, and would feature Ben Affleck's Batman, Henry Cavill's Superman, and Gal Gadot's Wonder Woman teaming with Jason Momoa's Aquaman (who had cameoed in *Dawn of Justice*), and two new heroes: Ezra Miller's The Flash, and Ray Fisher's Cyborg.

Justice League cost roughly $300 million to make, and was shot between April and October 2016. Reshoots were ordered after Warner Bros. apparently didn't like the film, and Joss Whedon was brought in to

Gal Gadot, off-screen, stars in *Justice League* (2017) as Wonder Woman.
John Muir Photo Archive

punch up the script. When Snyder suffered a personal tragedy, Whedon also stepped in to direct the reshoots, from his rewritten script. Ultimately, only Snyder got director's credit for the film, but Whedon was credited as one of the screenwriters. As many periodicals made note, a writer only gets credit when 33 percent of the script is his or hers. So while producers said publicly that Whedon's two months of reshoots (in L.A. and London) only accounted for 15–20 percent of the script, his writing credit suggested as much as a third of the film was "his," not Snyder's.

Jason Mamoa's Aquaman is reluctant to join the JLA in *Justice League*.
John Muir Photo Archive

And so begins one of the greatest controversies in superhero film history. Upon the film's release in November of 2017, critics began to openly speculate about ownership of the film, pointing to tonal inconsistencies to suggest a mishmash of Snyder and Whedon's unique and individual visions. The film was both praised and criticized for being too light. Those who felt it was too light, and didn't like it, saw *Justice League* as Whedon's attempt to make the JLA more *Avengers*-like. Those who liked the tone saw it as an improvement from the gloom-'n'-doom of earlier DCEU films (excluding *Wonder Woman*).

"This is a generic, uninspired and mind-bogglingly boring comic-book movie that's out to steal your money and time," wrote Calvin Wilson for the *St. Louis Post-Dispatch*. Meanwhile, Ignatiy Vishnevetsky, of *The A.V. Club*, stated that "the "new and improved" model" for the DCEU "looks claustrophobically like an overpriced TV pilot, and not in a good way. Say what you want about the tenets of brooding, art-school-fascist superhero worship, but at least it's an ethos."

The bad news kept coming, with the *Guardian*'s Peter Bradshaw dismissing *Justice League* as "ponderous and cumbersome," and the *Chicago Tribune*'s Kate Walsh's description as "breathtakingly bad."

As ownership of the film and discussions of the film's low quality were written about ad nauseum, *Justice League* went on to become a box-office failure, emerging as the lowest-grossing of the DCEU stable. After opening in over four thousand theaters nationwide, the film only grossed $229 million domestically. It earned roughly double that in the international marketplace. However, the film's total gross, approximately $650 million, left it just about a billion dollars short of the mark set by *The Avengers*. Many DC fans blamed Whedon for fundamentally altering Snyder's darker vision, and went to petition sites such as Change.org to demand that the "butchery" be undone through a Snyder cut of the film. One such petition got more than eighty thousand signatures. The feeling on the part of many was that Whedon's glib dialogue and banter was a poor match for Snyder's existing footage.

It was a situation that benefitted neither Whedon nor Snyder. Both talents were criticized for the film, and their work questioned relentlessly by fans and the press. While making *Justice League*, Whedon was attached to *Batgirl*, another superhero film in the DCEU, but shortly after its release he stepped away from the project, and many fans suggested he had actually been fired. The film itself seemed lost with all the inside-baseball commentary, and the real casualty was the property, the Justice League of America, which did not, for many, live up to the promise of its cast or budget.

People said the age of heroes would never come again.

Justice League tells the story of a storm gathering. A demonic/alien villain called Steppenwolf (Ciarán Hinds) sets out on a mission to collect three powerful relics known as "Mother Boxes," with the help of his flying minions, the Parademons.

One of these boxes has been hidden at Themyscira, the island kingdom of the Amazons, and home to Wonder Woman (Gal Gadot). Another has been held and guarded in Atlantis, the home of Arthur Curry (Jason Mamoa), the Aquaman. And another was gifted to the kingdom of Man, who hid it. If brought together, these Mother Boxes can bring about a state of "Unity," which will turn the Earth into a primordial hellscape.

Gotham City's hero, Batman (Ben Affleck), realizes the danger Steppenwolf poses, and knows that in the absence of Superman (who has died), the very planet is threatened. He joins forces with Wonder Woman, and recruits Aquaman to his cause.

Even this is not enough. So Wayne sets out to recruit young Barry Allen (Ezra Miller), the Flash, while Wonder Woman attempts to bring Cyborg (Ray Fisher), a half-man/half-machine, into the fold. This diverse team does not see eye-to-eye, but Batman believes that the Mother Boxes can be used to revive Superman, and give the planet Earth a fighting chance in the upcoming war with Steppenwolf.

As planned, Superman (Henry Cavill) returns to the land of the living, but is not himself. His unstable condition grants Steppenwolf the time he needs to join the Mother Boxes, and begin the ascent of Unity . . . in Russia. Now the Justice League must put a stop to him, or lose the planet.

I think something is definitely bleeding.

First things first: It is very difficult to watch *Justice League* and not think of the MCU. That just seems a fact. Wealthy Bruce Wayne with his incredible gadgets is a fine Tony Stark/Iron Man replacement, while the noble and true Superman seems to be of Captain America's true-blood ilk. Wonder Woman and Aquaman both fulfill elements of Thor's noble and otherworldly nature, while the over-enthusiastic and young Flash seems very much like the Spider-Man audiences encountered in *Captain America: Civil War*. The team dynamics feel very, very familiar. This isn't a fair assessment, admittedly, since many DC heroes predate the existence, even, of the Marvel heroes. But the feeling that the hero interaction in this film is derivative of the Avengers' interaction is difficult to shake.

The Infinity Stones, the *raison d'etre* of the first decade of the MCU have been replaced here by the Mother Boxes, and the Chitauri by the Parademons, who "eat" fear. But again, there are just so many similarities. Steppenwolf is a poor-man's Thanos, gathering the boxes, instead of the stones, and set on assembling them so he can fundamentally rearrange the nature of existence.

Finally, the climax of both *Age of Ultron* and *Justice League* focus on Eastern European families caught in the superhero crossfire. Call it the Sokovia Syndrome. The moments with the imperiled family in *Age of Ultron* were among the film's most unsuccessful, so it is baffling why the whole subplot gets lifted to another Eastern European country for *Justice League*.

Perhaps the greatest criticism against the film, then, is simply that *Justice League* doesn't seem to thrive on its own energy, but rather seeks to absorb the energy of the MCU. The lighter tone suggests the same mission, an attempt to rewrite a "darker" universe into the role of a jauntier, happier one. But those Marvel shoes simply don't fit on DC feet.

The derivative nature of the film established, there are some wonderful contextual touches in *Justice League* that bear examination. At one point, Jeremy Irons's Alfred notes sadly, "I don't recognize the world," and this line seems very apt following the election of Donald Trump to the presidency in 2016. Again and again, dialogue in the film acknowledges the fact that the world has fundamentally changed for the worse.

Likewise, a police detective tells Commissioner Gordon, for example, that "the world's gone crazy" and so, perhaps, has Batman as well. These sentiments have been made on *Agents of S.H.I.E.L.D.* as well, so they seem to be something that superhero productions are grappling with, post-Obama's presidency.

However, all is not gloom and doom, as *Justice League* points out. This film is also about how good people can respond to galvanizing threats, like one that lives on daily attacks and lies, or separates children from their parents in the name of security. "Darkness" the film reveals "is the conviction that the light will never return." And "hope" is knowing there are heroes in the dark, working together, for all our betterment. Thus the movie becomes a voice for resistance and optimism in a country that has fallen beneath the shadow of injustice, tyranny, and cruelty. "Men," Bruce Wayne tells the audience, act like "the Doomsday Clock has a snooze button." That line is a reminder for people to resist oppression now, rather than believing it can be done at a later date, or by someone else.

Taken together, all these dialogue cues suggest the post–2016 era, and a world in which hope seems lost. But instead of saying, "Down with the modern world" (as one terrorist does), the film suggests that there is still time to stop enemies, and the way to do it is by working together. The film itself is an argument for diversity as a millionaire, a woman, a sea dweller, a teenager, and a cyborg put their differences aside to strike back against an enemy who would rob the world of its diversity in favor of a false "unity." It isn't hard to read that unity as any American bugaboo of the moment, whether nationalism, white supremacy, the alt-right, or any of the other horrors loosed in the Trump era.

So *Justice League*, for all its problems, offers a coherent message, one that is appropriate for our historical context. That fact may not make the film good, but it certainly makes it more than a mere knockoff of a certain superior superhero universe. If it falls apart in any area it is in the fact that so much of the team is unknown to audiences at this point.

By the time *The Avengers* was made, audiences had seen Iron Man in two films, met Black Widow (in 2010's *Iron Man 2*), Thor, Captain America, and Hulk in their own features. Here, audiences know Superman, Batman, and Wonder Woman, but Aquaman remains largely a mystery. The Flash and Cyborg are introduced in this team film, and perhaps that is why they seem undeveloped to a certain extent. Audiences don't know how they will react to other characters, and when their reactions prove reminiscent of MCU characters, there is a strong sense that the film is a rip-off. Clearly, given the *Justice League*'s long life, that is not the case, and it is a shame the film suffers from this perception.

Justice League comments on the world in which we dwell with meaning and purpose, and yet its plot-points and characters feel disingenuous. How did that happen? Who is to blame? Zack Snyder? Joss Whedon? These are questions not easily answered, but the result is that, once again, the *Justice League* failed to achieve the success the property deserved. Readers know that this book has stressed in many chapters the found families of Joss Whedon, and the JLA is one such family. Is it right to compare any one family to another?

Justice League, for all its ups and downs, possesses some moments of glory. It is also blessedly short compared to some of the longer superhero team films. What it lacks in depth, the film makes up for in brevity. And despite the schizophrenic nature of *Justice League*, it still possesses more bounce than can be found in the long-winded and sullen *Age of Ultron*.

25

Is Joss Whedon Going to Write and Direct *Batgirl*?

The DC character Batgirl has had a long and somewhat confusing history in comics. This female crime-fighter was introduced in 1961 as a love-interest for Robin. Her name was Betty Kane. Then, in 1967, Julius Schwartz re-created the character as Barbara Gordon, daughter of Gotham City's Commissioner Gordon. This is the version most mainstream superhero fans remember best, and who formed the basis for Yvonne Craig's high-kicking TV heroine in the 1960s. Craig's Batgirl was introduced to boost the ratings of ABC's lagging *Batman* (1966–1968) series during its third and final season.

Following the resolution of the Crisis on Infinite Earths, Batgirl was re-booted yet again in DC comics as Gordon's niece/adopted daughter. And then, in 2011, DC rebooted its titles again as part of the "New 52" branding initiative, and yet another new version of Batgirl was featured. This thumbnail history of the character does not even focus on the instances that other individuals—Cassandra Cain, Stephanie Brown or Helen Bertinelli—adopted the cowl of Batgirl in comic books.

In the spring of 2017, Joss Whedon's involvement with the Batgirl property for the DCEU (DC Extended Universe) became public. At the premiere of *Guardians of the Galaxy 2* (2017), on April 20, the writer-director discussed the property. Apparently, Batgirl had not been part of Warner Bros. plans for the cinematic universe, but then joined the line-up when Whedon expressed his enthusiasm for the character to studio higher-ups.

The plan, according to these reports, was to feature a young Barbara Gordon as the Batgirl du jour, and to dramatize her story, in particular. What Whedon found fascinating about the character was clear, as he reported: "She came up and I started getting obsessed with how a young woman could get hard-nosed enough to need to put on the cowl," Whedon told *The Hollywood Reporter.* "Like, what's her damage?"

In this case, many fans can speculate about that damage.

One of the most famous comic tales involving Batgirl is *Batman: The Killing Joke* (1988), written by Alan Moore, which sees the Joker shoot Barbara Gordon, leaving her paralyzed. In some versions of *The Killing Joke*'s aftermath, Barbara remains paralyzed, but operates from a wheelchair as another superhero, Oracle, as seen in the short-lived WB series, *Birds of Prey* (2002). Dina Meyer played Barbara Gordon/Oracle for eight episodes in that series. In this case, Batgirl teams up with Huntress (Ashley Scott) and Black Canary (Rache Skarsten). The final episode of that series, "Lady Shiva (aired November 27, 2002), saw the paralyzed Gordon donning her Batgirl suit for the one-and-only time during the series.

Recent comics have altered the post-trauma story of Batgirl a bit, making her paralysis a temporary, three-year condition. Certainly, the idea of a female crime-fighter working her way back to fighting shape, overcoming physical adversity, plays into the character's "damage."

The news of Whedon helming *Batgirl* preceded his involvement in *Justice League* (2017) reshoots and came as a shock to many fans and insiders because of the director's previous involvement with Marvel's cinematic universe, directing both *The Avengers* (2012) and *The Avengers 2: Age of Ultron* (2015). But according to Kevin Feige, at Marvel, Whedon contacted him to let him know of his plans for Batgirl. Feige told *The Hollywood Reporter*'s Mia Galuppo that everyone at Marvel wanted "to see a Joss Whedon Batgirl film be awesome."

Following the release of *Justice League*, and its lackluster performance at the U.S. box office, rumors flew fast and furious on the internet that Warner Bros. had frozen Batgirl's development, and that, additionally, Joss Whedon would no longer be involved with the property. *Entertainment Weekly*'s James Hiberd reported, on November 22, 2017, that these rumors were unfounded and that Whedon was still hard at work writing a script, and preparing the film for eventual release.

A bigger question, perhaps, remained in the arena of casting. Who would put on the cowl of Batgirl for Whedon? He had expressed, back in April of 2017, a preference for someone who was not a household name.

Allison Keene, of *Collider*, reported that he said, "You need somebody who is just right," but that's as much information as was available.

By February 2018, the winds were turning another way for this latest Joss Whedon movie project. On February 22, 2018, it was announced that he had indeed departed from the film, and that, according to Chaim Gartenberg at *Verge*, it was because it took him months to realize he didn't have a story. The decision for Whedon to leave the project was termed mutual, and on February 28, the *AV Club*'s Sam Barsanti reported that the film was on hold, lacking both a director and story.

The departure of Whedon from the *Batgirl* project rattled Whedon fans around the globe. After the failure of *Justice League*, *Batgirl* looked like it could be the talent's triumphant return both to superhero storytelling, and to stories with a feminist bent. Much speculation occurred in the genre press that Whedon was let go from the project in the wake of the #MeToo movement after details about his marriage were published by his wife, Kai Cole, and it was feared that such bad publicity would follow the film. She had claimed that he used his marriage to her, both during and after the union, to deflect commentary about his feminism, or lack thereof.

Other writers pointed to a film released February 16, 2018, just short of Whedon's announcement. *Black Panther* (2018) was released on that day, and had a gigantic opening weekend, one that dwarfed *Justice League*'s. The film, concerning an African hero and king, was directed by an African-American man, Ryan Coogler, and so some writers suggested, again, that Whedon, as a white male, was not the right person to helm *Batgirl*. Under his guidance, it wouldn't have the same credibility or authenticity as a superhero film directed by a woman (like *Wonder Woman*), or a superhero film directed by a black man, about a black character (*Black Panther*), they insisted

There was also some commentary in the press that Whedon's unproduced script for *Wonder Woman* was sexist in nature, or as Whedon described it in April of 2018, not fully "woke," though he stood by it. After he left the project, Christina Hodson, scribe of the *Transformers* movie spinoff *Bumblebee* (2018), was hired by DC to write *Batgirl*. She had also been tagged to write the upcoming *Birds of Prey* movie to be directed by Cathy Yan.

When this book was being written, Joss Whedon's career seemed troubled. After two failures with DC, would he return to superhero-dom? Or would he return to the development of his own properties (such as *Buffy*, *Angel*, or *Firefly*)? In the age of #MeToo and diverse directors, was the age of Hollywood's preeminent geek/fan boy finally coming to a close?

One thing was for certain in the autumnal days of 2018: Joss Whedon's incredible career in Hollywood had taken its most significant downturn since *Alien Resurrection*'s premiere and negative reception in 1997. *Justice League* had failed at the box office, and by and large, he was blamed for it. Further, Whedon had stepped away from his next superhero project, *Batgirl*.

Finally, and quite unbelievably, many subscribers on Twitter in the summer of 2018 had even begun comparing Whedon's physical appearance to that of *Avengers: Infinity War*'s (2018) monstrous villain Thanos. Both men have goatees, for instance, and a meme started about Thanos being a "purple" version of Whedon.

In just six years, then, Joss Whedon had gone from being the geek-boy hero who first assembled the most profitable superhero team on the silver screen, to the ultimate villain of the MCU, and the galaxy itself.

It couldn't have felt good.

26

Does Joss Whedon Write Comic Books?

As many authors and scholars have noted, comic books and film (or TV series, for that matter) are actually very closely related in terms of their structure and creative nature. Comic books feature a "vocabulary, grammar and syntax all their own," according to Neil Cohn, a psychology professor at University of California at San Diego, and author of the *Visual Language of Comics*. He describes the specifics of this language in an interview in 2013 with David Robson of *The Observer*. But the long and short of it is that comic grammar and film grammar are not that far apart. Both depend on the borders of a frame; both use visual symbolism, and both can be colorful and fast paced.

To be more specific, as Mark Swain writes in his essay "Comic Book Films and Visual Style," published by The Sequart Organization in 2006, comic books are "a printed medium which use sequential images to tell a story. Films are a medium which uses sequential moving images to tell a story ... films quite often use storyboards in which a series of sequential images are used in order to aid the filmmakers to tell the story. These storyboards are much the same as comics in their design and construction."

Given these similarities between forms, it is no tremendous surprise that in addition to his film and TV work, Whedon has proven himself a fixture in the comic-book world, going back more than fifteen years.

Before he became a creative powerhouse in Hollywood, Whedon was a comic-book fan himself, with a particular interest in *The X-Men*, Marvel's team of misfit outcasts and heroes. The X-Men are uniquely American heroes, an underclass (of mutants) striving to overcome ingrained bigotry and discrimination, and even fighting among themselves about how to do that. The characters were born in the turbulent 1960s, the same era as the Civil Rights Movement, and this context is literally burned into their characters. When one is an outsider, is it right to use violence against oppressors? Or is it better to work within the system to effect change? These are not small, or "fantasy," issues, but the dynamics of real-life debate.

Across the decades, the X-Men team members have been compared to ethnic or racial minorities, homosexuals, and transgender individuals. Since Whedon has often categorized his artistic theme as "everyone matters," his interest in X-Men is part of his foundational creative gestalt. He himself noted this connection in an interview with *The National Post* in 2004 ("The X-Universe's New Master"). "It was pointed out to me," Whedon said, "how the 'Buffy' gang had sort of morphed into the X-Men, which is the ultimate alienated group of teens and grownups who feel that the world is against them and have more power than they know what to do with . . . . [L]ike *'Spider-Man,'* it is a classic text." Not coincidentally, the idea of a created or found family, so prevalent in Whedon's work, is also a theme that can be traced back to Marvel, and The X-Men specifically.

From 2004 to 2008, Whedon penned *Astonishing X-Men*, a Marvel Comics limited series featuring art from John Cassaday. The series ran for two-dozen issues and featured a series of mini-arcs, including one about a mutant "cure," a storytelling device later utilized in *The Last Stand* (2006), the third X-Men film, which, at one point, Whedon was rumored to direct.

Other mini-arcs in the *Astonishing X-Men* involved Sentinel, and Break-world. After the twenty-four-issue run shepherded by Whedon, a new creative team, including author Warren Ellis, worked on the series. But during his creative tenure, Whedon credited the X-Men character Kitty Pryde as being a source of inspiration for Buffy, and noted that "writing the comic . . . is the real payoff of the childhood dream," according to an interview he conducted with *Publisher's Weekly* in 2005 ("Astonishing X-Men: Gifted").

In terms of comic books, most casual fans tend to think in terms of the big "two" companies: Marvel and DC, as well as a perceived competition between them. Whedon has not only worked in each company's cinematic universe, but in each comic-book realm as well.

In particular, he contributed to an issue of *Superman/Batman*, a follow-up series to *World's Finest Comic Books*. Although the primary author of the series was Jeph Loeb, Whedon (again working with artist Cassady) worked on a special issue, #26, devoted to the memory of Loeb's son, Sam, who had died of cancer at age seventeen, and had been slated to work on the issue.

For Whedon fans, however, it wasn't the auteur's work for either Marvel or DC that felt the most significant to them, but rather his welcome return (for multiple publishers, including Dark Horse and IDW) to the Buffyverse.

Even while *Angel* still aired on network TV, Whedon was writing the next chapter of the universe in comic-form, a post-apocalyptic tale called *Fray*. Writing for Dark Horse, Whedon invented a future slayer, Melaka Fray, who fought the good fight in a ruined New York City, and used the same slayer weapon seen in season seven of the celebrated series.

Perhaps of more genuine interest, Whedon also oversaw, or as he reported, "executive produced" a comic-book seasons eight and nine of *Buffy the Vampire Slayer*, in some cases bringing series writers back to the fold to continue their previous work.

This comic series featured some surprise twists for the slayer, as she moved into a new, even more adult phase of life, and had to deal with a villain known as "Twilight," someone eventually revealed to be someone quite important from her own past. Season eight ran in comic-book form from 2007–2011, and season nine debuted in 2011. Angel, who played a crucial role in these comics, also had his own comic-book title from 2007–2009, IDW's, *Angel: After the Fall*.

Other Whedon-sponsored titles in the Buffyverse included 2002's *Tales of Slayers*, and 2003's *Tales of Vampires*.

Whedon's other property, *Firefly*, moved to comic-book form in 2006 to coincide with the release of a feature film, *Serenity*. The first comic out of the gate was "Those Left Behind," a tale which filled in the time between the events of the series and the film. Later stories, such as "The Shepherd's Tale," filled in background information about popular characters, and this one was devoted to Shepherd Book's mysterious backstory, which was never fully revealed in any live-action production.

Finally, later comic stories such as "Leaves on the Wind, "The Warrior in the Wind," and "No Place in the 'Verse," all took place in the continuity after the film, and following the tragic death of Wash.

Even *Dollhouse* briefly got into the comic-book business. In 2011, "Dollhouse Epitaphs" was published by Dark Horse, and penned by Jed Whedon and Maurissa Tancharoen.

For years—or at this point, decades—fans have clamored for the return of Whedon characters and stories, and these comics help to fulfill these desires.

Part V

Other Projects

27

Did Joss Whedon Adapt Shakespeare?

Much Ado About Nothing (2012)

Cast

Amy Acker:	Beatrice
Alexis Denisof:	Benedick
Nathan Fillion:	Dogberry
Clark Gregg:	Leonato
Reed Diamond:	Don Pedro
Fran Kranz:	Claudio
Jillian Margese:	Hero
Sean Maher:	Don John
Spencer Treat Clark:	Borachio
Riki Lindhome:	Conrade
Ashley Johnson:	Margaret
Tom Lenk:	Verges

Crew

Bellwether Pictures presents *Much Ado About Nothing*
Costume Designer: Shawna Trpic
Production Designer: Cindy Chao, Michele Yu

Director of Photography:	Jay Hunter
Music:	Joss Whedon
Film Editor:	Daniel S. Kaminsky, Joss Whedon
Produced by:	Kai Cole, Joss Whedon
Line Producer:	M. Elizabeth Hughes, Nathan Kelly
Adapted from a play by:	William Shakespeare
Written by:	Joss Whedon
Directed by:	Joss Whedon
M.P.A.A. Rating:	PG-13
Running time:	109 minutes

Let me be that I am and seek not to alter me.

Shortly after proving victorious in a vicious war against his illegitimate brother, Don John (Sean Maher), the noble Don Pedro (Reed Diamond), the prince of Aragon, and his men, visit Governor Leonato (Clark Gregg) of Messina at his lovely estate.

There, two sharp wits, Benedick (Alexis Denisof) and Beatrice (Amy Acker), bicker and fight incessantly, making exaggerated swipes at each other. At the same time, an officer, Claudio (Fran Kranz), falls in love with Leonato's virtuous daughter, Hero (Jillian Margese).

Tired of Benedick and Beatrice's ongoing quarrels, Don Pedro engineers a plan to end their disputes. With Claudio and Hero's help, he decides to convince each combatant, separately, that their opponent is in love with them. This plan works as intended, and Beatrice and Benedick fall for each other, putting aside their jibes and jokes.

Unfortunately, another far more serious deception is wrought. Don John conspires to make Claudio believe that Hero has cuckolded him with another man.

Claudio spurns Hero on their wedding day, as does Leonato, her very father.

Now Benedick and Beatrice must challenge Don John's story, and prove that it is a terrible lie. They are helped in their efforts to unravel the villainy by a buffoonish local constable, Dogberry (Nathan Fillion).

I do love nothing in the world so well as you—is not that strange?

In his review of *Much Ado About Nothing* in the *New Yorker*, film critic Anthony Lane writes: Once you have created 'The Avengers,' in which you lassoed a gang of Marvel characters, including Iron Man, Captain America, and Thor, and wound up with the third-highest-grossing film in history, what next? Easy: you make a black-and-white film of *Much Ado About Nothing*, shooting over twelve days, in the safety of your own home. The project is kept secret, there are no big stars, and the budget is probably less than what you spent on Thor's hammer."

This opening line from Lane explains perfectly *Much Ado About Nothing*, and why it looks the way it does. Chronologically, in terms of Whedon's career, this Shakespeare adaptation falls between *The Avengers* (2012) and *The Avengers: Age of Ultron* (2015), and therefore one can view it, if so inclined, as palette cleanser, or much-needed respite, between two instances of high-stakes blockbuster franchise filmmaking. Between bouts of wrangling green screens, stunt-people and CGI—all while attempting to keep nitpicking fans happy—Whedon seized the opportunity to adapt this Shakespeare play, one that is seen by many scholars as a necessary precursor to the Bard's most complex works: *Hamlet*, *King Lear*, *Othello*, and *Macbeth*.

Sometimes, as one can detect from the careers of both Whedon and Shakespeare, a small or seemingly inconsequential project must presage work on something bigger and more psychically exhausting.

However, to call *Much Ado About Nothing* inconsequential, in either case, would be to do the work something of a disservice. The play, believed to have been written in approximately the middle of Shakespeare's career, circa 1598–1599, is set in Messina, Sicily, and involves, albeit in fast-paced fashion, a meditation on the necessity of deception in social interactions. Specifically, the work juxtaposes two sets of lovers, and compares the deceptions that impact each. Benedick and Beatrice are deceived to fall in love with each other, but they already share a strong attraction for each other, so the deception engineered by Don Pedro, prince of Aragon, only brings to light that which already lurks beneath the surface. In the end,

Benedick and Beatrice are served by Don Pedro's deception, and they put aside their barbs and jibes for a chance at happiness.

This deception mirrors the one engineered by Pedro's anti-social brother, Don John, who seeks to convince Claudio that his chosen love, Hero, is unfaithful, and that, even before marriage, she has betrayed him. In this case, a deception creates conflict, and actually threatens lives and social amity at Leonato's estate. Some Shakespeare scholars even consider the deceptive Don John to be a kind of protean version of his more famous villain, Iago.

Regardless, *Much Ado About Nothing* is all about the lies people tell that make them happy, and the lies people tell that destroys happiness. "One deception leads to social peace and marriage, to the end of deceit," writes Richard Henze in his 1971 work "Deception in *Much Ado About Nothing*," while "the other deception breeds conflict and distrust."

Treading a bit deeper into the text, *Much Ado About Nothing* also concerns toxic masculinity, particularly the inability to put war aside, even in domestic situations, and seek power via the aforementioned deception. Don John's actions ruin Claudio's love for Hero, and nearly destroy Leonato's relationship with his own daughter. In both scenarios, men are unable to see the truth of a woman's character, even though they ostensibly love her, either as a spouse or as a child.

Similarly, Benedick is unable to acknowledge the superior qualities (namely wit and humor) in Beatrice, and instead attempts to paint her as a monster whom he could never marry. If the play concerns how Don Pedro is easily able to deceive Claudio and Leonato, then it is also about how men deceive themselves, and actually move away from happiness, out of either sheer stubbornness, or some constant state of military-readiness, embodied by the esprit-de-corps the reader sees among the male characters. Basically, these men have served together in war, and developed what, in modern terms, would be considered a "bromance." They don't easily put that friendship/relationship down in favor of marriage. They derive something ego-satisfying, something vain, from the male bonding. Perhaps it is a reinforcement of the us vs. them mentality inherent in the battle of the sexes.

If the men in *Much Ado About Nothing* are easily deceived by others and themselves, such is not the case with Beatrice, a surprisingly progressive female character, one whom scholar Nadine Page, in 1935, wrote as a "symbol of changing conditions." In her work, "My Lady Disdain," Page described how Beatrice was written at a time when the covenant of marriage was changing. Basically, leading up to the writing of the play, marriage seemed of sole benefit to the man, with young women often married off to much older (and unpleasant) men, and living unhappily due to such arrangements. However, society was beginning to move towards the acknowledgment that for women to be married they had to have some say in terms of who they considered an acceptable mate. They had to have, at least, the possibility of happiness.

Beatrice is a character who embodies this (then progressive) viewpoint, this shift in the societal understanding of the benefits of marriage. As Page writes, "She [Beatrice] is, in truth, not anti-matrimonial, as is popularly alleged. She offers every evidence, however, of exercising much discrimination in the choosing of her husband."

In other words, Beatrice is commendably discerning, and desires a voice in what is undoubtedly the most important decision in her life. When she notes, "So goes everyone into the world but I," she is commenting not about her resistance to marriage, but the utter unsuitability of any possible mates.

The two most powerful themes seen in *Much Ado About Nothing*, the deceptive manipulation of men (to others and themselves), and Beatrice's agency in her own life, are obviously perfect fits for Joss Whedon.

If one considers for a moment the men that audiences see in the works of Whedon, their talent for self-deception is prodigious. Angel allows himself to become entangled with Buffy, even though he knows they can never be together. Yet he lingers, with an almost Hamlet-like diffidence. He knows what he must do, but is slow to act. Spike makes the same mistake, engaging romantically with Buffy, even though he knows he is not good enough for her and that, finally, she can never love him. Meanwhile, Malcolm Reynolds in *Firefly* and *Serenity* fashions himself a bastion against totalitarianism and tyranny, even as he declares that, on his boat, it is not a democracy. He calls Inara a whore, when she has made a choice regarding her own independence of which he doesn't approve. Basically, he covets independence for himself but can't extend the principle of independence to anyone else in his social circle.

All these men have a talent—and penchant—to deceive themselves about what they want, and what they can have.

Contrarily, the women in Whedon's work boast feminist qualities that enhance their agency. Buffy ultimately discovers a way to be the person she wants to be, by activating all the potential slayers. Echo, in *Dollhouse*, actually overcomes computer programming to leap beyond the agenda of the Dollhouse patriarchy. Beatrice, in *Much Ado About Nothing*, feels very much of a piece with these Whedon women. She is clear and distinct in expression, and motivated not to settle when it comes to her future.

Thematically then, *Much Ado About Nothing* is the right Shakespeare play for Whedon to adapt. This does not mean that he doesn't hedge his bets. He populates his film with all his stalwart repertory players, meaning that he has infused the film with a guarantee that his fandom will seek it out. The film features Nathan Fillion, Amy Acker, Alexis Denisof, Gregg Clark—even Tom Lenk, for heaven's sake. Since these actors are well known in the Whedonverse, Shakespeare's drama actually takes on new meaning, as the actors bring forth echoes from their previous work with the director.

For example, the lovers Benedick and Beatrice are notably portrayed by Alexis Denisof and Amy Acker, two lead actors in *Angel*. In that series, Denisof's Wesley Wyndham-Price and Acker's Fred Birkle were deeply in love, but throughout the series, their joining was never possible, either because of romantic rivals such as Gunn, or because of demonic possession by Illyria. *Angel* went on for several seasons with the love story unsettled, and then the series ended with no happy ending. Wesley died while Illyria was in Fred's body. Fred's soul had, by that time, been completely destroyed.

Yet, in *Much Ado About Nothing*, the audience gets to experience a notable emotional "resonance" of this relationship. Once more, we have Denisof and Acker playing characters enmeshed in a romantic relationship that appears doomed, or at least troubled. When they join forces and marry, it is very much the happy ending that Wesley and Fred were denied in *Angel*. *Much Ado About Nothing* feels like an alternate universe resolution to the multi-season Fred/Wesley narrative, as well as a self-reflexive acknowledgment of it.

This self-reflexive aspect of the film plays out in other notable ways. Nathan Fillion plays Dogberry, the braggadocio constable of Messina. Inauthentic and incompetent, the character is very similar in qualities to Captain Hammer, Fillion's anti-hero character from *Dr. Horrible*. It's true, Dogberry is not as malicious as Hammer, but there are certain parallels. Both characters love to hear themselves talk, apparently, and boast a comic persona based on pomposity and verbal self-aggrandizement. By 2013, Fillion was also well-ensconced in another TV series: *Castle* (2009–2016). That series, a procedural that featured Fillion in the titular role (as an author working with the police), also seems related to his role as Dogberry. Delightfully, Whedon has updated all the Dogberry scenes for the surveillance state and technology of the twenty-first century. This means that his scenes in *Much Ado About Nothing* play as, basically, a comic police procedural, with shades of the aforementioned TV series.

The casting of Fran Kranz as Claudio similarly lends to the undercurrent of intertextuality in the film. Kranz had already played two important roles in the Whedonverse by the time of this adaptation. First, he is Topher, from *Dollhouse*, a man who has blindly created technology to deceive others: both the Dolls, and the clients of the Dollhouse. His form of deception—though he does not recognize at first—is overtly of the kind Don John practices. It destroys life.

Secondly, Fran Kranz plays Marty in *The Cabin in the Woods*, a character who, alone among his peers, is able to sense that he is being deceived. All around him is deception, and yet he won't play along with the deception, or the role the world demands that he take. In the ultimate switcheroo from Marty, Kranz's Claudio is a man incapable of seeing any deceit at all; falling headlong for Don John's lies about his would-be bride, Hero. He is a foolish, easily swayed man who cannot discern truth from lies. All these roles hinge on a character's lack of or penchant for self-deception.

Joss Whedon's decision to shoot *Much Ado About Nothing* in stark black-and-white is also an intriguing, but illuminating, touch. Of all the Bard's plays, *Much Ado About Nothing* is the one that modern Shakespeare critics most often compare (pedantically) to a contemporary "rom-com." Yet the crisp black-and-white imagery and chiaroscuro lighting of the Whedon film undercuts that kind of lightness, making the film, instead, something akin to a noir, at least in terms of visualization. This choice, and the focus on light and shadow, heightens Don John's malevolence. He is a smoking, scowling villain whose plan is not harmless or funny at all, and which nearly brings about the death and dishonor of Hero.

Instead of playing the story as a light, colorful comedy about quarreling lovers, Whedon's choice to lens the film monochromatically enhances the idea of the dangers of deception and self-deception. Many scenes in the film feature handguns, again adding to the feel of danger and militarism, and supporting Shakespeare's theme of men who are unable to find peace outside of the camaraderie of war.

The film's first scene embodies the noir aspect of the film, and turns on its head Shakespeare's line that "silence is the perfectest herald of joy." The film's opening scene is of a disorderly bedroom, with clothes sprawled on the floor. It then captures Benedick leaving Beatrice alone in a disordered bed. Her eyes are open and aware, as he skulks out after their assignation, and the feeling here is not of romantic love, or even sexual satisfaction, but shame and guilt. One may say that silence is the perfect herald of joy, but that does not make it so. The silence here is deafening. Something is amiss between these lovers.

A main character in *Much Ado About Nothing* is the setting, which is Joss Whedon's home with his wife at the time, Kai Cole. The entire film was shot at that location, and Whedon told Rebecca Keegan, of the *Los Angeles Times*, that it was the perfect location for this story: "The house informs what the movie is. It has a combination of sunny spaciousness and dark labyrinthine intrigue," he observed. With the black-and-white photography, it is that dark intrigue which becomes a crucial player in the film's thematic framework. Smart, fast-paced, and featuring dazzling imagery, *Much Ado About Nothing* explores fully Shakespeare's world of twin deceptions. The returning-from-war heroes are billeted, jarringly, in a children's bedroom, for instance. That domestic space is replete with such childish toys as teddy bears and other accouterments of the young and carefree, thus offering an ironic commentary on how a place of domesticity is spoiled by machismo posturing and trickery.

In terms of reception, *Much Ado About Nothing* was greeted warmly by many film critics, despite the fact that, from a certain perspective, it was a step well outside the comfort zone of its creator. *The Washington Post's* Ann Hornaday wrote, for example: "Whedon finds unexpected meaning in this famously saucy "skirmish of wit," the opposites-attract story upon which myriad modern-day rom-coms have sprung. Not only does the spiky verbal sparring between would-be lovers Beatrice and Benedick still crackle with convincing sting and verve, but Shakespeare also turns out to have plenty to say about an era when, more than ever, someone is more apt to be destroyed by fast-moving rumors and strategic leaks than by an act of brute physical aggression."

She makes a great point about why this story remains relevant today. The Age of the Internet has permitted for the creation of such things as catfishing, and even revenge porn. A love affair gone wrong can destroy someone publicly and swiftly today, just as Hero was almost destroyed in Shakespeare's tale. In fact, there are myriad instantaneous ways available, in our world, to ruin a reputation, or strike out at those who reject us.

Peter Travers, of *Rolling Stone*, agreed on the virtues of the film, noting that "Whedon, without skimping on the tale's tragic undercurrents, has crafted an irresistible blend of mirth and malice." That alliterative description captures perfectly the duality of Shakespeare's (and now Whedon's) work. We all deceive ourselves and each other every day, but is that deceit the thing that makes society possible (and endurable), or is it something that destroys bonds, and love? While this film is hardly typical of Whedon's oeuvre, it shows off the same values as the majority of his works, wrapping up social commentary in an entertaining and witty affair.

28

Did Joss Whedon Write a Horror Movie?

The Cabin in the Woods (2012)

Cast

Kristin Connolly:	Dana
Chris Hemsworth:	Curt
Anna Hutchison:	Jules
Fran Kranz:	Marty
Sigourney Weaver:	The Director
Jesse Williams:	Holden
Richard Jenkins:	Sitterson
Bradley Whitford:	Hadley
Brian White:	Truman
Amy Acker:	Lin
Tim DeZarn:	Mordecai
Tom Lenk:	Ronald the Intern
Dan Payne:	Matthew Buckner
Dan Shea:	Father Buckner
Jodelle Ferland:	Patience Buckner

Crew

Lionsgate, Mutant Enemy, Metro-Goldwyn-Mayer, and United Artists present *The Cabin in the Woods*

Casting:	Anya Colloff, Amy McIntyre Britt
Costume Designer:	Shawna Trpic
Production Designer:	Martin Whist
Music:	David Julyan
Director of Photography:	Peter Deming
Film Editor:	Lisa Lassek
Executive Producer:	Jason Clark
Produced by:	Joss Whedon
Written by:	Drew Goddard and Joss Whedon
Directed by:	Drew Goddard
M.P.A.A. Rating:	R
Running time:	95 minutes

You think you know the story.

Five young adults—the sensitive Dana (Kristin Connolly), the hunky Curt (Chris Hemsworth), sexy Jules (Anna Hutchison), stoner Marty (Fran Kranz), and scholar Holden (Jesse Williams)—go on vacation at a remote cabin in the woods.

They are unaware, at least at first, however, that they are pawns in a giant game, a game that could have repercussions for every living human being on Earth. In particular, they are the latest in a long line of youngsters to be sacrificed to the Ancients, malevolent gods who demand tribute from the human race.

Meanwhile, a group of technicians in a subterranean headquarters, led by Sitterson (Richard Jenkins) and Hadley (Bradley Whitford), plan the demise of the kids with a workaday attitude, certain that all will go as planned. These workers, however, have not counted on the fact that Marty somehow senses "the puppeteers" pulling his strings. And he really dislikes authority.

We work with what we have.

The year 2012 was a great one for Joss Whedon. He directed the block-buster of the year, Marvel's *The Avengers*, and shot *Much Ado About Nothing*. He also saw the release of *The Cabin in the Woods*, a long-gestating horror film that he had co-written with its director, Drew Goddard. The screenplay was reportedly written in just three days, and production of the $30 million film took place in Vancouver. The U.S. release was delayed (because of M.G.M.'s bankruptcy) to April of 2012, just before the release of *The Avengers*, and critics immediately raved about the film, as it offered a new and insanely smart take on old horror film tropes.

"The film's virtue, a large virtue indeed," wrote Lawrence Toppman in the *Charlotte Observer*, "is that it does not give anything away before its shockingly apt time." The *Tampa Bay Times* critic, Steve Persall, went further, noting "'The Cabin in the Woods' isn't merely another 'Scream' exercise in self-awareness, or a 'Scary Movie' spoof of the same. It's a wick-edly smart hybrid mutation, biting the severed hand feeding the genre."

NPR's Ian Buckwalter noted that the film is a "horror-movie attic sale" and "an attempt to exorcise the genre of its formulaic possession by stuff-ing the movie full of its most overused and predictable elements—and then dumping through clever skewering."

Although the film was the subject of a $10 million copyright lawsuit that was ultimately dismissed, *The Cabin in the Woods* feels like another perfect "geek" storm for Whedon. It gazes at every aspect of horror as a genre, even horror film viewership, and then ties those things together in a postmodern, incredibly amusing—and still scary—effort. More than five years after its release, the film is still discussed and debated by critics and fans.

The Ancient ones see everything.

The Cabin in the Woods (2012) is simultaneously a clever genre outing that presents a "unified theory" of horror films and a deeply cynical work of art. The film concerns stories we choose to amuse ourselves, and the reasons why we choose them.

Writers Joss Whedon and Drew Goddard have fashioned a witty, surprising, and intellectually engaging movie here, but they have also made one that is deeply, *irrevocably* hopeless about the current state of mankind, and, in addition, the state of art in the (modern) form of the twenty-first century horror movie. This underlying cynicism makes the film a far cry from other Whedon works in that there is no hope at the end of the day that the battle against dark forces can be won by a committed individual, or team of individuals.

When using the term *cynical* here, this writer doesn't assert that *The Cabin in the Woods* is a craven cash grab, or somehow dishonest in its desire to achieve audience approval. Rather, he asserts that this movie actually adopts *a cynical point of view* as its central thematic terrain. What is cynicism? "A state of mind characterized by general distrust of others' apparent motives or ambitions, or a general lack of faith or hope in the human race." Or at least that is Wikipedia's definition.

For this book's purposes while discussing *The Cabin in the Woods*, the section of that definition above that remains most pertinent describes cynicism as "a general lack of faith or hope in the human race." The same definition goes on to suggest that cynicism is a product of "mass society," and can manifest itself as a result of "frustration, disillusionment, and distrust."

This definition fits *The Cabin in The Woods* perfectly. It is a movie that sees man as a hopelessly corrupt creature, and therefore one who does not deserve continued dominion over Earth. It views modern horror movies in a not entirely dissimilar way: as a collection of familiar elements or ingredients to be shuffled around, again and again, in the hopes that the re-shuffling and re-arrangement of the familiar will be mistaken as original or fresh.

Hit the jackpot of ingredients, and you get a blockbuster! In some way, *The Cabin in the Woods* suggests, this philosophy explains the current glut of remakes, reboots, and re-imaginations.

In some perverse and even paradoxical way, Joss Whedon and his director, Drew Goddard, present their cynical view of the world and the horror film with absolute sincerity and clarity in *The Cabin in the Woods*. They aren't being glib or half-assed about their film's social critique. One can't fault the filmmakers for, first, possessing a powerful vision, and second, presenting it with such merciless, jaw-dropping effectiveness, but one can still quibble with the philosophy espoused.

Take a closer look at the film's worldview. *The Cabin in the Woods* is a well-made, articulate, meaningful horror film that says something important about our times. It offers a *unified theory*, one that explains the fundamental forces in a single system or area. Very craftily, and with tongue in cheek, *The Cabin in the Woods* explains why so many aspects of diverse horror films appear alike, from the crazy old coot who warns youngsters "You are going to die," to the young, beautiful virgins, to the nature of the monsters themselves.

The basis for the unified theory is, simply, that *reality is not as we know it*. Man doesn't call the shots on Earth; the Ancients do. And the human sacrifice rituals of ages past have now—*in the twenty-first century*—morphed into the very conventions we all know and recognize from decades of horror movies.

These conventions include familiar locations like the iconic cabin of *The Evil Dead* (1983), or the one featured in *Cabin Fever* (2002), and the "Last-Chance" gas station viewers remember from such films as *The Texas Chainsaw Massacre* (1973), *The Hill Have Eyes* (1977), and *Wrong Turn* (2003), among others.

In terms of the central cabin locale, it is a realm of isolation, where help is not available. It is an unexplored place, and often in horror films even a representative home of a minority culture (mountain folk) or of a previous time period (an age passed, for example). In exploring the cabin as a setting, Whedon and Goddard make direct visual and thematic comparisons to *The Evil Dead*, Sam Raimi's first motion picture.

In *The Evil Dead*, five kids (again) go to a cabin in the woods. In both films, that cabin is a small, one-story affair. In both films, the door to the basement seems to magically blast open at an unexpected moment, and in both films, the most sensitive female character is depicted as an artist with a sketchbook. The transgression, or act, which unleashes the evil in both *The Cabin in the Woods* and *The Evil Dead* is the speaking aloud of words in another language.

Where the two films diverge, however, is in the precise role of the "Evil" in the very similar scenario. In *The Evil Dead*, the demons do all the hard work and attack the living victims themselves (with a little help from an "Angry Molesting Tree," as *The Cabin in the Woods* describes it). Conversely, in *The Cabin in the Woods* man himself has become the agent who greases the wheels for horrible deaths to occur, while the demons are reduced to being mere audience members below, in hell.

To break this down succinctly, *The Cabin in the Woods* suggests that *man has created a factory or industry out of committing atrocities.* Either horror films exemplify that atrocity—the postmodern reading of the film's perspective—or our very culture—replete with war, poverty, and reality TV shows—is the atrocity. Either way, humanity is doing the dirty work: arranging for victims and trapping them, so they can be sacrificed.

Another important setting that appears in *The Cabin in the Woods* is the Last-Chance gas station, the last place of human civilization and safety before the danger, chaos, and wildness of the frontier beyond. This setting possesses a well-established presence in horror films of the last fifty years. It is has been seen in every "backwoods" horror movie, from *The Texas Chainsaw Massacre* (1973) and *The Hill Have Eyes* (1977) to the more recent *Wrong Turn* films. Audiences recognize it as the place where the worlds begin to overlap, for The Last-Chance gas station stands at the border between civilization and savagery. Again demonstrating a canny understanding of the horror lexicon and its imagery, *The Cabin in the Woods* recognizes an important quality of this location. It's the last place where the protagonists and future victims can step back, contextualize their experience, and decide to reverse course and return home.

Invariably, the protagonists do not take that step.

Instead, they blunder forward and pay the consequences for their bravado. In the film, the last stop at the Last-Chance gas station is contextualized as a "choice," and the screenplay brings up the idea that freedom of choice must be involved in the ritual sacrifices to the Ancients. In other words, the characters have been warned, and yet they still go forward into danger. This crossroads in horror films is almost universally populated, or presided over, by another horror convention or element from the lexicon: *The Threshold Guardian/Herald of Death.*

This character (and symbolic representation), seen in *Friday the 13th* (1980) as Crazy Ralph and in many other examples of the genre, is the clear human symbol of danger. The Herald carries knowledge of something vital, and he physically embodies a quality of derangement or menace. And yet he's often a despicable person, possessing racist views or even allied with evil.

Because the character's important message—*Go Back or Die!*—comes from an old, crazy, and/or disfigured person, however, it is often ignored. The Threshold Guardian/Herald of Death isn't recognized for what he is, and is instead demeaned, his cause is invalidated. It is easy for young, beautiful, carefree people to disparage and dismiss the guardian as a backwoods hick. But the truth is, *they should listen.* They should see below the surface and recognize that the Herald of Death's message is crucial to their survival.

Even in terms of its specific evil, *The Cabin in the Woods* boasts a very recognizable movie archetype: the demon who brings pain and pleasure to the living as these victims wade into terror and select their own fate. In the *Hellraiser* films, that evil force is represented by Pinhead, a hellish "scientist" who combines sensuality and agony. During the climax of *The Cabin in the Woods*, we see a figure very much like the famous Cenobite, though he boasts circular saws perforating his skull instead of nails. But both creatures hold puzzle-boxes, wear leather outfits, and seem to live by the motto: "Hands don't call us; desire does."

What this means is that those who hold the puzzle *determine* the nature and shape of their own demises. This aspect of the "monster" ties in with the Last-Chance gas station, and the film's notation regarding free will. The human characters must choose their own fates, through their actions, inaction, and choices. Their behavior summons the evil.

Another important character type is the *stoner* or *fool*, as represented by the character of Marty. He is truly the film's wild card. At first, an audience member might mistake Marty for the same goofy character seen in so many slasher films: the guy who takes a hit off the bong and is so spaced out that—*vice preceding slice and dice*—he gets killed early in the action.

But in *The Cabin in the Woods*, Marty breaks out of his assigned "role" in the ritual, and begins to unravel everything. He is, thus, something of a villain in the scheme of things. He is the Loki character, the *mischief maker*, not actually the fool. Either that or he is the unexpected hero, depending on one's perspective on authority.

Clearly then, *The Cabin in the Woods* assembles many elements, conventions, and archetypes from the horror film genre, and then re-purposes all of the disparate ideas for the purpose of its unified theory, which, interestingly, serves the same purpose as ... a *myth*. A myth might be defined as a brand of story that reveals how mankind came to exist in its present form, and, furthermore, explains some mysterious aspect of nature (like thunder, lightning, or natural disasters).

The Cabin in the Woods qualifies as a modern myth because it assiduously explains why horror films across the decades hold so many important conventions in common, like the cabin, the gas station, or the herald. Underneath the surface of "reality," malevolent creatures await tribute and appeasement, and our very entertainment suggests the shape of that tribute, subtly preparing us for the «truth» lurking just beneath the surface.

There's a term for this kind of surreptitious preparation in conspiracy circles: *predictive programming*. It's the effort of the "mass society"—*remember the stated cause of cynicism in our definition above*—to ready its populace for catastrophic changes in not quite above-board, not-quite-direct fashion.

The Cabin in the Woods embodies a unified theory of horror—this myth that explains the "whys" of modern horror movie and connects them all together into a meaningful "story" about human nature—represents more than enough brilliance to rate the film a "thumbs-up" moviegoing experience. The familiar story of teenagers/victims at a cabin in the woods fighting monsters is blown-up, re-assembled, and re-invented to seem fresh in an age where the tale is no longer fresh at all.

In a sense, this is very much what *Scream* (1996) accomplished for slasher films of the Clinton era. That film made audiences think differently about slasher film conventions, and after *The Cabin in the Woods*, one can't quite look at *The Evil Dead* in the same way as before.

As impressive as the unified theory of horror movies remains, *The Cabin in the Woods* offers a commentary on that theory that is—again, like *Scream*—postmodern. Much of the film involves the duo of Sitterson and Hadley, two aging middle-management functionaries who, basically, "engineer" creative deaths for human beings so as to please and appease a monstrous audience (the Ancients) that, if angered, could rise up and destroy humankind.

Dig beneath the surface of that scenario just a little bit and you will see that Sitterson and Hadley represent the "underneath" of horror films. Not a psychological or subconscious underneath in this case, but, literally, the *creative* underneath of the genre. The two men sit at a giant control panel with monitors, the equivalent of a writer's laptop, and help to select from a series of elements which horrific scenario the human sacrifices should face.

The Merman, or Angry Molesting Tree? The redneck Zombies, or the Japanese Water Girls? The evil clown, or the ballerina with a face of teeth?

Since the setting, the cabin in the woods, and the character archetypes are already established, all these writers can do, according to the film's commentary, is vary the monster and the manner of killing the protagonists. This is a new expression of a very old argument about horror films that goes something like this: Each *Friday the 13th* or *Halloween* movie or *Saw* movie is merely a recycled plot, but one featuring new and inventive ways to kill people.

To put it another way, this film suggests that the modern horror film has become a mindless regurgitation of old elements, with the only new element each time being a different murder weapon or particular victim. As a longtime aficionado of the horror movie, the author doesn't agree with this critique any more than he agrees with the film's cynical outlook on human nature, because horror—*right now*—is as healthy as it has been in decades. If this film's argument had been made circa 1987–1989 (after eight *Friday the 13ths*, five *Halloweens*, and five *Elm Streets*), that would be different.

But in 2012, the horror genre was back at the top of its game, courtesy of independent and foreign films, and the infusion of life brought about by the found-footage subgenre. It was the age of *The Bay*, *Sinister*, *American Mary*, and many more interesting films. And that milieu gave way to even more prestige horror, like 2014's *Honeymoon*, or *The Babadook*, or *It Follows*.

Still, even while disagreeing with the movie's premise, the author can appreciate how *The Cabin in the Woods* forges its arguments. In a beautiful example of form mirroring content, the audience follows the film's survivors into a subterranean underground where every kind of nightmare monster is trapped in a transparent cage, a gigantic Rubik's Cube of "choices." This gorgeous image represents *the puzzle dynamic of modern screenwriting* (let's fit this monster, or element, in here) and also suggests the modern writer's paucity of imagination. He or she can choose from *what already exists* (ghosts, goblins, aliens, demons, slashers, zombies), but he can't, it seems, pick something that hasn't already been selected at least once before. In other words, no originality exists, just that constant shifting or re-shuffling of the established deck (or puzzle box).

The leader of the film's underground Monster Initiative, not coincidentally, is called The Director (Sigourney Weaver), and this is the individual "upstairs" who makes sure the writers get everything right so the product is met with appreciation from the Ancient audience. So we're really talking about the movie director here, not just the project director. In the film's overriding postmodern metaphor, those Ancients might represent us, the very people watching horror movies in the real world. When the Ancients rise at the end of the film—disappointed by the unexpected finale—the comment seems to be one about viewer expectations.

Horror movies actually condition predictability, the filmmakers seem to be saying, and anything unpredictable will be met with audience outrage and anger. Viewers are, therefore, victims of their own viewing habits, going back to see the same thing, again and again and again, and drawing life, not from fresh meat, but from warmed-up leftovers.

Again, this commentary applies splendidly to the context of what *The Cabin in the Woods* means on an intellectual level. The film is multi-layered, and wants to reveal something important to the audience about itself. In particular, if the screenplay's "unified theory" explains why horror movies look the same, it also explains why audiences want the same thing over and over again. It has something to do with the inherent contradiction of seeking a scary cinematic experience, but one whose boundaries we already understand, going in. Audiences desire fear, but not *too much* fear. Audiences want terror, but it must be acceptable terror, within established and familiar parameters.

The author's grave concern with the film—and the thing that makes *The Cabin in the Woods* so cynical in its telling—involves the characters, those existing in the story who don't possess the perspective granted to viewers, and who therefore can't see or interpret the events as, essentially, postmodern.

For instance, early in the film, the stoner, Marty, opines that "society needs to crumble. We're just too chicken shit to let it happen." At the end of the film, he is given the opportunity to either save the world, or let it be destroyed by the Ancients. Remembering his comment from earlier in the film, it's not a stretch to guess which path he chooses. He's got free will . . . and he uses it. Chicken shit he is not.

Although the Director begs Marty to sacrifice himself so that everyone else on Earth may live, he refuses to play along with authority. He believes it is better to blow it all up than to save the (corrupt) human race. He sees society as worthless because the secret overlords have moved in the shadows to shape his destiny without his knowledge. Disillusioned, he responds, cynically. And the Ancients rise.

It's a dick move on Marty's part, and a deliberate comment on what a hopeless piece of work is man. Earlier in the film, however, Marty mentions his mom, fearing she would consider him a "burn-out." So, he doesn't even want to save the world for his mom? Are viewers to believe there is not one person in Marty's life—*one person in the world*—he deems worthy of his saving the planet? It would be nice to claim that this is just the movie's commentary on Marty. He's a selfish, indulged prick. But sweet, kind Dana gets the opportunity to kill Marty and save the world in the process, and she doesn't act either.

Again, this would be a fairly easy decision for any one of us, I suspect. Do *you* have loved ones? Children? Parents? Siblings? Friends?

Among that circle, is there at least *one* person you love, who is worth saving the world for?

It seems there would be such a person in Dana's case, if not Marty's. So, in a sense, this ending doesn't ring true on an individual, human level, even if it rings true on a philosophical one, on the level of cynicism as governing individual philosophy. Joss Whedon's work usually functions effortlessly on two tracks: as drama, and as social commentary, or postmodern reflection. In *The Cabin in the Woods*, the commentary is strong, but it doesn't ring true in conjunction with the characters as they are presented.

The judgment of *The Cabin in the Woods* is that man deserves to die, apparently, for turning matters of life and death—*human sacrifice*—into a workaday job where people get drunk, wager cash on outcomes, and crack cruel, thoughtless jokes. The image projected is of a callous race that cares nothing for his fellow man. Mary and Dana's decision not to spare the world at the end of the film, however, reinforces this notion. They are both just as rotten as Sitterson and Hadley. They are so selfish and narcissistic they can't even think of sacrificing themselves for the "greater good." In *The Avengers*, Steve Rogers defines heroism as "the sacrifice play," and doesn't think Tony Stark is up to it. He proves that he is. Here, there is nobody to embody that heroism.

So cynical, in fact, is the film about man, that it even audaciously, if sincerely, suggests blood-loving, "giant evil gods" will do a better job with the Earth than we have. Dana says words along the lines of "Humanity . . . it's time to give someone else a chance," and, well, simply, this author calls *bullshit* on that line. Dana would never think it, let alone speak it. It doesn't feel true to her character.

And her line gets the dynamic wrong. This isn't a battle between "humanity" and "someone else" in a kind of hopeful sense, like choosing between candidates for high office. It's a choice between humanity . . . and giant evil gods who, as the story reveals, have been using human sacrifices since the dawn of time. The ones who, from the very beginning, rigged the system, are going to do a better job?

It is easy to understand why people are cynical and disillusioned. When this film came out, America had been through a terrible recession, witnessed gridlock in Washington, and watched the greedy 1 percent take more and more while the other 99 percent holds the bag. We've seen the election of narcissistic morons who want only to raid our national coffers and pat themselves on the back while doing so. In a sense, believing in the American dream today is like kissing that stuffed, mounted wolf on the wall in *The Cabin in the Woods*, and hoping it won't bite us when we tongue it.

A lot of folks say, "The system is rigged," and—let's face it—what Dana and Marty learn in *The Cabin in the Woods* is that *the system is indeed rigged*. They aren't in control of their lives, and they have been manipulated in terrible ways. But *The Cabin in the Woods* doesn't take the necessary step of deciding what the right response to a rigged system is. Things don›t get improved by blowing up everything, by destroying the human race.

As soon as people stop believing that they can each make a difference, and surrender to chaos, we're in real trouble. The great thing about the human race is that it keeps renewing the well of hope, and it keeps re-asserting the belief, generation after generation, that the best days remain ahead. People might get depressed or discouraged, but they have a responsibility—to the children, at the very least—to pull themselves out of that funk and keep moving forward. Cynicism accomplishes *nothing*. It never has, and it never will.

The author realizes this is his personal issue with the film, but has a very difficult time enjoying *The Cabin in the Woods* on an emotional level, even if it is easy to appreciate it and admire its craft on an intellectual basis. It is difficult, however, to buy into a worldview which says it is better to destroy *everything now* than to keep trying to make the world better. The system is rigged . . . *okay*. But the response still matters. It has to matter, or everyone can just stop working, stop having children, and stop trying.

Do you think that would make this world a better place, or a worse one?

For all its intelligence and wit, *The Cabin in the Woods* answers that vital, final question with a lack of vision. Unlike Marty in *The Cabin in the Woods*, Buffy Summers or Malcolm Reynolds would have saved the world for everyone else.

This author is with those guys.

Buffy gave her life (in the fifth-season finale of that series), to save an imperfect world for all families. In *Serenity* (2005), Mal Reynolds sacrificed his ship and nearly his entire crew to get the "signal"—the truth—out to a listening galaxy, because he believed that people still cared about the truth.

The Cabin in the Woods is glib, ironic, and smart, like so many Joss Whedon entertainments, but it is totally and irrevocably lacking in hope or belief, and that makes the film, for all its brilliance, deeply sad.

29

Did Joss Whedon Write a Love Story?

In Your Eyes (2014)

Cast

Michael Stahl-David:	Dylan Kershaw
Zoe Kazan:	Rebecca Porter
Mark Feuerstein:	Phillip Porter
David Gallagher:	Lyle Soames
Jennifer Gray:	Diane
Steve Howey:	Bo Soames
Nikki Reed:	Donna
Kayde Currier:	Jack
Preston Bailey:	Clay
Reed Birney:	Dr. Maynard
Steve Harris:	Giddons

Crew

Bellwether Pictures and Night & Day Pictures Production

Casting:	Angela Demo, Barbara J. McCarthy
Music:	Tony Morales
Costume Design:	Mirren Gordon-Crozier
Film Editor:	Steven Pilgrim
Director of Photography:	Elisha Christian
Producers:	Michael Roiff, Kai Cole

Written by:	Joss Whedon
Directed by:	Brin Hill
M.P.A.A. Rating:	PG-13
Running time:	105 minutes

Sometimes when I'm with you, I forget myself.

An unhappily married and very insecure young woman, Rebecca Porter (Zoe Kazan), living in snowy New Hampshire, and a hot-tempered ex-con, Dylan Kershaw (Michael Stahl-David), living in sun-baked New Mexico, unexpectedly begin to experience strange psychic flashes of each other's lives. They begin to see, essentially, through each other's eyes. Although at first this proves inconvenient, and nearly causes Dylan to drive his truck off the road, the duo soon begins to feel connected.

As they communicate meaningfully over vast distances, Rebecca and Dylan become fast friends, and realize that their paranormal bond goes back years, even decades, to a wintry sleighing accident Rebecca had in childhood. Their friendship becomes increasingly intimate, and Rebecca even tries to help Dylan date a woman named Donna (Reed), and hold down a steady job, leaving behind his life of crime. Dylan, meanwhile, helps Rebecca to grow more confident in her relationships.

Rebecca's icy, selfish husband, Phillip (Mark Feuerstein), however, believes that Rebecca is mentally ill, and when he grows embarrassed by her public "seizures" (really her communication with Dylan), he thoughtlessly hands her over to Dr. Maynard (Reed Birney), an expert in "schizophrenic narcotherapy."

Rebecca is thus incarcerated in a mental institution, which means that Dylan must break his parole, flee his parole officer (Steve Harris), and race to the other side of the country to spring the woman he realizes is the love of his life.

As the police track Dylan, and authorities from the hospital pursue Rebecca, the lovers meet in the flesh for the first time on a train box car. Eye-to-eye, they look at a future together for the first time.

I've never met anyone I didn't disappoint.

In Your Eyes is a low-budget film from Bellwether Pictures, the production company that brought *Much Ado About Nothing* to life. Because of its low-budget, independent nature, the film features no big stars, and no real special effects sequences. Instead, *In Your Eyes* is a kind of intimate romantic film in the literary school of magical realism, from a script that Joss Whedon wrote in the 1990s.

Magical realism is a genre of writing in which the overall setting is largely realistic, or true to life, but some element of the paranormal seeps into that reality. Typically, in literature of the magic realism school, there is very little, if any, explanation of the supernatural in the everyday world. This quality is often described as authorial "reticence," meaning that something out of the Earthly norm occurs, but the author deliberately holds back knowledge that would clear up points about the story.

Another important quality of magical realism in terms of literature and film is its hybrid nature. It often occurs on multiple planes of meaning, or in opposing, mirror locations. The opposing locations, the mirror imagery, is key to an understanding of the characters and their plights.

In Your Eyes perfectly fits the many elements of this definition. The story is set in a "kitchen sink" (or consensus) reality everyone recognizes as our world. It is one of personal isolation and regrets, failed marriages, lost opportunities, and the eking out of a living from an unfulfilling job. It is a world of human foibles, failed relationships, and the quest to find meaning primarily through connection with others. Most notably, *In Your Eyes* is determinedly not a world of superheroes, vampires, future-tech, or other superhumans.

However, this kitchen sink reality is stretched a bit when its two primary characters, Dylan and Rebecca, discover that they possess an inexplicable ability to see through each other's eyes. No explanation, however, is provided for this out-of-the-norm ability, or why it impacts these two particular characters and not others. The power is questioned, briefly, but never explored or explained in scientific, supernatural, mythological terms. Joss Whedon demonstrates the authorial reticence of the form, refusing to offer answers. Instead, the film merely concerns how this unusual communication ability impacts Dylan and Rebecca.

Finally, the hybrid setting is one of its most powerful virtues. The script, and the film's visualization itself, set up opposing, mirror-reflection worlds and characters. Rebecca is inward-directed, uncertain of what she desires from life, and lives in the frozen Northeast. She has an abiding passion for art, but keeps this buried, as if under feet of snow, in part to maintain her marriage to her unemotional, shallow husband.

Rebecca and her wintry settings are directly juxtaposed with Dylan's world. He is a man who lives life too "hot." He lives in the sweltering southwest of New Mexico, and keeps making mistakes because of his impulsive nature. He is an ex-con who has had frequent trouble with the law, the result of too many bad decisions.

Only in connection with each other through the auspices of their unusual, possibly paranormal abilities can the extremes of cold (Rebecca) and hot (Dylan) succeed. Their connection may come about if one reads into the scenario, because of their opposing natures. They need the balance the other person brings.

This is going to be so weird.

In Your Eyes was produced by Joss Whedon's wife, Kai Cole, and directed by Brin Hill, a writer and filmmaker who had worked on many independent shorts going back to 1999, including *Glance Away*, *Morning Breath*, and *The Ecology of Love*. His first full-length feature was 2008's *Ball Don't Lie*. "We did the table reads at Joss's house," Hill reported about the making of the film, in Jennifer Vineyard's interview with him, "How Whedonesque is Joss Whedon's New Film, *In Your Eyes*?"

"So we were walking on the ghosts of *Much Ado*. He watched dailies every day. He was weighing in on things. He was in and out of the edit room." And of course, he commissioned a dance party. "You have to have a dance party if you're working with Joss."

Hill was a good choice to direct the film, and he visualizes it in a fashion that reinforces the magical realism approach to the romance. He told *Moveable Fest*'s Steve Saito: "It's funny, the first time I read the script, I saw the film in two different color palettes. I knew that I always wanted to identify each environment by a colorscape. It's much more subtle than, say, a traffic [light], but it's there, and it was [there] to root them in the ground and know where they are at any given time. Then [there was] the intimacy of camera and having it move a little bit because there is a talking nature to this. It's about two people who are exploring each other through dialogue, so there's a challenge of how you keep that energetic."

With no real special effects, *In Your Eyes* unfolds with a kind of neoclassicist style, focusing on faces and locations, and strongly supporting the written word.

Sometimes when I'm with you, I forget myself.

In Your Eyes possessed an unusual release strategy. Joss Whedon announced at the Tribeca Film Festival in 2014 that after the film premiered there, it would also premiere, virtually simultaneously, online, on Vimeo. This meant critics and viewers would have concurrent access to it. Unfortunately, reviews were largely negative. *Indiewire*'s Sam Adams wrote: "*In Your Eyes*, which was written by Joss Whedon and financed by his personal microbudget studio, Bellwether Pictures, made news Sunday night with the announcement it was available for online rental immediately after its world premiere at the Tribeca Film Festival. Unfortunately, it turns out to be noteworthy for another reason: It's the worst production with Whedon's name on it in years, and arguably decades. Whedon likes to joke about the *Avengers* movies being his "little passion project," but they're far more infused with his distinctive wit than this flavorless mush."

The Guardian's Tom Shone awarded the film just two out of five stars, and likened it to a romantic version of Stephen King's *The Shining*. He felt that very little cleverness was exercised in the central conceit of telepathic communication. "There's nothing here for the conceit to bounce off, no way of distinguishing between these characters' insides and their soft-focus outsides. Whedon's idea of getting behind into someone's eyes and into their head involves no shocks, no revelations, no new information. How can that be?"

Variety's reviewer Peter Debruge did not like the film much either, and likened it to a writer's drawer-cleaning exercise. "For anyone who's ever wondered whether "the right one" might be somewhere out there waiting for you, Joss Whedon has the answer in the form of a supernatural soap opera so first-drafty, only the faithful need apply. In 'In Your Eyes,' two complete strangers on opposite sides of the country discover they can see and feel whatever the other is experiencing, which naturally leads them to conclude that they belong together. Scripted by Whedon and helmed by Brin Hill, this low-budget quickie plays like something unearthed from a junior-high creative writing journal, partly redeemed by a pair of compelling lead performances."

Not all reviews proved so overwhelmingly negative. Kurt Loder termed the film a "radiant romantic comedy," and Witney Seibold, of *The Nerdist*, commented that *In Your Eyes* "is a bit padded, and the ending is trite." He concluded, however, that it is "a sweetly realized and moving fantasy romance."

Why such a rough reception, overall, for a film that, indeed, feels rather sweet? Above all, Whedon is renowned by his admirers and critics for his edgy, subversive overturning of tropes, or questioning of forms and formats. *Buffy the Vampire Slayer*, with that "Dark Alley Story," undercuts decades of vampire stories. *Firefly* turns over the "Technology Unchained" paradigm of future, or space-age, stories, such as *Star Trek*. And *The Cabin in the Woods* acidly takes on the formulaic nature of modern horror films. Even the *Avengers* films feature a knowing sense of humor about themselves.

There is simply no comparable edginess, or cleverness, about *In Your Eyes*. The film is sentimental and straight-forward, never accomplishing anything unexpected with the material, or putting a twist on it that feels genuinely Whedonesque. One feels that in the cinema and TV of Joss Whedon, *everything* is questioned, and yet no form, no character, no idea is questioned or deeply gazed at in *In Your Eyes*. The dialogue, instead of seeming knowing and smart, feels schmaltzy and trite. At one point, Dylan notes, "The best thing about myself. The only thing I like ... is you." It is such a trite, rom-com Hollywood line.

Similarly, the film's plot development depends on supporting characters who are not three-dimensional, and have no real motivation for their behavior. This seems abundantly true in Rebecca's tale. Her husband, Phillip is a veritable moustache-twirling, one-dimensional villain. The fact that her husband is so clearly an antagonist and a bad person makes it easier for Rebecca to leave him, and to pave the way for a happy ending. But Phillip is a cold-as-ice, selfish bastard, who takes away, in some sense, the film's attempt to portray (magical) reality. He is a cruel, sadistic person, and it is never clear why Rebecca would have married him in the first place. And it is convenient how he happens to know a sadistic doctor, who is willing to incarcerate Rebecca, and do tests on her. It's all a bit simplistic and obvious.

The film's ending is even more predictable. Leaving aside the lack of any third-act twist or turn in the story, *In Your Eyes* ends with a hackneyed chase. Dylan flees parole and is chased by the police as he tries to rescue Rebecca from the hospital. Meanwhile, Rebecca flees from her husband and the doctors. They run through the woods, and guide each other to a reunion on a railroad. They board a train, and the movie ends, as they finally see each other in the flesh.

But the story is not over, and all the conflicts of the tale have not truly been resolved. Rebecca was apparently legally incarcerated in the hospital. And Dylan has broken the conditions of his parole and committed new crimes, too. So yes, they have gloriously met face-to-face on the train, but where are they going to go from there? Are they going to live together, on the run? Will they flee to Canada? Dylan might be able to make a go of that, but the buttoned-down Rebecca?

So many bad Hollywood movies end when things aren't resolved, after an escape, or action sequence, and *In Your Eyes* falls into that category. Just because the physical action is resolved doesn't mean that the character story achieves meaningful closure.

The final chase might have felt more than merely mechanical if there had been a final twist to the tale. And what should that final twist have been? The movie is about an intimate link, and sharing a kind of deep communication between two people. What if Dylan had been shot and killed in the effort to save the love of his life, Rebecca? What if Rebecca had seen death, through her lover's eyes, and learned, in the process of losing him, to live her life fearlessly?

That (admittedly sad) denouement might have provided the punctuation, emotional zenith, or surprise twist the film needed to make it feel more challenging, and that the journey actually reveals something deep and meaningful about human nature. Connection in love is one thing, but what about connection through tragedy? *In Your Eyes* is inoffensive and sweet, but also, in some way, unambitious.

On the other hand, the film commendably conforms to the above-referenced magical realism tenets described earlier in this chapter. The hot-and-cold visual opposition in terms of location and character traits is clever, and well-wrought, and the main performances are very good. And, even if the film is not edgy, it features a typical Whedon metaphor worthy of examination.

"I think that all of Joss's supernatural writing is a way at getting really human problems," star Zoe Kazan told reporter Valentina Valentini in "Tribeca Interview: Zoe Kazan, Michael Stahl-David Talk Whedon's 'In Your Eyes.'" "Like 'Buffy the Vampire Slayer' is about puberty and people's bodies becoming strange to themselves and how to deal with this scary adult world, there is something similar in this film. I think he's using the supernatural element to talk about connection and about self-love—discovering a new part of yourself."

Kazan's comment about self-love is on the mark, and this author is not simply referring to the film's oft-discussed masturbation scene. Instead, *In Your Eyes* concerns self-concept, and the ways that it is wrought, or changed, through experience and connection. Rebecca and Dylan each grow and become stronger as they see themselves in the eyes of their counterparts. For individual and personal reasons, both characters suffer from low self-esteem and are unable to actually see themselves in an accurate way.

They begin to see, through each other's eyes, how beautiful and worthwhile they are. It is a lovely concept, even if the film is unambitious, unchallenging, and often trite. The question, one supposes, is whether aid concept is weighty enough to support a feature-length film, or complex enough to please Whedon admirers and critics at this juncture in his career. His fans are ready to embrace postmodern, intertextual, self-reflexive explorations of created families, diversity, and the value of women in modern society A simple love story about two lost souls who discover each other may simply not be enough to garner the love of the artist's fans.

Part VI

Politics and Personnel

30

What Are Joss Whedon's Politics?

Joss Whedon's political beliefs and activism are well known. Although many right-wing individuals and scholars have interpreted *Firefly* (2002–2003) as the ultimate expression of libertarianism, Whedon actually identifies as a liberal, or left-leaning, and it is that viewpoint and ideology he often expresses both through his art and in life, particularly as it applies to feminism, poverty, and even universal healthcare.

In 2012, at the height of Whedon's visibility in the press due to the success of Marvel's *The Avengers*, Whedon created and posted to YouTube a memorable two-minute-twelve-second video that went viral and garnered over seven million views. It was a parody, explaining why voters in the November presidential election should choose Republican nominee Mitt Romney over Democrat and President, Barack Obama, who was running for re-election at the time.

The "Whedon on Romney" ad is set in an upscale kitchen (in Whedon's home). In a well-staged medium shot, the audience sees Whedon washing dishes at the sink as he pivots to address the audience in friendly fashion. At this point, Whedon reminds viewers of 2008, and the historic election of President Obama. He then observes that, in 2012, times have changed. Candidate Mitt Romney, Whedon declares, would officiate over deep rollbacks in the nation's safety net, and guarantee poverty, unemployment, and other social ills. Worst of all, Whedon suggests, a Romney era will see the rise of ungoverned corporate privilege, making way for the zombie apocalypse.

"Money is only so much paper to the undead," Whedon reminds his audience.

The ad is marked as a vintage Whedon piece by a few elements worthy of closer inspection. First are the deliberate genre overtones, suggesting that a Romney administration would usher in an age of zombies. Instead of a straight advertisement arguing why Romney is not the right choice for the country, Whedon connects his hypothetical administration to a topic (the zombie invasion) that had moved into the national consciousness in a powerful way because of the success of the hit AMC series, *The Walking Dead* (2010–). Whedon is famous for his genre love, and this commercial demonstrates that alongside the politics.

Second, Whedon's ad knowingly drops a number of careful literary and movie allusions, acknowledging their cultural importance and relevance. Right-wing author (and role model) Ayn Rand is name-checked at one point, which is also timely, since just a few weeks before this political ad was posted, a movie based on Ayn Rand's best-known work, *Atlas Shrugged Part I* (2012), was released theatrically. Rand's ideas about self-interest were again coming into the political mainstream, and Whedon is ready here with a response to their resurgence.

Another production called-out is Danny Boyle's 28 *Days Later* (2001). This is a horror film featuring the fast-moving zombies of the new millennium, rather than the old-fashioned, slow ones of the George A. Romero era. But as always, this video proves that Whedon's finger was on the pulse of pop culture.

In the lead-up to the next presidential election, in 2016, Joss Whedon was again active in politics. He formed a Super PAC for Democratic candidate Hilary Clinton called "Save the Day" and raised over a million dollars for the candidate in her (ultimately doomed) quest to defeat Republican nominee Donald Trump. To the ire of many conservatives, Whedon recruited a number of his friends in Hollywood to help the cause.

Whedon's first "Save the Day" video had more than thirty-five million views in forty-eight hours, and featured *Avengers* stars including Robert Downey Jr., Scarlett Johansson, Mark Ruffalo, and Don Cheadle. Other Whedon stalwarts appearing in the short ad included Nathan Fillion, Clark Gregg, Neil Patrick Harris, and Tom Lenk. Others featured were Julianne Moore, Keegan-Michael Key, and Stanley Tucci.

Like his video from 2012, Whedon's "Save the Day" video employed humorous content, rather than mere political maneuvering. While some of the stars appearing discussed the election as a "tipping point for the country and the world," others insisted that if Clinton won, Mark Ruffalo would do a nude scene in his next movie. The video's tagline quickly became "Make Mark naked," much to Ruffalo's discomfort.

Typically, the reception to "Save the Day" was dependent on the ideology of the watcher. Those who were left-leaning appreciated it, while many on the right revived their old "shut-up-and-sing" argument, suggesting that the stars involved, and Whedon himself, should drop politics and simply do what they were supposed to do: entertain us.

The problem with this line of debate, of course, is the hypocrisy. Conservatives are supposed to be champions of free speech, even if it is free speech counter to their own views. That right to express one's self extends to movie stars and writers/directors. Second, "shut up and sing" seems to be a tenet conservatives only wish to apply to left-wing entertainers.

Historically speaking, it is actually the right that has frequently depended on entertainers and TV stars to popularize their political viewpoints. After all, Ronald Reagan was a movie actor before being elected to the presidency in 1980, and Donald Trump was a reality TV star on *The Apprentice* (2004–2017) before becoming commander-in-chief. Arnold Schwarzenegger, of course, was the biggest movie star of all before becoming the Republican governor of California. And at Trump's 2016 convention, prominent speakers included actor Scott Baio, Antonio Sabato Jr., and Will Robertson. No conservative pundit has ever explained, cogently, why it is acceptable for celebrities such as those listed above to run for and hold office, or talk politics, but it is somehow deemed unseemly for the likes of Whedon to do so, or for actors of the caliber of Downey, Moore, or Ruffalo to join in.

Another "Save the Day" PAC ad that ran before Election Day 2016 was called "Verdict" and it featured a Latino girl waiting to learn who had won the presidency. If one candidate—Clinton—won, she and her family could stay in the United States and build a future here, as Americans. If the other candidate —Trump—won, it was likely she and her family would be deported.

Just days short of the election, on November 1, 2016, Patrick Caldwell interviewed Whedon for the internet periodical *Mother Jones* in a piece called "Joss Whedon Explains Why Donald Trump is America's Scariest Big Bad," adopting the terminology of *Buffy the Vampire Slayer* to explain the stark choice facing voters.

As Whedon noted in the piece: "The world is scary, and things are overwhelming, and there's a lot at stake . . . . But this voting thing is actually beautiful." In the same article he discussed how he was turning voting in the election into a hero narrative, not unlike one of his beloved projects.

Of course, come November 8, 2016, Election Day, Donald Trump carried the Electoral College, even as Whedon's candidate, Clinton, carried the popular vote by roughly three million votes. After such a defeat, Whedon's words about a Trump victory were more relevant than ever. Back in September, he had told *The Hollywood Reporter:* "I'll tell you what you don't do [if Trump wins]. You don't move to Canada or any of that bullshit. You don't give up on the world."

And, of course, Whedon didn't.

Instead, he embraced his next challenge, which at the time was taking the reins on another superhero team movie: *Justice League*. After Trump's election, however, Whedon stoked controversy again with a tweet that expressed his exhaustion with the new administration. "Die, Don. Just quietly die," he wrote. Twitter then suspended him for a short time before he returned with—*surprise!*—a movie reference. Specifically, Whedon alluded to *The Breakfast Club* (1985), thus contextualizing his "time out." from the social networking site.

In May 2017, well into the Trump era, Whedon directed a political short film about Planned Parenthood called *Unlocked*, which followed three women of different generations through a dystopian future in which the organization had been made illegal. Delving into the topic of abortion made Whedon public enemy number one with conservatives, but Whedon did not seem bothered by it. Instead, he championed the value of supporting Planned Parenthood and wanted to share it with the public. He told *Entertainment Weekly* that if "politicians succeed in closing down Planned Parenthood, millions of people lose access to basic health services, STD testing, birth control cancer screening . . . how can those be at risk?"

Meanwhile *Breitbart*, *Red State*, and other right-wing sites took Whedon to task for a Mother's Day tweet in 2017 in which he claimed he was glad his mother was not alive to witness Trump's disastrous presidency. The right-wing sites twisted his words to mean that Whedon was happy his mother was dead, when his point was actually quite different. The idea he expressed was that it was better for his mother not to know the regressive, misogynist indignities of the Trump era.

Whedon's politics have been judged and found wanting not just by those on the right side of the political spectrum, but by those on the left, who have deemed his work and commentary neither feminist nor progressive enough. Following the release of *Avengers 2: Age of Ultron* (2015), the artist faced harsh criticism from the left over the character of Black Widow, and her desire to have children.

As noted in the chapter about *Age of Ultron*, Some left-wingers felt Natasha's description of herself as a "monster" was based on her sterilization, her inability to bear children, though the dialogue in that scene (and the many references to "monsters" in the film's screenplay) suggests that was not the point. Frankly, some of the same people attacked Chris Carter over his *X-Files* reboot in 2018, over the fact that Dana Scully (Gillian Anderson) desired to have a child with Mulder. Again, people argued that this desire to be a mother somehow made Scully only the sum total of her reproductive organs and their capacity.

In both cases, the point was missed. Feminism has always been, and will always be, about the right of women to make their own choices. Black Widow was robbed of that choice by those who "raised" her to become an assassin. And if Scully, with all her degrees, abilities, and genius, decides she wants to be a mother, why would anyone else judge that an invalid choice? It is her decision to make.

It is ironic, not to mention extremely sad, that Joss Whedon spent his own fortune, time, and creative genius, on two succeeding presidential elections to help the liberal candidate succeed, and yet, in short order, he was pilloried for not being sufficiently liberal himself. He made himself a target for conservatives, but then was also targeted by liberals.

In terms of politics and art, Joss Whedon has done precisely what right-wing people in Hollywood—including Charlton Heston, Arnold Schwarzenegger, and Bruce Willis—have done before him: used his megaphone to try to make the world a better place, at least from their own ideological standpoint. It is fascinating that Heston starred in leftist material such as *Planet of the Apes* (1968) and *Soylent Green* (1973), and that Joss Whedon launched the libertarian-tinged *Firefly*.

Perhaps these are good reminders not to paint people in broad strokes, or to dismiss their art because we disagree with a viewpoint on one issue or another. Artists like those listed above are more than just the "R" or "D" that you find on their voter registration card. They are people who see the world through their own experience, and with nuances and shading. Modern left vs. right, blue vs. red binary selections don't begin to tell the whole story.

31

Is Joss Whedon a Feminist?

F*eminism* is a hot-button word (and issue) in today's hyper-aggressive, hyper-partisan society. It is also a term that is defined incorrectly, often intentionally so by those who oppose it. Feminism is, basically, the advocacy for women's rights in terms of *equality* of the sexes. This definition does not mean that feminists believe women should be raised above men in the eyes of the law or society. It does not mean that women should hate men. It does not mean that men should be subordinate to women, like, at all. Feminism is simply the belief that men and women should be treated equally under the law in America, and so long as that is not the case, injustice exists in society. Yet feminism is often treated as a dirty word, because people have been misinformed about it, or don't know its actual definition. They have been persuaded by those who argue incessantly about "feminazis," or the need to put on a pedestal traditional values.

Joss Whedon defines himself as a feminist, and was raised a feminist by his mother, Ann Lee Stearns. Accordingly, his films and TV programs are feminist to their creative core. This means they demonstrate that women can act as heroes. They can be courageous, mythic, iconic, and flawed—just like men. In the realm of fantasy and science fiction this is an especially big deal. More treatises and academic books and papers have been written about *Buffy the Vampire Slayer* than any other pop-culture hero in the history of television. And when viewing Joss Whedon's works, it is impossible not to recognize that he pays special attention to the cause of feminism: equal rights. For those who understand and appreciate feminism, this focus makes Whedon a welcome voice in the genre. For those who don't appreciate feminism, it makes Whedon wrong, an enemy, or even a *libtard*. For such people, Whedon should leave politics and social issues outside his entertaining work.

In 2006, Joss Whedon made his viewpoint on feminism plain when he was acknowledged for his "representation of female characters in film by the organization Equality Now," according to the article "Whedonesque Women: One Man's Quest for Positive Gender Representations." At that event, Whedon declared that equality is not a concept. "It's not something we should be striving for. It's a necessity. Equality is like gravity, we need it to stand on this Earth as men and women, and the misogyny that is in every culture is not a true part of the human condition."

Instead, Whedon opined, such anti-woman forces represent "life out of imbalance . . . sucking something out of the soul of every man and woman who is confronted with it." He finished by demanding equality "kinda now."

Alas, events in Joss Whedon's personal life in the year 2017 gave cause to feminist allies to question the writer's credentials in that realm. From 1995 through 2012, Whedon was married to Kai Cole, and their divorce became official in 2016. In August 2017, *The Wrap* published an article Cole wrote, one explaining the dissolution of their marriage. She describes in the piece, at length, Whedon's history of alleged marital infidelities and lying to her. She uses the article, in her words, "to tell my truth." And that truth consists of the assertion that Whedon used his marital status "as a shield . . . so no one would question his relationships with other women, or scrutinize his writing as anything other than feminism."

Cole also writes in the same article about a diagnosis, following their divorce, of "Complex PTSD." What this comes down to is an accusation of gaslighting on Whedon's part. That term is defined as the manipulation of someone by psychological means into questioning their own sanity. Apparently, according to Cole, Whedon had been having extramarital affairs since the days of the *Buffy the Vampire Slayer* TV series, and not telling her the truth, and in fact, deflecting the truth.

When published, the article created an incredible stir in the media, and among the writer/director's fans. Whedon's terse response to the piece was that it contained some "inaccuracies," but that out of respect to his wife and children, he would not contest in public its substance. In terms of Cole's writing, she also reported in *The Wrap* another item that drew the ire of Whedon's fans and former fans. In his explanation of his infidelities and lies, according to Cole, Whedon described the difficulty of working consistently with "beautiful, needy, aggressive young women." This explanation seemed to shift the blame for the marital indiscretions from Whedon—a man—to the women in those dalliances.

This did not sit well with many.

Writing for *The Mercury News*, journalist Martha Ross described Whedon's explanation (again, relayed by Cole's piece) as the "solipsistic rationalizations of a man who preaches male sensitivity while serving his own needs." *The Mary Sue*, a genre periodical, went further. Vivian Kane wrote: "Joss Whedon helped make feminism a mainstream talking point, and we paid close attention as he did so. So you're going to be damn sure we'll do the same thing when his behavior undermines those same values on a huge scale."

The article describing his behavior was damaging to Whedon's reputation, so much so that professional associates were asked to respond to its content. Referring to Cole's essay, *Buffy the Vampire Slayer* producer Marti Noxon told journalist Lindsay Kupfer in *Page Six* that *The Wrap* article "broke" her heart and that she "never experienced" Joss Whedon in "that way."

Without going into much further detail about this matter, Kai Cole's essay paints the picture of a man unwilling to take responsibility and, in fact, blaming others for his actions. So great was the fall-out that the long-standing Whedon website, Whedonseque, shut down shortly after publication of the story, though the moderator admitted that the story was but one reason for doing so, not the *only* reason.

And, of course, Whedon's political enemies on the right came out in force on Twitter to lambast him and discredit a powerful progressive voice in the media. To this day, trolls will respond online to any tweet from Whedon that supports the feminist cause, by pointing out his own alleged treatment of his wife.

There are two sides to every story in a marriage, but it is difficult to view this situation as much other than a self-inflicted wound on Whedon's part. Regardless of all the facts and details surrounding the collapse of his marriage, Whedon has, in the age of #MeToo, fallen into the category of artist who creates great work, but whose work must be separated, in some sense, from his personal life. This is a not-entirely unfamiliar predicament for admirers of Alfred Hitchcock, Woody Allen, Gene Roddenberry, or even Rod Serling. They are legitimate artistic geniuses all, but imperfect men who ended up disappointing people, and not living up to the high ideals expressed in their works.

In short, Kai Cole's article caused critical damage to the perception of Whedon as one of the "good guys" in the battle for equal rights for women. Every time he speaks on issues of feminism now, his voice is neutralized, and it shouldn't be. Not a one of us is infallible. But in the age of social media attacks, a public tarnish such as this is difficult, if not impossible, to rub away. Whedon's enemies hate him for his progressive views on feminism, the environment, health care, gay rights, and other issues, and now they have the ammunition to neuter Whedon's input in the discourse. His fans continue to love his work, but many have lost their unswerving faith in him. And Whedon's feminist allies, by and large, have a document at the ready to suggest that Whedon has failed egregiously to live up to his ideals.

So the question of this chapter is a difficult one to answer definitively. *Is* Joss Whedon a feminist? The undeniable answer is that his work is unabashedly and rewardingly feminist. But Joss Whedon is also a human being who has made mistakes and hurt those he loves, mitigating the power of his feminist viewpoint.

It's a sad fact that as of this book's writing, Joss Whedon's feminist credentials are indeed in question, for many fans and non-fans alike.

32

The Joss Whedon Repertory Company

If one surveys the many TV programs and films of Joss Whedon, one finds that several actors and actresses appear frequently. Throughout his career, Whedon has worked with this "stock," ad-hoc company, again and again.

To qualify as a Joss Whedon repertory company member in the listing below, the performer in question must appear at least three times, or in three separate productions, in the Whedon canon. For the record, *Firefly* and *Serenity* count as two productions, since one is a TV series; the other, a film.

The repertory company members are listed below in alphabetical order.

The Company

Amy Acker

This actress has portrayed a number of heroic and lovable characters in the Whedonverse, and sometimes dramatized multiple personalities in one character! She played Winifred "Fred" Birkle in the TV series *Angel* and finished off the five-season series as Illyria, an ancient demon who possesses Fred's body.

Acker also played a recurring character, Dr. Claire Saunders, in both seasons of Fox's *Dollhouse*. She also played Saunders's active incarnation, Whiskey.

In 2012, Acker appeared both in the horror film *The Cabin in the Woods* (as Lin) and *Much Ado About Nothing* (as Beatrice). Her most recent

Amy Acker is one of the key actors in Joss Whedon's Repertory Company, having starred in Whedon TV series and films.   *John Muir Photo Archive*

appearance in the Whedonverse was in a 2014 *Agents of S.H.I.E.L.D.* episode, "The Only Light in Darkness," in which her character's name is Audrey Nathan.

Felicia Day

Although best remembered as the tragic, if noble, Penny in the Whedon web series, *Dr. Horrible's Sing-A-Long Blog* (2008), Day has appeared several times in the Whedonverse. She starred as "Mag" in two post-apoc-alyptic episodes of *Dollhouse* ("Epitaph One," and "Epitaph Two: Return") and got her start in the Whedonverse as Vi, one of the potential slayers in the seventh, and final, season of *Buffy the Vampire Slayer*.

Outside the Wedonverse, Day reunited with Dr. Horrible himself, Neil Patrick Harris, in an episode of Joel Hodgson's *Mystery Science Theater 3000: The Return* (2017–).

Alexis Denisof

This actor began his career in the Whedonverse as the prissy, stuffy Wesley Wyndham-Price during the third season of *Buffy the Vampire Slayer*, in 1998–1999. Following that stint as a "watcher," he returned to the 'Verse, as a tougher, more likable version of Wesley, following Doyle's death in the first season of *Angel*. He played that role until the series cliffhanger, "Not Fade Away."

In 2009, Denisof played Senator Daniel Perrin, a tool of the villainous Rossum Corporation, in *Dollhouse*. Finally, in 2012, Denisof worked with Whedon again in *Much Ado about Nothing* as Benedick, the sparring lover to Amy Acker's Beatrice.

Reed Diamond

This actor entered the Whedonverse playing the apparently villainous Laurence Dominic in *Dollhouse*. As the series revealed more information about Dominic, it was learned that the character was not the monster Echo believed him to be.

Reed returned to the Whedonverse to play Don Pedro, the "good" prince in *Much Ado About Nothing*, and then completed a multi-episode guest-stint on *Agents of S.H.I.E.L.D.* as Daniel Whitehall.

Eliza Dushku

The star of her own sci-fi TV series outside the Whedonverse, *Tru Calling* (2003–2005), Eliza Dushku also made a significant mark on Whedon's

Eliza Dushku, Echo in *Dollhouse* and Faith on *Buffy*, has appeared many times in the Whedonverse.   *John Muir Photo Archive*

many television series. She played Faith, a rogue vampire slayer, beginning in the third season of *Buffy the Vampire Slayer*. She returned to that role throughout the remaining four seasons of the series, and then brought the character to a story-arc in *Angel*'s first season.

Ten years after her first performances as Faith, Dushku headlined her own Whedon series, *Dollhouse*. There, she portrayed Echo/Caroline, a woman whose mind and identity were "wiped," and served a five-year stint as an "active," for the Rossum Corporation's *Dollhouse*. While operating as an active, "Echo," she began to develop memories of her engagement/missions, despite the fact they were wiped from her mind.

Nathan Fillion

Captain Mal Reynolds remains one of the most unforgettable figures one will find in Joss Whedon's canon. Nathan Fillion plays that role to perfection throughout the TV series, *Firefly* (2002–2003), and in the film *Serenity* (2005).

But Fillion has also played some villainous roles in the 'Verse too. He guest-starred as the misogynistic fundamentalist preacher, Caleb, in the seventh, and final, season of *Buffy the Vampire Slayer*.

Whedon's go-to-leading Man, Nathan Fillion.   *John Muir Photo Archive*

Fillion also played the vapid, arrogant Captain Hammer in 2008's *Dr. Horrible's Sing-Along Blog*, and the laughable constable Dogberry in *Much Ado About Nothing*.

Summer Glau

This beloved cult-TV actress has starred as a Terminator in *Sarah Connor: The Terminator Chronicles* (2008–2009), but her TV career began in the Whedonverse.

In particular, Glau played the prima ballerina "cursed" to dwell forever in a time-loop in an episode of *Angel*'s third season, "Waiting in the Wings," written and directed by Whedon. In 2002, Glau was cast as River Tam in *Firefly*, a role she reprised in *Serenity* (2005).

Finally, in 2009, Summer Glau returned to the Whedonverse as the brilliant Dr. Bennett Halverson, a recurring character on *Dollhouse*.

Ron Glass

This former *Barney Miller* (1975–1982) star made a splash in the Whedonverse by playing the Reverend Shepherd Book, a pious man with a mysterious past, in both *Firefly* and its feature film counterpart, *Serenity*. Glass later guest-starred as a surgeon on episodes of *Agents of S.H.I.E.L.D.*

Clark Gregg

Gregg joined the Marvel Cinematic Universe at its inception, appearing as Agent Coulson in early entries such as *Iron Man* (2008), *Iron Man 2* (2010), and *Thor* (2011). He reprised the role for writer-director Whedon in *The Avengers* (2012). Sadly, Agent Coulson was murdered by Loki in that film, before returning from the dead to headline the popular ABC series *Agents of S.H.I.E.L.D.* (2013–).

Gregg also starred in *Much Ado About Nothing*, as Leonato.

Chris Hemsworth

Known by the civilized world as Thor, the god of Thunder, in *Thor* (2011), *Thor: The Dark World* (2013), and *Thor Ragnarok* (2017), Hemsworth reprised that role for Whedon's *Avenger* films, both the 2012 original and 2015's *Age of Ultron*. In 2012, he also starred in *The Cabin in the Woods*, as Curt, a dumb, horny jock.

Fran Kranz

This actor has often played characters in the Whedonverse who are put in positions to save the planet Earth, and the human race. Kranz's Topher Brink sacrifices his life at the end of *Dollhouse* (in the climactic episode, "Epitaph Two: Return") to undo the apocalypse for which he blames himself, as the developer of the active architecture technology.

In *The Cabin in the Woods*, Kranz plays Marty, a stoner who can sacrifice himself and save the world, or attempt to survive, and bring about the apocalypse in the process. By choosing to live, Marty dooms the world.

Fran Kranz also plays Claudio in *Much Ado about Nothing*, a character who loses his moral compass and betrays his true love, Hero, when he believes her to be inconstant.

Tom Lenk

This actor is the voice and face of geekdom (or maybe) nerd-om, and as well as awkward social interactions in the Whedonverse. Lenk played Andrew, one of the Nerds of Doom in the sixth and seventh seasons of *Buffy the Vampire Slayer*, and carried that role over to an episode of *Angel*. Later, Lenk appeared as a gullible intern in *The Cabin in The Woods*. He also had a supporting role, as Verges, in *Much Ado About Nothing*.

Sean Maher

This actor played the consummate good guy, Dr. Simon Tam, in *Firefly* and *Serenity*. He then undercut that gentle, good-guy image, rather dramatically, as the cunning and deceitful Don John in *Much Ado about Nothing*. As Don John, he is the architect of Claudio, Leonato, and Hero's suffering. Maher plays the character with a seductive, noir edge.

Gina Torres

Before recent roles in *Hannibal* (2013–2015) and *Westworld* (2015–), Torres was a Whedon stalwart. She played Zoe, the soldier and wife, in *Firefly* and *Serenity*. Then, in a complete change of pace, she was cast as the demonic Jasmine in several episodes of *Angel*.

Alan Tudyk

This actor is a leaf on the wind. Watch him soar.

Tudyk is loved by *Firefly* fans for his role as Washburn—Whedon's individual voice—in the cult-TV series. He was mourned by those fans because of the character's brutal death scene at the hands of Reavers, in *Serenity*.

In 2009-2010, Tudyk returned to the Whedonverse as a schizophrenic active in the *Dollhouse* episode "Alpha." Recently, Tudyk played a droid in another space opera, *Rogue One* (2016), as the sarcastic droid, KS20.

33

Deaths in the Whedonverse

Joss Whedon films and TV programs are famous for their creator's trademark wit, feminist slant, and references to pop culture, particularly comic books. However, they are also known for one very dark thing: the often-brutal and surprising deaths of beloved characters.

Why kill off characters, including fan favorites? Whedon has made it clear, in more than one interview, that fighting evil must bear a cost. The death of a hero is something that pays for that cost, and makes the battle seem more believable. Disbelief is suspended when the heroes conquer a villain, because there is a grave price to be paid for that victory.

There is an important corollary, too. Several characters who have been killed have also been resurrected, to allow their journeys to continue. However, a resurrection also comes with a price. Characters such as Buffy and Coulson could testify at length about the cost of returning to this mortal coil.

One quality that makes the Joss Whedon universe so popular is the fact that everyone living there still worries about their mortality. Super powers, or even apparent "immortality," are not givens in a chaotic universe, or one where a Big Bad lurks around every corner.

Finally, a note about the deaths written about below. They are included in chronological order. Whedon's horror films—*Alien Resurrection*, the theatrical *Buffy the Vampire Slayer*, and *The Cabin in the Woods*—are not included. After all, horror movies are designed to feature character deaths as a key element, and Merrick's death in the *Buffy* movie is expected as part of the hero's journey (the death of the wise elder, or mentor), so it does not conform to the "surprise" twist under discussion.

Ripley reborn, a character resurrected by Joss Whedon in *Alien: Resurrection* (1997).
John Muir Photo Archive

The deaths in the Whedonverse are also organized below in terms of the (apparently) permanent ones, and those that came to include resurrections. A resurrection in the comics, please note, does not qualify for this list.

The Deaths (Permanent)

Jenny Calendar

This *Buffy the Vampire Slayer* character, played by Robia La Morte, was Sunnydale High School's computer instructor, and a love interest for Rupert Giles. She was also, secretly, an agent sent by gypsies who had been tasked with spying on Angel.

Calendar was introduced early in the series' first season (in the episode "I Robot . . . You Jane"), so her death in the second season, at Angel's hands no less, in the episode "Passion" was a shock. Her death showcases the fact that the Angel that Buffy knows and loves is truly gone, replaced by the soulless Angelus. Calendar's death also creates tension and conflict between Buffy and Giles about whether Angel is worthy of being saved. Jenny's death was permanent, and the character was never resurrected. However, the First Evil did take the form of Jenny Calendar to taunt and torture the (re-souled) Angel in the third-season Christmas episode, "Amends."

Doyle

This half-human, half-Brachan demon hero works with Angel in the first season of the series' spinoff. Doyle is the conduit from the Powers-That-Be to Angel, providing the "visions" Angel needs to locate those in Los Angeles who need rescuing.

So he should have been safe, right?

Wrong.

In the ninth episode of the series, Doyle sacrifices his life, and passes on his visions power to Cordelia, to save a group of oppressed demons from Nazi monsters called the Scourge. Nobody foresaw this character dying virtually right out the gate, but Doyle's meaningful (and early) sacrifice put the steel in Angel's spine, and makes him realize that his long journey to redemption (and worthiness) will not be an easy one.

Joyce Summers

In the opening moments of the fifth season *Buffy the Vampire Slayer* episode "The Body," Buffy returns home to find her mother, Joyce, dead on the sofa in the family's living room. She has suffered a brain aneurysm, and despite Buffy's sincerest, most emotional wishes, there is nothing to be done. She is dead and gone, and now everyone must cope with the loss.

"The Body" is the single-most devastating episode of the series in part because it is very much about the finality of death. For Joyce, there was no pain, and her suffering is over. But for those she leaves behind, there is only the reckoning that she is gone, and that they will never see her again.

Tara Maclay

The love of Willow's life is Tara Maclay, a fellow Wiccan. In the episode "Seeing Red," Tara is caught in a crossfire when the very human Warren (Adam Busch) literally comes gunning for Buffy. While talking to Willow in an upstairs bedroom, Tara is accidentally shot in the chest.

And since her death does not come about by supernatural means (like Buffy's or Angel's deaths, in "Becoming," or "The Gift," respectively), there is no way for Willow to bring Tara back. This totally meaningless (and unintentional) death serves an important purpose, dramatically speaking. It is the turning-point that transforms the magic-addicted Willow into the season's Big Bad.

Anya

When Charisma Carpenter's Cordelia left Sunnydale for Los Angeles (and jumped *Buffy*'s ship for *Angel*'s), Emma Caulfield's former vengeance demon, Anya (or Anyanka), became Buffy's voice of callow sarcasm. And what a job the character did.

Unfortunately, Anya falls in battle against the First Evil in the series finale, "Chosen." Of all the character deaths in the series, this is the weakest and most poorly handled. After four seasons as a regular character, and a delightful one at that, Anya deserves a better sendoff than an anonymous death in a huge battle. This is especially true given her close relationship with Xander, and friendship with Giles, at the Magic Box. Anya's death, in "Chosen," feels like an unnecessary and poorly thought out effort to give the finale a final tug at the heartstrings.

Cordelia

Really, who *is* Cordelia Chase? The superficial rich girl? The well-meaning but sarcastic young woman? Angel's love interest? A conduit to the

Powers-That-Be? Connor's mother? Saint Cordy, willing to sacrifice every-thing for Angel and the world at large?

To *Angel's* everlasting detriment as a series, the writers never stuck with one character arc for long, and so Cordelia was a different person in nearly every season of the series. That fact established, the character's sendoff in the fifth-season episode "You're Welcome" is deeply affect-ing, even heartbreaking. Cordelia wakes up from a coma to help Angel overcome one more existential crisis (his work with Wolfram and Hart), as well as defeat his nemesis, Lindsay (Christian Hart). After the mission is done and all seems happy, Cordelia unexpectedly says a final goodbye. Angel gets a call in his office informing him that Chase is dead, having never awoken from her coma.

In real life, some fans have suggested that Cordelia's absence from season five, and ultimate death in "You're Welcome," is some form of punishment for the actress's pregnancy late in the series run. Cordelia's onscreen treatment is often brought up as another chink in Whedon's pro-feminist armor.

Winifred "Fred" Birkle

In "A Hole in the World," a fifth-season episode of *Angel*, a parasitic Old One, a demon named Illyria, takes possession of Fred's body, hollowing her out, and liquefying her organs. As Illyria takes over her body bit by bit, Fred disappears into oblivion. By episode's end, Illyria is in control, and Fred's very soul has been annihilated. She is lost forever, destroyed by an evil plot, and even the other series regulars can't undo her demise.

The death of Fred, an innocent, sweet character, is heartbreaking, in part because she has just found happiness in her relationship with Wesley. The loss of Fred is devastating to Wesley, and the audience as well, and helps set the stage for Angel's climactic act, the final battle against Evil.

Wesley Wyndham-Pryce

A character who started out as a prig and a jerk grew into one of the most soulful, and important, characters on *Angel*. In the series finale, Wesley is killed by a demon called Vail (Dennis Christopher). In his dying moments, Illyria becomes Fred one last time, so that his last moments on Earth are spent in the company of the woman he loves.

Shepherd Book

One of the most intriguing elements of *Firefly* involves the background of the mysterious Shepherd Book. Mal Reynolds frequently queries the enigmatic character about his history and background, and almost universally gets frustrating non-answers in response.

Many fans believe that Book, because of his knowledge of the Alliance, must have been an operative at some point, but is now a man who seeks redemption. This plotline seems in keeping with other Whedon characters, such as Angel and Spike. Book's storyline, however, is never resolved. Instead, he dies in the film *Serenity* when another operative launches an attack on his colony, on the planet Haven. This assault is done as an attempt to destroy any home base that Mal may have.

When *Serenity* lands on Haven, Book is mortally injured, and barely alive. He speaks briefly to Mal before dying, giving the captain the impetus to continue his fight against the Alliance. No questions about the character's backstory are answered. Instead, he is gone, and his secret history goes into the Great Beyond with him.

Wash

The death of Wash is arguably the most upsetting and dramatic of any character in the worlds of Joss Whedon. There are two reasons for this.

First, Wash's death—the result of being impaled while sitting at the helm of *Serenity*—is so damned shocking and sudden. It comes out of nowhere. More significantly, Wash undeniably represents the voice of Joss Whedon; the voice of glib humor and light wit. And in the future, high-tech world of *Firefly* or *Serenity*, Alan Tudyk's Wash is undeniably the audience's link to the present, expressing audience concerns about dangerous plans, or a crew-member's odd behavior. Wash's light tone and funny way of talking remind the audience that we are in Joss Whedon's playground. When he dies, suddenly, that voice is abruptly silenced, and that connection to the author is lost.

Paul Ballard

Throughout *Dollhouse*'s two seasons, this character played by Tahmoh Penikett, is a dogged hero. First, he stops at nothing, as an FBI agent, to find the Dollhouse, and those women (like Caroline/Echo) he believes are enslaved there. Then, he falls in love with Echo, and joins her battle. This is no easy task, as the technology to erase and rewrite human minds falls into unscrupulous hands, and civilization is destroyed.

In the post-apocalyptic world, Ballard fights at Echo's side, clearly expressing his feelings of love for her. During the final battle, after just acknowledging that Echo is lonely, and refuses to "connect" with him, Paul dies randomly, shot in the head by a crazed person near the Los Angeles Dollhouse. His journey . . . just ends. Echo realizes Paul's observation about her was correct, and that she has lost the only person in this world who truly knew her.

Significantly, Paul doesn't get a traditional resurrection. However, he doesn't exactly stay dead, either. In the final moments of "Epitaph Two: Return," Echo takes the cartridge that holds all of his memory and personality, and uploads it into her own brain, becoming one with the man she loves, permanently.

Topher Brink

Driven to madness—to the brink or edge, as his name implies—by his role in the apocalypse, this *Dollhouse* character makes things right with a noble sacrifice. In the final episode of the series, "Epitaph Two: Return," Brink develops a "pulse" bomb that can restore all the minds (and identities) in the world. He must activate it manually, however, which means that he dies in the ensuing blast. The cost of redemption is his own death.

The Deaths (with Resurrection)

Angel

In the closing moments of the *Buffy the Vampire Slayer* episode "Becoming Part II," Willow works her magic, and Angel's soul is restored to his body. But it is too late to save him. The evil Angelus has already opened the portal to hell, via the statue of a demon called Acathla. Only his blood can seal the portal.

Realizing this, Buffy kisses the love of her life, tells him to close his eyes, and then, while he is still confused about what is happening, runs him through with a sword, spilling his blood and closing the portal. She has saved the world once again.

Angel dies and goes to hell, but in early season three, he returns to Earth as a kind of feral, animal man ("Beauty and the Beasts"). Buffy nurses him back to health, but he must cope with the memories of spending time being tortured in hell. The cost of his resurrection is an even more tortured life than he experienced before. Later in the third season, the torture grows even more harmful, as the First Evil attempts to make him feel guilt for all the blood Angel has spilled during his long life.

Buffy Summers

In the climactic moments of the fifth-season finale, "The Gift," Buffy sacrifices her own life to seal the portal to a hell dimension, and saves her sister Dawn's life. The episode ends, shockingly, with scene transition and an unexpected push toward Buffy's tombstone.

The gravestone reads: "She saved the world. A lot."

This ending for the beloved slayer proves all the more upsetting because of the age when it occurred in the history of the series. It was known at the time of the shocking season finale that Buffy was leaving the WB, and it had not yet been renewed on UPN (which became the CW).

So, for all intents and purposes, and for one very long summer, Buffy really was dead, and the future felt uncertain.

When Buffy was resurrected in the sixth season on the CW ("Bargaining Part I," and "Bargaining Part II,") it was at quite the cost. Specifically,

Buffy didn't want to return to this mortal coil at all. She had been at peace in the afterlife, and found life on Earth to be miserable and painful. She sought to alleviate this pain with a sometimes degrading sexual relationship with Spike.

Spike

James Marsters's punk vampire Spike (introduced in the *Buffy* second-season story "School Hard," a riff on 1988's *Die Hard*), sacrifices himself to save the world in the series finale, "Chosen." He makes this choice because he loves Buffy, though he knows she does not, and perhaps should not, love him.

However, his final act of sacrifice makes him worthy of Buffy, or someone like Buffy. As was the case with Buffy and Angel, however, Spike's death is not permanent, though there is a cost for his resurrection. The character returns to life, after a fashion, in the fifth season of *Angel*, as an incorporeal ghost haunting the offices of Wolfram and Hart.

About midway through this final season, Spike is restored to flesh and blood, and resumes his "life," believing himself, not Angel, to be the champion of the Shanshu prophecy.

Agent Phil Coulson

This agent for S.H.I.E.L.D. is true of heart, as his fan love for Captain America (he collects his trading cards) implies. A loyal deputy for Nick Fury, Coulson is dispatched on numerous dangerous missions to help save the world.

However, in *The Avengers*, Coulson rushes in where angels fear to tread, and confronts Loki, one-on-one, only to be killed in one of the Asgardian's trademark tricks. Coulson's demise then becomes the glue that holds the diverse group of Tony Stark, Bruce Banner, Steve Rogers, and Natasha Romanoff together long enough to take on Loki's forces in New York City.

In the first episode of *Agents of S.H.I.E.L.D.*, however, Coulson is resurrected. He thinks he faked his death to help the Avengers bond as a team. In fact, he was resurrected using strange alien blood, as part of a project called T.A.H.I.T.I. Even that, however, is not the end of his journey. He learns that those who have taken the alien blood become insane, cutting and injuring themselves. Later in the series, he learns that, in a very real sense, his body *did* die in that confrontation with Loki, and that he is now living on borrowed time.

34

What's Next for Joss Whedon?

Following up on his lengthy and troublesome "post-Marvel malaise," as *Den of Geek* called it in July of 2018, Joss Whedon suddenly had several new projects to announce. These announcements came nearly a year after the damning Kai Cole–penned article proved to be a (self-inflicted?) stake through the artist's professional heart, and splintered his fan base.

In mid-June of 2018, for example, it was announced that Whedon would executive-produce a new TV series called *Pippa Smith: Grown-Up Detective*. This comedy project, created by Siobhan Thompson and Rebecca Drysdale, originates at Freeform, the outfit behind Marvel's latest hit, *Cloak & Dagger* (2018), and *Grown-ish* (2018). The series concept, according to online news website *Coming Soon*, is "a dark comedy that follows Pippa Smith, a twentysomething who played a former kid sleuth on television as she deals with relationships, addiction, and being too dang old for the detecting game." It sounds a little like the brilliant *Veronica Mars*, though with a more Hollywood/celebrity-centric approach. Like previous TV projects with which Whedon has long been associated, this effort looks to be female-led onscreen and behind-the-scenes as well.

The second new project on the horizon sounds even more promising. On Friday the 13th of July, 2018, HBO announced that Whedon would be serving as writer, director, and showrunner of a new "prestige" sci-fi drama called *The Nevers*. Apparently, HBO prevailed during a bidding war with Netflix for the right to air the series, and proved so enthusiastic about the possibilities that *The Nevers* got a straight-to-series order, meaning that no pilot episode was deemed necessary.

Although the premiere date was not set when this book went to press, *Daily Variety* described the premise of *The Nevers* as a "sci-fi epic about a gang of Victorian women who find themselves with unusual abilities, relentless enemies, and a mission that might change the world."

Tellingly, this project sounds more like a superhero fantasy (in keeping with *Buffy the Vampire Slayer*) than it does actual science fiction (*Firefly*, *Dollhouse*). Like *Buffy*, the series is going to be a female-centric series, and the period-setting promises that fight for feminism will likely be front and center. With the announcement of this new series, some speculated that HBO was looking to shore up its TV ratings (and history for prestige programming) because of the conclusion of *Game of Thrones* (2011–2019).

The hiring of both Whedon and J. J. Abrams (on different projects) seems to suggest as much.

Almost immediately after HBO announced *The Nevers*, Whedon's alleged past behavior with his wife came back into the press with a vengeance, with *Salon* posting an article about an author (and former Whedon fan) moving beyond his work, and being "done" with him because of his treatment of his wife in the age of the #MeToo movement.

Another Whedon project was announced during the writing of this book. At San Diego Comic-Con, on July 20, 2018, it was announced that Whedon would write a *Dr. Horrible* comic book to coincide with the tenth anniversary of his celebrated web project.

And then the bomb dropped.

It was announced that *Buffy the Vampire Slayer* was to be rebooted, and that Joss Whedon would be an executive producer on this new series. And in this new version of the familiar myth, Buffy would be a woman of color.

Almost immediately, fans complained and worried about the idea of a reboot unwriting more than ten years of stories regarding Angel and Buffy on TV and in comic books. Many fans had no problem with the idea of a new slayer story, or with a slayer of color. They only had a problem that Buffy's story—so thoroughly and beautifully dramatized from 1997 to 2003—was going to be undone and then redone. How could the classic TV series be improved upon?

As criticism of a reboot spread like wildfire, the new series showrunner/producer, Monica Owusu-Breen, took to Twitter to affirm her creds as a *Buffy the Vampire Slayer* fan, noting that the original series was her *Star Wars*. She also declared that, after twenty years, it was time to meet a new slayer, meaning the new series would be a twenty years–later sequel, *not* a reboot. So the series would either focus on a different Buffy, or a vampire slayer with a different name. But, like its predecessor, it would focus on more than just horror. She told *Verge* on July 26, 2018 that "like our world, it [the new series] will be richly diverse, and like the original, some aspects of the series could be seen as metaphors for issues facing us all today."

By August of 2018, the new series seemed to be moving forward, and Joss Whedon told the press that Dark Horse Comics, after finishing its latest *Buffy the Vampire Slayer* run, would lose the rights to the franchise, and they would revert to Fox.

This switch of rights likely means that *Buffy the Vampire Slayer*—or at least her universe—is returning to our TV screens, sooner rather than later.

Although fans will, no doubt, complain again, this reboot may represent the way that Joss Whedon will truly achieve a kind of pop-culture immortality. His greatest story will survive and change and grow for the next generation.

Into each generation a slayer will be born.

Bibliography

Burkhead, Cynthia, and David Lavery. *Joss Whedon: Conversations.* (Jackson: University Press of Mississippi, 2011).

Coombs, Danielle Sarver, and Bob Batchelor. *We Are What We Sell: Volume 3: Advertising in the Contemporary Age.* (Santa Barbara, CA: Praeger, 2014).

Frankel, Valerie Estelle. *Joss Whedon's Names: The Deeper Meanings Behind Buffy, Angel, Firefly, Dollhouse, Agents of S.H.I.E.L.D., Cabin in the Woods, The Avengers, Doctor Horrible, In Your Eyes, Comics and More.* (Online: Lit Crit Press, 2014).

Giamo, Genie Nicole. "Memory, Brains, and Narratives? The Humanities as a Testing-Ground for Bioethical Scenario-Building." *Literature and Medicine.* (Spring 2016).

Klein, David. "Emmy-Worthy *Buffy* Musical Slays This Critic." *Electronic Media.* July 8, 2002, p. 6.

Kowalski, Dean A., and Evan S. Kreider. *The Philosophy of Joss Whedon.* (Lexington: University Press of Kentucky, 2011).

Muir, John. *The Encyclopedia of Superheroes on Film and Television, Second Edition.* (Jefferson, NC: McFarland and Co., 2008).

——. *Singing a New Tune: The Rebirth of the Modern Film Musical.* (New York: Applause Theatre and Cinema Books, 2004).

Pascale, Amy. *Joss Whedon: The Biography.* Foreword by Nathan Fillion (Chicago: An A Capella Book, 2014).

PopMatters. *Joss Whedon: The Complete Companion—the TV Series, the Movies, the Comic Books and More.* (London: Titan Books, 2012).

Sterba, Wendy. *J. J. Abrams vs. Joss Whedon: Duel for the Media Master of the Universe.* (Lanham, MD: Rowman and Littlefield, 2017).

Szebin, Frederick C. *Cinefantastique.* "Horror on Television," October 1997, page 119.

Time Magazine. "Television: The Best Television of 1997," December 29, 1997, page 137.

Tucker, Ken. *Entertainment Weekly*: "Ouija Broads." (November 6, 1998).

Matt Roush, *TV Guide*. "Roush Review," January 2–8, 1999. page 23.

Wilcox, Rhonda, Tanya R. Cochran, Cynthea Masson, David Lavery (editors). *Reading Joss Whedon*. (New York: Syracuse University Press, 2014).

Index

Pages with photographs are marked in **bold** type.